AGONY IN NEW HAVEN

The Trial of Bobby Seale Ericka Huggins and the Black Panther Party

DONALD FREED

Simon and Schuster / New York

First printing
SBN 671–21284–2
Library of Congress Catalog Card Number: 72–83929
Designed by Irving Perkins
Manufactured in the United States of America
Printed by Mahony & Roese, Inc., New York, N.Y.
Bound by H. Wolff Book Mfg. Co., Inc., New York, N.Y.

The publisher wishes to thank the following for permission to quote
   certain material:

Robert Lantz-Candida Donadio Literary Agency, Inc., for the excerpt
   from *An Open Letter to My Sister* by James Baldwin. Copyright ©
   1971 by James Baldwin.
Monica McCall, International Famous Agency, for the excerpt from the
   biography *Willard Gibbs* by Muriel Rukeyser. Copyright © 1942,
   1969 by Muriel Rukeyser.
Bobby Seale, for excerpts from *The Black Panther Newspaper*.
Stronghold Consolidated Productions, Inc., for all selections signed
   "Ericka," copyright © 1972 by Stronghold Consolidated Productions,
   Inc. All rights reserved.

AN ACKNOWLEDGMENT

There is no way, actually, to describe one's indebtedness—in a book like this one—to those with whom one worked and shared the remarkable events at New Haven. One can only mention a few memories at random.

Jan von Flatern and the Liberation News Service; Peter O'Connell and the Coalition for Defense of the Panthers; Martin Kenner and the Committee to Defend the Panthers; Vivian Noble, Phil Runner and Carey Kirking and the Task Force for Law and Justice; Michael Avery and the Connecticut Civil Liberties Union; Pat Gallyot and the People's Committee; John and Ann Froines; Delmarie Fieldhammer and Michael Rubinovitz for painstaking research, manuscript work and editing on the spot; Yale Masters Kai T. Erikson and John Trinkhaus, exceptions to the rule; Phyllis Grann, Greg Armstrong and Daniel Moses, committed editors; and most of all, of course, the Defense.

DONALD FREED

West Los Angeles, California
June 1972

FOR BARBOURA MORRIS FREED

Ag'o-ny (Gr. *agon*):
A struggle or contest . . . a match
between combatants . . . the argument
introducing a classical tragedy. . . .

PART I

THE

JURY

"A body of men for judging and awarding prizes at a contest or exhibition"

CONTENTS

Ag'o-ny (Gr. *agon*):
A struggle or contest . . . a match
between combatants . . . the argument
introducing a classical tragedy. . . .

PART I

THE

JURY

"A body of men for judging and awarding prizes at a contest or exhibition"

THE BOBBY SEALE and Ericka Huggins affair was a sleeping giant. The case would be history before it was news.

One George Sams testified that in May of 1969 he tortured one Alex Rackley and then ordered one Lonnie McLucas and one Warren Kimbro to kill Rackley. Sams told the Federal Bureau of Investigation that he had been ordered to do what he did, by one Bobby Seale—a man indistinguishable from George Sams to most of the nation until the agony was all over; the "difference" between Seale and Sams was part of what the trial was about.

Of the many people arrested for conspiracy to commit this crime, an unknown young woman, Ericka Huggins, was selected by the State of Connecticut to stand trial for her life alongside Bobby Seale.

All actors in the agony were young and black. They were not only black, they were Black Panthers.

A constellation of issues was to be raised around this strange trial, which did not seem to exist for the news media because there "were no angles." The media did not recognize the fateful issues: jury of peers, systematic racism, secret-police and political repression, death-penalty scruples, presumption of innocence and pre-trial detention, the rights of bail and due process, and prison conditions.

The issue of issues, the Black Panther Party's charge of genocide and their "right of revolution" was on the mind of every potential juror, but the media told a different myth. The angle of refraction of "the news" was set on the first day and was never really changed, even when individual reporters began to awaken and see things differently.

The New Haven *Register,* Thursday, May 22, 1969:

8 PANTHERS HELD IN MURDER PLOT

Eight members of the Black Panther Party here were arrested on murder charges early this morning in connection with the discovery of a mutilated body in Middlefield Wednesday night.

The eight were charged specifically with murder and conspiracy to murder as a result of the investigation which reportedly promises to have widespread ramifications. . . .

The arrests were made within eight hours after the discovery of the body of a man, burned and mutilated, in a shallow river in Middlefield. The victim had also been shot twice.

A heavily armed team comprised of uniformed and plainclothes officers smashed its way into the Party's headquarters at 365 Orchard St. shortly after 1 A.M. today to effect most of the arrests . . .

The team seized a number of weapons, a large amount of ammunition and tape recordings of a "kangaroo trial" which police said preceded the victim's murder.

Authorities said there is a direct link between the murder and the arrests several weeks ago of 21 New York City Black Panthers who were charged with conspiring to blow up several big department stores. . . .

The New Haven *Journal-Courier,* Friday, May 23, 1969:

SECOND "VICTIM" SOUGHT IN PANTHER CASE

. . . Ahern said Thursday that practically the entire plainclothes division—about 50 men—is involved in the investigation as well as State police and the Federal Bureau of Investigation.

The New Haven *Register,* Friday, May 23, 1969:

8 SUSPECTS IN KILLING TO FACE HIGH COURT

Superior Court bench warrants are expected to be issued today in connection with the "trial" and murder of a Black Panther Party member from New York . . .

[Where] members . . . were arrested several weeks ago for plotting to blow up several large department stores. . . .

It was also learned that Mrs. Huggins, whose husband, John, was killed during an intra-party dispute in California two months ago had been a high-ranking member of the Black Panther Party in Los Angeles. She and her late husband were said to be closely identified with Bobby Seale, a top ranking Black Panther in the San Francisco area.

The names of Ericka Huggins and Bobby Seale were being singled out, by the police and the press, and linked, although Seale was not to be accused or arrested for many months, until George Sams, Jr., became a government witness. The Panthers claim that an obvious frame-up can be observed in the first twenty-four hours. The newspapers live only in the present—like wild beasts— and their perspective of the Panthers was one of almost mythic violence.

So, what the public, the people, saw first was: a New York–New Haven axis of murder and bombing. Later, in 1971—after 1,550 people, the size of a small American town, the largest jury selection in history—it would be clear that those big headlines and the mug shots of the Panthers under them would continue to hang over Bobby Seale and Ericka Huggins like a legend. And that no jury of peers ever would or could be chosen. (When the defense had used up its challenges and the twelfth juror was forced on them it took nine men to hold Bobby Seale down.)

Was the five-year-old Black Panther Party—created on the streets of the Oakland ghetto by Bobby Seale and Huey P. Newton—the gang of thugs and killers that J. Edgar Hoover, Spiro Agnew and, finally, even *The New York Times,* after the acquittal of the New York "Panther Twenty-one," and much of the Establishment called them? Or were they, as they called themselves, "servants of the people," the vanguard of the new American revolution?

Liberal America, with its fast-growing "educated class," would watch the case, looking for a coherence to the stunning violence that seemed to be sweeping up out of all the American ghettos and into their living space.

At the same time, Bobby Seale and Ericka Huggins, because they were black, were only a little worse than, but not much different from, Lieutenant William Calley—or, rather, Charles Manson and his girls—to the disorganized, more traditional middle-American public of 1970–71 which was reporting at the New Haven Municipal Court for jury duty in November, 1970.

So the Black Panther Party was on trial too, and not just before white people but to the almost 70 percent of the black population (cited by "white" polls) that supported their program of "survival pending revolution."

Before the agony in New Haven was over not only the country, but the Black Panther Party itself, would be split on the course of black liberation and the "second American revolution."

The Black Panthers—who consider themselves prisoners of war—make out these events in New Haven to be only one increment on the short road toward American fascism. The government's conspiracy against the Panthers cannot be understood, the Panthers argue, apart from their political world view at this time.

In January of 1969, the leaders of the Los Angeles Black Panther Party, Alprentice "Bunchy" Carter and Jon Jerome Huggins, were assassinated on the campus of U.C.L.A. This was not a "shoot-out" between "rival black militants" as the press to this day insists. It was a bloody example of what happens when "cultural nationalism" is confronted by "revolutionary nationalism."

In every prerevolutionary period, certain political phenomena are inevitable. Following a period of civil-rights demands and passive resistance to felt oppression, there arises a longer or shorter phase of a separatist and militant "cultural nationalism."

In the United States, Dr. Martin Luther King, Jr., led the nonviolent, *Negro* civil-rights drive, which began to give way in the early 1960s to the militant *Black* nationalist movement. The agrarian, religious, Southern base shifted to an urban, Northern, cultural focus. The transitional figure was Malcolm X. Stokely Carmichael, LeRoi Jones and Ron Karenga represented different accents in the changing pattern of Black Culture.

According to revolutionary historical theory, at a given moment in time this cultural nationalism comes to a dead end and must freeze into a kind of reactionary racial separation or rise to the higher level of mature *revolutionary* nationalism, where class begins to supersede caste or race and go on from there to internationalism, or what Huey P. Newton calls "intercommunalism." The life and death of Malcolm X was a personification of this identity struggle between the past and the future, the religious and the material, the national and the international.

Malcolm X is the link in the long black chain of rebellion as old as slavery itself. Expunged from white, Western "history," the reports of the slaves' resistance have begun, lately, to come in. The movement for civil and human rights in our time builds on all the unnamed fighters and those, later, like Denmark Vesey, Gabrial, Nat Turner, Sojourner Truth and John Brown's men, who shot their way into that same majority history.

The Black Studies movement of the middle 1960s was an attempt to rescue this minority history. The cultural nationalist movement played a part in bringing the past of black America to the fore. At U.C.L.A., as elsewhere, a conflict flashed over the direction of the Black Studies program: the Panthers wanted to look ahead to struggle and power, the nationalists backward to "identity."

The modern human-rights movement in America has gone through three stages. In its first stage, to use a psychological schema, it was "infantile." It was a Southern, agrarian, Christian, matriarchal movement; it was nonviolent; it depended on trust; like a good child, it put itself at the mercy of those who hold power. It was transcendental—"truth crushed to earth will rise again"; "we shall overcome *someday.*" It was metaphysical, and political only in its implications.

In the early 1960s, that movement began to be replaced by what we now know as the "cultural nationalist" movement. This was urban, male, adolescent, and it was a psychological movement. The first movement had been religious and infantile; the second was to be psychological and adolescent, but no longer transcendental. It was existential—"Freedom now"; "Hell, no! We won't go!" The politics were those of *petit-bourgeois* rebellion.

When the cold-war liberals and the crackpot pragmatists sold out the Southern nonviolent movement in Atlantic City in 1964, young men like Stokely Carmichael took off their L.B.J. buttons, put quotes around the word *nonviolent* (Student Nonviolent Co-ordinating Committee) and went North. Malcolm was a star that was rising. The voice that spoke for the deracinated urban masses was authentic, while the Biblical rhetoric of the preachers was becoming an anomaly. Out of the ruins of the Negro stepped the first generation of black men. Black was power, black was beautiful. The existential leap had been made. The ghetto was purged of the White Devil. Time passed.

It was a swindle. Suicide and genocide hung over the urban concentration camps like a plague. The psychological, adolescent, black-nationalist movement was playing out. The riotous rebellions were co-opted by ministers and magicians. There was a vacuum of power.

Suddenly the heir of Malcolm X appears in the streets. Huey P. Newton—the armed intellectual who could, as Eldridge Cleaver was later to say, "bring out the niggers who were *under* the mud"—stands there with his gun and his love.

The third phase of the American human-rights revolution has now gotten into clear view. The birth pangs are over. The psychological, adolescent cultural nationalist movement is giving way inexorably to the mature, political, revolutionary internationalist and, now, intercommunalist movement.

The new phase represents an enormous challenge. The cultural nationalism of the psychological movement is forever a part of the American version of the human-rights movement, whether it be in names, hairstyles, dress, or a sense of African historical identity. It is subsumed now in the new movement, just as the idea of radical Christian love and soul, from the first, infantile, religious movement, is subsumed in the revolutionary core of the new vanguard. (For instance, Panther free clinics and food for children are "non-violent.") The movement has come out on the other side.

Once again it is "black and white together," but this time not on a parent-infant basis, but on a revolutionary level of equality, of suffering and risk together. But now it is the vanguard that is black! With Huey P. Newton, the genetic agenda advanced fatefully; the "manhood" and "womanhood" of the movement had begun. Religion and psychology have given way not to guns but to *politics*. Revolutionary politics—that is, that exact calibration of love and hate in action which can liberate the *renaissance* locked in the unconscious of the dumb; Newton refers to it when he says, "The spirit of the people is greater than Man's technology."

The new politics of black liberation is a revolutionary dialectical materialism: Marxism, psychoanalysis, existentialism, and Huey P. Newton's "intercommunalism."

Before the trial was over, public criticism of the Black Panther Party would be in full cry, but the most far-reaching of the criticisms would come from Newton and Seale themselves.

"When you make men slaves you deprive them of half their virtue, you set them in your own conduct an example of fraud, rapine and cruelty . . . and yet you complain that they are not honest or faithful," wrote an eighteenth-century slave.

Caliban is taught the ruler's language, and he rewards the generosity with curses. These curses are the literary movement of *Negritude* in Europe, and the primitive nationalism of Haiti's Papa Doc. But the old white face soon bleeds through the beautiful black mask of Negritude, and voodoo nationalism soon enough becomes fascism.

To the Panthers the adolescent movement of black nationalism is the subjective minor term in the dialectical process toward a classless community of character in the same way that the old nation is now ready for translation into the world of "intercommunalism."

It is Frantz Fanon who gives the last word on this ordeal. "To believe that it is possible to create a black culture," he wrote in 1961, "is to forget that niggers are disappearing just as those people who brought them into being are seeing the breakup of their economic and cultural supremacy." The Panthers had exposed the masks, both black and white, and there were many who would never forgive or forget.

If a national minority is not driven past its cultural identity it becomes as politically impotent as a St. Patrick's Day parade or a Purim festival. All that is left are the once powerful symbols, now merely children's rattles. If a majority cultural nationalism, as opposed to the American black minority, should come to power,

then one would see the metaphysical State, Nazi Germany or
Duvalier's Haiti. Nostalgia and fascism—nationalism is suicide
because it insists on a "master race."

It was Huey Newton and Bobby Seale who in 1966 began to
build on the last revolutionary avatar of the murdered Malcolm X.
(He was murdered because he gave up cultural and racial sepa-
ratism, the Panthers argue.) From studying the writings of the
Third World prophet and depth psychologist, Frantz Fanon, the
early Panthers were able to predict that revolutionaries, simply by
their existence, would soon expose the nationalists as failed middle-
class intellectuals and elitists. The adolescent metaphysics of the
cultural phase would break before the dialectical materialism of
the revolutionary; the juvenile clothing, symbols, slogans and
pseudo history of the cultural-identity struggle would be replaced
by the master symbol of technology—the gun—in the hands of the
"bad niggers," the wretched of the earth, the black communists.
The adolescent phase gives way, painfully, to the manhood (and,
sometime later, *womanhood*) of the movement.

So, in 1968, the "beautiful" black unity began to shred. Not
much longer could dashikis and black leather jackets coexist. At
U.C.L.A. the large cultural-nationalist organization, US, was moving to control the important Black Studies program. Poor black
students, having read their fill of African princes, kings and
Swahili, were now responding more and more to the revolutionary
concept of class-plus-color as the determining factor for liberation.
Bunchy Carter and Jon Huggins won the hearts of many uncom-
mitted students by insisting that the chairman of the new department be chosen by the students themselves (local control) and
not by the off-campus US leadership. At the same time the *Wall
Street Journal* reported that Ron Karenga, the head of US, had
held meetings with the Rockefellers, the Governor of California,
and the Mayor of Los Angeles! Karenga was booed off the
U.C.L.A. campus when he tried to take over the voting for
chairman.

The next day, high-ranking US members shot and killed Bunchy
Carter and Ericka Huggins' husband, Jon.

There were to be other killings, and sometimes only verbal violence, as when Stokely Carmichael resigned from the Panthers,

giving his antipathy to socialism as his reason. Rootless, he was to go in search of that oldest of chimeras, the Pan-African Movement. "It's not a question of Left or Right, it's a question of black."

Over and over, the Panther leadership has explained its position. For example, Huey P. Newton in an interview:

> We don't suffer in the hangup of a skin color. We don't hate white people; we hate the oppressor. And if the oppressor happens to be white then we hate him. When he stops oppressing us then we no longer hate him. And right now in America you have the slavemaster being a white group. We are pushing him out of office through revolution in this country. I think the responsibility of the white revolutionary will be to aid us in this. And when we are attacked by the police or by the military then it will be up to the white mother-country radicals to attack the murderers and to respond as we respond, to follow our program. . . .
>
> The resistance by white radicals in Berkeley during the past three nights is a good indication that the white radicals are on the way home. They have identified their enemies. The white radicals have integrated theory with practice. They realize the American system is the real enemy but in order to attack the American system they must attack the ordinary cop. In order to attack the educational system they must attack the ordinary teacher. Just as the Vietnamese people to attack the American system must attack the ordinary soldier.

Bobby Seale at a "Free Huey" rally:

> We're just waiting for this racism to break down when we see the poor white Appalachians up in the mountains copy our same Ten-Point Platform and Program and go forth to destroy the Nixons, the Reagans, and the pig Aliotos. When the Party says "Power to the People," we ain't jiving a pound!

All to no avail; the majority press seldom missed a beat in pumping out stories about the "separatists," "nationalists" or "black racists."

Against Pan-Africanism the Panthers pose their new "intercommunalism," world communism; against a beautiful black aristocracy in long and straight descent from kings, the Panthers proclaim the hectic imagery of "niggers under the mud," the marginal workers and fateful *lumpenproletariat,* and their hot breakfasts for children (that fed 15,000 a day before the big raids and arrests), free clinics, visiting programs for prisoners' families and liberation schools.

There were no warrants for the arrests in New Haven, or for the search or the seizure of property. The seven people arrested were taken to the police station and held incommunicado. Lawyers who tried to reach them that night were physically prevented from doing so.

The Fourth Amendment to the Constitution states: "The right of the people to be secure in their persons, houses, papers and effects against unreasonable searches and seizures, shall not be violated, and no warrants shall issue, but upon probable cause, supportd by oath or affirmation, and particularly describing the place to be searched, and the persons and things to be seized."

It had all been predicated, the police argued, on information supplied by a "trusted ten-year informant." If authorities can convince a judge to take their "informant's" word on faith, the name of the "informant" (to use the law-enforcement agency's ungrammatical euphemism) need never be revealed.

The hot summer saw six more Panther arrests. Loretta Luckes was arrested in New Haven; Landon Williams and Rory Hithe in Denver, where they were still fighting extradition as the Seale-Huggins trial began; Lonnie McLucas in Salt Lake City; George Sams, Jr., in Toronto, Canada. Bobby Seale, chairman of the Black Panther Party, was last. George Sams's confession was the only bit of evidence linking Seale to the case.

During the search for these defendants, police and F.B.I. agents raided Panther Party headquarters all across the country. Police stormed into the headquarters in Washington, Denver, Indianapolis, Salt Lake City, Des Moines, Detroit, San Diego, Chicago; and in nearly every case they smashed or confiscated office equipment, literature, supplies and money, and arrested whoever was there on charges that were often dropped later. The Chicago office underwent a series of attacks. The F.B.I. conducted an armed raid on

June 8 and confiscated, among other items, a petition with nine thousand signatures for the release of Illinois Party Chairman Fred Hampton. As the events of December 4, 1969, have shown, Hampton may have been safer in prison. On that awful night, police shot Fred Hampton and Mark Clark to death. Fred Hampton was still in his bed. By the time of the New Haven trial, hundreds of Panthers were dead, in exile, or in prison. The exact body count was to become a poisonous controversy during jury selection.

As George Sams traveled around the country, spending large sums of money, certain things began to happen to the Panthers. Each city he visited was thereafter subjected to predawn raids by combinations of city, state and federal police. But Sams was never caught; he always managed to leave before the raids were made. In Chicago, he said that he had walked, armed, through the police and F.B.I. lines.

When Sams came to New Haven, in May of 1969, he found a young and inexperienced group, none of whom were actually Panthers except Ericka Huggins. Later, Huey Newton begged the pardon "of the people for our inexperience" and detailed that the sick Sams could not even get psychotherapy in a society "as depraved as America." The Panther leader said that he "pitied" Sams, he didn't hate him.

As it turned out, George Sams, Jr., was a victim as well as a murderer. Everyone connected with the death of Alex Rackley, however tenuously, paid dearly for being who they were.

After the state's conspiracy, then, as the Panthers theorize, the local police and courts became the mortal instruments.

The Panthers operate amphibiously: they explain phenomena in revolutionary political terms but are quite capable of speaking the traditional legal language of the Constitution as their chairman had done so insistently in Chicago when he faced charges of conspiracy to riot—charges that eventually were dropped.

The Party's rapport with attorney Charles R. Garry and Huey Newton's early interest in the law had brought this double approach of the Panthers to a high pitch. They see their tactics as dialectical and not contradictory. The Panthers believe in a full-dress legal defense in the courtroom and a large and, at the same time, disciplined crowd in the street adjoining. So, when Alex Rackley was murdered the Black Panther Party announced a reasoned legal analysis of the state's actions in the more narrow or criminal sense that the authorities themselves use. While the revolutionary propaganda was broadcast to the movement and to the world, the legal dialogue was joined in the courts. The two sides of the dialectic could be fused, if at all, only by Charles R. Garry, later in New Haven at the trial's climax. But first the Newton-Garry strategy would be unleashed—"Exhausting all legal means."

The great division which was to come in the Black Panther Party during the trial was, in some measure, between the extra-legal underground and the aboveground with its strategy of using the law and the courts politically. Charles Garry was to be damned as one of the architects of this "revisionist" approach.

It is Marxist canon that the revolutionary exhausts the legal means and ideals of a society and that then the State is forced to violate its own laws in order to repress the will of "the people." The State must be brought to the point of breaking its own laws to cause the public to disassociate, in its mind, the idea of the nation from the illegal government. The revolution becomes the nation, and the former rulers are now the outlaws. Thus the trials take on a supreme dialectical importance.

The Panthers insist that they are and will continue to be a legal, public, political party. They dread being forced underground. Anyone breaking into the New Haven courtroom with guns would doom the Panthers' hopes of being the vanguard party of liberation. They believe that when they have "exhausted all legal means" and the government has repressed them in a criminal fashion, then "the people" will rise, as Huey Newton predicts, "like a mighty storm." For the Panthers believe in the *People* of History the way the revolutionaries of the Enlightenment believed in the God of Nature.

The only "truth" is the people; and only the people, they say, can set them free.

Back in New Haven, the grand jury met to issue indictments against the fourteen defendants. Grand juries meet in secret; they can compel testimony from a witness in the absence of his attorney and deny cross-examination and discovery of state's evidence. The selection of the grand jury is not random. In New Haven County, Sheriff Slavin, the same man responsible for the custody of prisoners, selects the members of the jury. Slavin had stated in the New Haven *Register* that he picked persons whom he "knew." He added that he kept no records of when a person last served. In other words, he was free to pick his political friends and allow them to serve as often as they liked. A *New York Times* article carried the "amusing information that the median age of the grand jury members was over sixty and that one of them was the Sheriff's barber and another, the owner of the barbershop. One member had served fourteen times."

This body handed down indictments for murder, kidnapping, conspiracy and binding with criminal intent against Warren Kimbro, Lonnie McLucas, Bobby Seale and George Sams, and for being an accessory to murder, for kidnaping, conspiracy and binding against Ericka Huggins, Frances Carter, George Edwards, Margaret Hudgins, Loretta Luckes, Rose Smith, Landon Williams and Rory Hithe. Murder, accessory to murder and kidnaping are all capital crimes, punishable by death. Conspiracy to kidnap carries a penalty of fifteen years' imprisonment; conspiracy to murder, fifty years; and binding, twenty-five years.

In January, 1970, the state arranged what the defense claimed was a secret and illegal visit to Warren Kimbro by his eldest brother, a police officer. A few days after the visit, on January 16, Kimbro pleaded guilty to second-degree murder. He may have been convinced that a fair trial was impossible, and, under pressure from his family, made a deal with the prsoecution to save his life. Then his sentence would depend on how cooperative he was in testifying at the trials.

George Sams's bitterness toward the Black Panther Party is hard to pinpoint. He gave the grand jury two reasons why Rackley was murdered. The first reason was to put a scare into the New Haven chapter and the second was to avenge the "New York Twenty-one."

Sams admitted, every time he testified, to initiating the torture of Rackley, but he said that Rackley had the power to leave whenever he wished.

Then, in August of 1970, Lonnie McLucas was convicted of

conspiracy to murder; maximum penalty fifteen years. The other charges of kidnapping, conspiracy to kidnap and binding with intent to commit a crime were dropped. The New Haven community proclaimed it a "fair trial." All the other arrested Panthers, except Bobby Seale and Ericka Huggins, were set free for undisclosed reasons.

The New York Times said that Lonnie McLucas broke into a radiant smile when Huey P. Newton came to his trial and gave him the clenched-fist salute. Who was McLucas?

Lonnie McLucas was born in 1945 in Wade, which is twelve miles from Fayetteville, North Carolina. In describing his early life, he says, "My father used to work all day behind two mules, from sun-up until sun-down, then work half the night in the sawmill. At twenty-five cents an hour, there were lots of times when my father, working at two jobs, could not make five dollars in twenty-four hours. There were a lot of times when there was no food at home."

According to his mother, "Lonnie was known as one of the best kids in Wade. He was always a leader. He was in the Boys Club and the Boy Scouts." As Lonnie puts it, "People were always coming to me with their problems, and for them to do this was like food for me, because this was and still is what I want to do more than anything else, 'Serve the People.' "

He had come North, of course, joined the Panthers and begun his training for death or prison. His New Jersey notes read:

Things accomplished while in Morristown: saved a policeman's life, directed traffic, dealt with personal problems, stopped street fights, saved a young boy's life, helped three people from going to jail, got jobs for lots of people.

Lonnie McLucas was separated from the others, tried and convicted. This was done, the defense claimed, to poison the atmosphere, to make selection of a fair jury impossible and to ensure the conviction and execution of the chairman of the Black Panther Party, Bobby Seale, who had been the target all along, and with him Ericka Huggins.

Charles Garry poked his gray head out the door of the Yale Law School. He started toward the court, walking fast. He always walked, to court as well as in court, hardly ever stopping. Across the street from the school, flowing past him, was the big cemetery. Over the gate was the declaration *The Dead Shall Rise.* "Balls," muttered Garry, striding toward the Municipal Court and seven months of ordeal.

THE FIRST DAY (NOVEMBER 17, 1970)

It begins.

THE STATE OF CONNECTICUT
VS.
BOBBY G. SEALE

Arnold Markle, State's Attorney for the County of New Haven, accuses Bobby G. Seale of: 1) Kidnapping; 2) Conspiracy to commit kidnapping; 3) Murder in the first degree; 4) Conspiracy to commit murder.

THE STATE OF CONNECTICUT
VS.
ERICKA HUGGINS

Arnold Markle, State's Attorney for the County of New Haven, accuses Ericka Huggins of: 1) Kidnapping; 2) Conspiracy to commit kidnapping; 3) Murder in the first degree; 4) Conspiracy to commit murder; 5) Binding with intent to commit a crime.

On the steps a few young black women are singing softly to their children, "The revolution has come, time to pick up the gun."

On the first day of the trial of Huey P. Newton in Oakland, California, three years before, ten thousand partisans roared the singsong battle cry. . . . Today, in New Haven, a handful of supporters walk diffidently into the murky old courthouse, there in the hall to be outnumbered by the press. The Seale-Huggins case, perhaps the most political trial since that of Sacco-Vanzetti or of Rosenberg-Sobell, is starting with a whimper.

It seemed like France on the eve of the Dreyfus Affair, as an English visitor reported.

There began to be discernible a distaste for life, an incapacity for effort, a renunciation of ideals. It was a period of fatigue and decline, of mysticism and sensuality in literature and the arts. The heroic ages were past, and the country had lost faith in its destiny.

Or, as some of the Panther *lumpen* put it, "the motherfuckers [the white peace or antiwar movement] have split again."

If there had been any extra observers they might have echoed the English journalist, George W. Steevens, who complained in 1898 that, "I looked out for the keen little knots of journalists, gendarmes, anti-Semites, Dreyfusards, and secret agents, who, as I knew, keep Argus-eyes on Rennes railway station from midday to midnight and on to midday again. There was apparently not a single journalist, gendarme, anti-Semite, Dreyfusard, or secret agent in the place."

Though there are a few of each in New Haven, it is uncannily like 1950 and unlike what had been predicted for the 1970s.

The now irrelevant sign in front of the courthouse was the only testimony of the last May's thunder on the Left.

By the order of the Superior Court there shall be no demonstrations, pickets, parades, or the like in the Courthouse, 121 Elm Street, New Haven, or within 500 feet in any direction of the Courthouse. The above excludes the confines of the New Haven Green.
April 9, 1970.

The crowd waits for an hour and a half in the radiator-stifling municipal hall. Outside, the Yale Green shines in the clear, cold air and sunshine. Police and agents are everywhere; the CBS television artist has his four sketches of people waiting in line confiscated; there is no place to sit. In all the public buildings—walls covered with quotations about Democracy and Justice—there is never a place to rest. In these halls of justice the poor seem to stand in an endless corridor from birth to death, from the county hospital in the beginning to the coroner's anteroom in the end. Everything is stone and marble, Romanesque columns, vaulted arches; and balconies, high up in the echoing half-light, from where guards and plainclothesmen peer down on the foreshortened shufflers waiting in the gloom for the Man, with his obligatory official piece of paper. There is no rest in these edifices that are dedicated to "the people." Later, sheriffs would actually pass out scraps of paper to the first people in the waiting line, and the immemorial bureaucratic mime would be complete.

The municipal labyrinth always as Allen Ginsberg called it, "Malach! Malach! Nightmare of Malach! Malach the loveless! Malach, the heavy judger of men! Malach the crossboned, soulless jailhouse and Congress of sorrows! Malach whose buildings are judgment!" Malach disguised as the "City of Elms" or the "School of Churches" or, better, the "Model City." The building sits facing the Green like a mausoleum. It is always under police surveillance, and at night it is guarded by state troopers armed with rifles.

Here, the radicals had predicted, the entire movement would come to demonstrate its new strength, flex its young muscles and set the Chairman and Ericka free; here in New Haven the toughs of the tender Left would—in the words of the poet of the concentration camp, Nellie Sachs—take the ball out of the hands of the terrible players. But the throngs of May Day had melted away, and the first childish worship of the Panthers had given way to an equally childish ambivalence toward yesterday's heroes who had proved human and had dared to fail. The bad blacks had, of course, drawn the lightning, and the beautiful students had taken a step backward and stopped, at long last, their echolalia of "Power to the People!" and "Right on!"

But on May Day, the previous spring, *everything* had seemed possible.

An anonymous National Guardsman later wrote that the Guard had been promised that they would "not be prosecuted if you shoot someone while performing a duty for the State of Connecticut." There was not much violence beyond a bomb that exploded after an antidemonstration telephone warning and a fire in the Center for New Politics, a reform-Democratic site. The Panthers circled the crowds constantly calling through loudspeakers for a disciplined, legal demonstration. Even the police paid them credit for the climate that led, the chief said, to "fewer arrests than on an ordinary weekend." When the new governor of Connecticut reminisced about May Day, almost a year later, he had forgotten the part played by the Panthers.

The newspapers and politicians, local and national, did their worst, but provocation was avoided; armed force, however, was in evidence, a huge systemic wave on which the rational, abstract legal trial was merely a chip.

Civil libertarians formed a "Coalition to Defend the Black Panthers." By November 10, 1969, they were ready to act: "This morning the Coalition attempted to meet with the State's Attorney. He refused to see us, asserting that he was so prevented by the recent court order. The purpose of our visit was to request that he release the three pregnant Panther women immediately, on their own recognizance, and grant reasonable bail for the other jailed Panthers.

"The continued denial of bail prevents the preparation of an adequate defense, violates their right to the presumption of innocence, and punishes them without trial.

"The Coalition clearly does not come under the recent court order, prepared without consultation with the defense attorneys. Our intent was not to discuss any factual aspects of the Panther case. Our sole purpose was to demand that the Panthers receive the fair treatment which the Constitution guarantees them."

The Human Relations Council was also visible. The New Haven *Register,* in an editorial, took notice of this ethical intervention.

The Human Relations Council of Greater New Haven in one of its contradictory and confusing publicity releases has attempted to defend and explain the Black Panthers by a smear attack upon the press.

The press is said to have sensationalized what the Council calls in quotation marks "evidence" against the Panthers. This and the claim that "the press must act more responsibly" is an outright distortion.

New Haven's newspapers, and other channels of information, have presented the official facts, as officially released by the FBI, the State Police and New Haven police, on the Black Panther murder charges. It is our public responsibility to do so—unless we are to have secret trials and secret decisions. The Human Relations Council's intervention at this point in the case is far less responsible than the things for which it criticizes the press.

The Council also claims that "an atmosphere now exists in this community which makes it all but impossible to find jurors who are not convinced of the guilt of the defendants."

This, of course, is sheer bigotry.

Since no trial is yet under way the Council has no more knowledge than any other person or agency about the ease or the difficulty of finding an unprejudiced juror. And in any event a change of venue, or removal of the trial to another community, is a standard consideration in such a case. The Human Relations Council, not content to accept such standard legal procedures, itself seems out to manipulate public opinion and to influence justice in this matter.

The official charge in this case involves murder. A man is dead.

An expression of proper regard for the rights and the position of the indicted Black Panthers is wholly within the scope of the Human Relations Council's community role. To extend this concern to an attack upon the press for fulfilling its separate and independent duty to provide public information in a criminal case of this gravity is unfair, incorrect, and in itself irresponsible.

On October 20, the Council pointed out "two dangerous elements of this arrest and the factors surrounding it," which, it said, must be considered by everyone in the area.

They are, "the pretrial publicity, which seriously jeopardizes the possibility of a fair trial, and the emotionalism about the Black Panthers, which is being used as an excuse to undermine the entire movement toward racial justice and equality.

"We believe that concern about this case transcends the question of the guilt or innocence of the defendants, and also transcends the question of whether we accept or reject the tactics and programs of the Black Panther Party," the Council said.

The Council also believed that "all too many people are using their feelings about the Black Panthers as an excuse for 'copping out' of this country's responsibility to provide freedom and justice for all people.

"It is clear that the situation of black people becomes more desperate each day," the Council warned. "Many of us are under the impression that great progress is being made towards equality of opportunity, simply because we talk about it." The Council quoted the Urban Coalition as saying that on the contrary, there is "not even a serious start toward the change in national programs, priorities and institutions" which would bring about a change in black people's lives.

"Here in our urban center," the Council continued, "we have known for years that one of every three inner-city residents lives in overcrowded conditions, that one of every four black and Puerto Rican residents lives in substandard housing. One result of these simple statistics is that the minds of children are being destroyed by lead poisoning from the criminally decrepit walls of the disaster areas which they are forced to occupy. While these conditions fester, America's vast energies are spent elsewhere."

The movement came to the New Haven Green for May Day, but the groups of concerned clergy and individuals from the local environs stayed on to work in their modest way long after the heroes and heavies, the toughs of the tender Left, had gone home.

As May 1 drew near, the campus became a rumor mill. Francine du Plessix Gray, in the *New York Review of Books,* reported that

There were rumors that Boston radicals planning to attend the rally had been purchasing guns in Massachusetts; that some 300 Minutemen had reserved rooms in motels adjoining New Haven; that a machine gun had been posted on the tower of Calhoun College; that in the bloody fray caused on Harvard Square the previous week by the November Action group, young radicals dressed as policemen had beaten up kids to incite provocation and were planning to repeat this tactic on May Day. The most ghoulish speculation heard was that if the virology lab on Wall Street was bombed, all its Lassa Fever viruses might spread through town.

But the guns were at Kent State, later that spring, and when the Seale-Huggins trial opened in November the movement seemed to have vanished.

To 20,000 people on the Green on May Day, Jean Genet delivered a frugal, lucid message that concluded:

As for Bobby Seale, I repeat, there must not be another Dreyfus Affair. Therefore, I count on you, on all of you, to spread the contestation abroad, to speak of Bobby Seale in your families, in the universities, in your courses and classrooms: you must contest and occasionally contradict your professors and the police themselves.

And, I say it once more, for it is important, what is at stake are no longer symbolic gestures, but real actions. And if it comes to this—I mean, if the Black Panther Party asks it of you—you must desert your universities, leave your classrooms in order to carry the word across America in favor of Bobby Seale and against racism.

The life of Bobby Seale, the existence of the Black Panther Party, come first, ahead of your diplomas. You must now—and you have the physical, material, and intellectual means to do so—you must now face life directly and no longer in comfortable aquariums—I mean the American universities—which raise goldfish capable of no more than blowing bubbles.

The life of Bobby Seale depends on you. Your real life depends on the Black Panther Party.

The one who announced himself as the first witness at the trial of Bobby Seale had to send his deposition from somewhere in the Third World. Eldridge Cleaver's manifesto gave a core of desperation to the thing that Seale and Huggins would undergo, that was insoluble.

CONCERNING: The pre-planned political murder of Bobby Seale, Chairman of the Black Panther Party, in the electric chair in the state of Connecticut. . . .

Black people will never accept this premeditated decision of the fascist power structure to murder Chairman Bobby Seale in the Electric Chair. So that the question is now posed, pure and simple: Is America going to have a Class War or a Race War? . . .

So if the so-called freedom-loving White people of America do not stand up now, while there are still a few moments of time left, and put an end to the persecution of Chairman Bobby Seale, then Black people will have to go it alone and step forward alone. This will mean the end of our dreams for the Class War which America needs and the beginning of the Race War which America cannot endure. This is the political consequence which America faces because of this unspeakably evil attempt to murder Chairman Bobby Seale in the Electric Chair.

But Cleaver's famous voice was not heard again during the trial.

When Huey P. Newton came out of prison in 1970 and visited

Harlem for the first time, people poured into the steets. One
brother off the block embraced Huey and insisted that "I back you
a hundred percent. I can't go for no socialism, but I'm with you all
the way." "Why do you support me," Huey asked, "if you don't
believe in socialism?" "Because you killed a cop!" "But, I
didn't." Huey faced him; the man did a little dance with his hands,
"I know you have to say that, brother."

There are millions of these men whom the Panthers hope to
inspire with "revolutionary love" to "serve the people." These
lumpenproletariat, Cleaver is predicting, will turn away in fury
from the Panthers if their white coalitions prove to be just one
more impotent "jive," and that the Seale-Huggins trial is the litmus
test of the class strategy versus the race strategy.

The press files in to sit against one wall facing the empty jury
box. Thirty-three spectators are searched and passed in to sit in an
alcove, where they can see only a fraction of the courtroom. The
setting is in miniature, the sheriffs are in plain clothes, the style is
New Haven, a small university town. The reason given for the tiny
courtroom is something about "air-conditioning" but the operative
word here is control.

It is also difficult to hear. The prosecution sits behind the defense. Only Judge Harold M. Mulvey can be seen full face; sometimes his lips move, but his voice does not carry. Sometimes,
suddenly, as if a large fan had been turned off, the vocal exchanges
ring out clear, there is no pattern. The big Roman clock over the
press section runs a quarter hour behind and sometimes—again
without pattern—a series of reportlike superticks intrudes noisily.
The two windows behind the jury box are newly bullet-proofed.

Bobby Seale and Ericka Huggins are led in quietly, almost
before anyone has noticed. He has flashed the sharp smile and
snapped the tight-fist salute to the Panthers in the front row whom
he, once seated, will hardly be able to see. Facing the judge, from
left to right, it is Charles R. Garry, Bobby Seale, David Rosen,
Catherine Roraback and Ericka Huggins. Nearly six feet tall, very
thin, leashed in, in a plain and random dress, Ericka Huggins is
unforgettable. The Panther women, three pregnant, had been in

isolation in floodlighted cells and on low-vitamin diets until Womens Liberation and a number of doctors forced the issue sharply. Now Ericka Huggins is alone, the others plea-bargained away to "freedom."

Bobby Seale bristles with energy—vital, tall and lean, in smooth greens and blues. He had said of Bunchy Carter, murdered with Ericka's husband, Jon:

We all have some sharp clothes, but Bunchy was always sharp—clean, with a sharp suit, pimp socks and shined knobs. Little Bobby would see Bunchy with his big natural that was kept very neat, a big moustache, a sharp suit, and some clean clothes on, and he really dug the way Bunchy looked.

(Knobs are up-to-date, stylish shoes, with well-shined toes. Pimp socks are men's socks you can almost see through; they are usually nylon.)

Who is this "Chairman" of the Black Panther Party? The nation had perceived him as a madman in Judge Julius Hoffman's Chicago courtroom. The movement had seen him as the apotheosis of American black protest, chained and gagged, staring with outrage and grief at the pictures of George Washington and Benjamin Franklin that hung above Judge Hoffman. Bobby Seale is an American.

(As the camera pulls back we see it is BOBBY SEALE, and he is running. He hurdles a fence, picks up six red bricks in the back yard, carries them to a street corner and breaks them in half. He waits, breathing heavily, sweating, and when the first car driven by a white person passes he throws the half brick at it. The brick hits the car on the side door. The driver looks, sees BOBBY, and drives off quickly. He waits, another car, this time the brick goes through a back window. The driver stops the car and stares at BOBBY. BOBBY stares back. The driver, a white man in his early fifties, drives off. BOBBY sits on the curb, his head in his hands and begins to cry. Two young black men approach him. One speaks.)
KEN: Bobby.
(BOBBY does not answer. His crying, however, subsides considerably.)

KEN: Bobby, c'mon. It's me, Kenny.
(BOBBY stands. He holds a half brick in each hand. The man puts his arm around BOBBY.)
BOBBY: Get away. You niggers are all crazy.
KEN: C'mon Bobby.
BOBBY: Malcolm's dead.
KEN: We know.
BOBBY: You know?
KEN: Yeah.
BOBBY: What the fuck are you gonna do?
(KEN shrugs his shoulders as if to indicate that nothing can be done. BOBBY drops both bricks. He walks over to a store on the corner.)
BOBBY: Fuck it. I'll make my own self into a motherfucking Malcolm X, and if they want to kill me they'll have to kill me.
(BOBBY smashes his fist through the store window. It is a small pane of glass. His hand begins to bleed.)
OTHER MAN: What the fuck did you do that for?
BOBBY: You don't understand?
KEN: I don't understand either.
BOBBY: Then that's your problem!

So he is the risen phoenix from the ashes of Malcolm X. But he has many identities, because Bobby George Seale is legion, a gifted actor, an artist of metempsychosis: when Huey P. Newton, another of his souls, was in prison, Bobby Seale would invoke his presence so that a multitude knew what Huey's soft voice sounded like before they ever heard him in person. He would bring the murdered Bunchy Carter and Fred Hampton back to life; or suddenly a white liberal sociologist would pop out of his mouth talking about "socioeconomic determinants of . . . ," and preachers, professors, Panthers were always available to his gift.

But most of all he was the apotheosis of a little-known black archetype called "Stagolee." Stagolee is a many-sided mythic image. Stagolee is, first, a continuous genetic human bridge stretching over almost half a millennium from his half-man status in the new world to the black cadre of America's new national-liberation struggle. Seale was predictable when he said of his book *Seize the Time:*

I dedicate this book to my wife, Artie, to Ericka, the widow of Jon Huggins, to my son, Malik Nkrumah Stagolee Seale, and his brother.

One of my son's names derives from the lumpen proletarian politically unaware brothers in the streets. Stagolee fought his brothers and sisters, and he shouldn't have. The Stagolees of today should take on the messages of Malcolm X as Huey Newton did, to oppose this racist, capitalist oppression of our people and other peoples are subjected to.

Malik must not fight his brothers. One is named after revolutionaries of our times, and me, who loves both of them. Power to the youth; all power to the people and power to the latest-born in the Black Panther Party, little Huey Bunchy (Li'l) Bobby Jon Eric Eldridge Seale, whose mother is Rose Mary. Brothers and sisters will struggle together in unity from generation to generation for liberation and freedom with the love we fathers and mothers who brought our young ones into the world.

The name is a touchstone for all the new Panther children, the flesh and blood of the first generation of martyrs and heroes, the future being molded in the crucible of revolution and rebellion and repression.

Stagolee and his female counterpart, "fast-talking Fanny," are also the "field niggers" that Bobby Seale always talks about so proudly, that the Panthers love as much as they despise the "boot-licking house nigger." It must be Stagolee.

When my wife, Artie, had a baby boy, I said, "the nigger's name is Malik Nkrumah Stagolee Seale."

"I don't want him named that!" Artie said.

I had read all that book history about Stagolee, that black folkloric history, because I was hung up on that stuff at the time, so I said, Malik Nkrumah Stagolee Seale."

"Why Stagolee?" Artie asked.

"Because Stagolee was a bad nigger off the block and didn't take shit from nobody. All you had to do was organize him, like Malcolm X, make him politically conscious. All we have to do is organize a state, like Nkrumah attempted to do."

Nkrumah was a bad motherfucker and Malcolm X was a bad nigger. Huey P. Newton showed me the nigger on the block was ten motherfuckers when politically educated, and if you got him organized. I said, "Stagolee, put Stagolee on his name," because Stagolee was an unorganized nigger, to me, like a brother on the block. I related to Huey P.

Newton because Huey was fighting niggers on the block. Huey was a nigger that came along and he incorporated Malcolm X, he incorporated Stagolee, he incorporated Nkrumah, all of them.

"The nigger out of prison *knows*," Huey used to say. "The nigger out of prison has seen the man naked and cold, and the nigger out of prison, he's got himself together, will come out just like Malcolm X came out of prison. You never have to worry about him. He'll go with you." That's what Huey related to, and I said, "Malik for Malcolm, Nkrumah Stagolee Seale."

Stagolee is transformed by an existential miracle into Huey P. Newton.

Huey P. Newton, Minister of Defense of the Black Panther Party, the baddest motherfucker ever to set foot in history. Huey P. Newton, the brother, black man, a nigger, the descendant of slaves, who stood up in the heart of the ghetto, at night, in alleys, confronted by racist pigs with guns and said: "My name is Huey P. Newton. I'm the Minister of Defense of the Black Panther Party. I'm standing on my constitutional rights. I'm not going to allow you to brutalize me. I'm going to stop you from brutalizing my people. You got your gun, pig, I got mine. If you shoot at me, I'm shooting back."

Huey Newton does not use the term *pig* very often now, he is shooting over the head of the police at the state and is working out an ideology for "Babylon." The years have passed, and Bobby Seale, too, has written an authentic work that is sheer American picaresque wherein "Bobby and Huey" become a kind of Tom and Huck in hell.

(BOBBY, HUEY and LI'L BOBBY HUTTON sell the Red Book.)
LI'L BOBBY: How do you say it, again?
HUEY: "Quotations from Chairman Mao Tse-tung."
BOBBY: Hey, all you white radicals get it together with Chairman Mao!
LI'L BOBBY: Hey, get your little Red Book.
(They hawk and sell at a great rate. A white radical walks up to LI'L BOBBY.)
RADICAL: Hey man. Where do you get those books?
LI'L BOBBY: That's for us to know and you to find out.

State's Attorney Arnold Markle and his detective Walter Schultz at his right hand must sit in back of the defense table. Both of them too small of stature to see over the heads of their opposition. They continually appear to write, but Mr. Markle's quick objections show that he is listening closely and only making markings on his paper most of the time, while pretending to work incessantly, never looking up. These two are stuck in the back area that, until Charles Garry made it an issue, was reserved for the defense. However, that is the New Haven way. (In the original seventeenth-century meeting-house every person had a place based on his standing in the community: those who did not need to work were called "Mister" and had first place; next came the "Brothers and Sisters"; and after them came those who were referred to as "Goodman and Goody"; no seats were assigned to the servants and slaves or anyone below the rank of Goodman or Goody.) And now, thanks to Garry's early contesting of each and every issue, including the seating arrangement and the *placing of the furniture* (just like a "communist"!), here are Mr. Markle and Schultz straining in vain to see over the Afros of the six-foot, one-inch Seale and this six-foot woman.

Charles Garry asks that the artists be allowed to sketch the proceedings. Denied. For the record he echoes Miss Roraback's observation that the absent jury panel is old—"my age," he says. They had all been introduced to the prospective jurors before, to make sure that no one knew any of the principals in the trial. This is a key to Western law—that the defendant is a stranger to the jury. It is the informal justice of all poor people that firsthand knowledge and judgment are inseparable. But here there would be Latin and numbers and the noises of strangers thrown together in a fateful word salad that rumor insisted would go on from 10 A.M. to 5 P.M., four days a week, for four months.

The sheriff's men seem to be Irish or Italian; the judge is Irish; the prosecutor is Jewish. The "ruling circle" itself, with its pale, far sea-look of New England, as Muriel Rukeyser called it, is not actually in attendance.

Bobby Seale, the same age as Bartolomeo Vanzetti when he

stood trial, found himself in Judge Mulvey's courtroom in New Haven, sitting at the table nearest the bench. Even this did not happen without a fight. Charles Garry, in his pretrial trip to New Haven, had demanded to know why the state had the favored table, while the defense was relegated to the rear. He fought, and the point was won. Arnold Markle and his investigative assistant Corporal Schultz were consigned to the back table, a change in *mise-en-scène* that Mr. Markle did not seem to appreciate as he shouted his questions and objections, from then on, toward the judge and witness box some twenty-five yards away in front of him. Mr. Markle's short stature insured that his line of vision, when he sat, was always trained on Bobby Seale's thick, tight black hair, forcing him to jump up whenever he wished to see the judge or the witness, and when the defense stood he could not see over them even when he stood.

Leonard Weinglass, a lawyer from the "Chicago Conspiracy," sits in the empty jury box, but there are no other notables. The trial is beginning with a strange silence, almost anonymity. In the preceding spring and summer, huge crowds on the Yale Green had made national news, now much of the movement had turned its attention to the Black Panther–sponsored Revolutionary People's Constitutional Convention to begin in Washington, D.C., after Thanksgiving. They would give the Panthers one more chance to fulfill white adolescent revolutionary dreams.

A sheriff raps on the jury door, and a Wallingford production foreman is guided to the witness stand to begin the *voir dire,* the "open speaking" that is one of the glories of Anglo-Saxon law.

Five hundred judges ("You will be a judge," Garry will tell them, "if you sit on the jury") have been abstracted from the surrounding Italian and Irish shore towns and the economically hard-hit Naugatuck Valley from Southbury and Seymour and Beaconfalls, North Haven, North Branford and Wallingford, West Haven, Cheshire and Guilford. Not from New Haven the "model city" or the Yale University community, lying behind a wall of class and power, but from Ascension Church, St. Boniface, Church of the Blessed Sacrament, St. Frances Cabrini, The Holy Infant Rectory, St. Mary's Church, Dominican Fathers, Our Lady of Mount Carmel, St. Stanislaus, Our Lady of Pompeii, Sacred Heart, and St. Vincent de Paul's.

Out of the past to sit and stare big-eyed at the unbelievable black future waiting for them at the defense table, then out again, helped by the sheriffs back into the corridor from where they came. Frightened, hard-working religious people. They are a tragedy whose first act was the Great Depression.

The defense table is, from left to right as it faces the judge, David Rosen, Seale, Garry, Catherine Roraback and, at the end corner, Huggins. At week three the order will be changed so that Ericka and Bobby can talk to each other—David Rosen, Bobby, Ericka, Katie Roraback, and Garry at the end. This black-and-white line of faces in the echoing and reduced chamber is a gantlet that each rejected retreating juror must pass on the way to safety outside the courtroom. They crawl along the floor of the arena—between the upraised bench and the strangers at the bar—at the mercy of the sheriffs who guide them silently back into the world, and as they leave, their hands still clasp and twitch in unconscious and unremitting supplication.

These talesmen are terrified. The great chain of being has been smashed flat, and every man (there are only men in this arena; juror after juror will say "sir" to Katie Roraback, who is very obviously a woman) is an insect, a Dostoevskian louse brought in here to be tortured by the glaring Seale and the mad beautiful woman who is writing poems left-handed, and who, when she does look up, stares right through a person.

Now everyone is watching the famous lawyer from San Francisco. He stands, intervening between the architecture and the ideology; the judge and the jury; the victims and the executioners.

Charles R. Garry. "The Lenin of the courtroom," Bobby Seale calls him.

"Goddamn Armenian" is what his schoolmates in the San Joaquin Valley of California called Charles Garabedian. He fought every day then; he has never stopped. Lean, tough, sixty-one years old at the time of the trial, he brought an original sense of physical combat to the courtroom.

His father, Hagop Robutlay, came to America from a mud cottage in Asia Minor. A Protestant and, thus, a religious rebel, he changed his name to Garabedian, his father's first name, as the son would change his to Garry. Thus, in English, Garry was Charles son of Charles. And Garry rebelled, ran away, rode the rods. The father led a strike against his own brother's shop! The son drove his motorcycle through fire and left Massachusetts after the Sacco-Vanzetti execution. He had been born there, in Bridgewater, in 1909.

His schooling was uneven—like that of Clarence Darrow, to whom he is often compared—because of poverty. He worked as a tailor and at odd jobs; when he passed the bar he took every kind of case, for experience, becoming a recognized authority in a wide range of practice from labor law to forensic medicine. As a member of the law firm of Garry, Dreyfus, McTernan and Brotsky, Garry was bringing in over $100,000 a year until, in 1967, he undertook the case of Huey P. Newton. Since then he has been out of the political courtroom only for an operation, during the "Chicago Conspiracy."

His father survived the 1897 Turkish massacre. Garry acts as if he is surviving his "beloved America." He worked in a cannery and at two other jobs at once and went to law school at night in conflict whether or not to go to Spain to fight for the Republic. Interrogated about Communist Party membership after the war, he replied, "Thou sayest." It was during this period that he accused big labor of "forgetting the masses . . . the unorganized, the unwanted, the undesired." In 1967 he met Huey P. Newton, the Minister of Defense of this same damned but no longer forgotten or invisible underclass. Now he grieves that when he debated Spain "American fascism was raging a mile away, in the Oakland black ghetto."

There are people who hold revolutionary beliefs and practice law, but they are not revolutionary lawyers in the same way as Charles Garry. Most political lawyers of the Left have no faith in the system or its courts; so their relationship is in sharp contradiction to the process of justice and their attitude is profoundly ambivalent. Garry is revolutionary because he, perhaps more than any other, rises above ambivalence to a dialectical stance. The lines of force run from the prisoner, with whom he stands, to the judge, and again to the jury, and finally to the street. It is this last line of dialectic that distinguishes Garry's tactics and thrust.

He has, for instance, a simple but all-encompassing theory as to why there should be no prisons, as we know them. First, because most "crimes" fall into what Garry calls the "Jean Valjean category." These are acts of survival based on a criminal system of property and class where prison only seals the victim's fate. Secondly, there are the "crimes" of "diminished responsibility." Sick people are treated and tortured moralistically by a blind and archaic system. Thirdly, there are the "political criminals" whom history, later, always credits with the necessary new ideas and new ideals of the time-bound age in question. And fourthly, yet to come in America, there are "prisoners of war." "The time is coming," says Garry, "when I'm going to have a client who shoots it out with the police or army, and the defense will be 'Civil war; self-defense.'" So he moves amphibiously from the courts to the street and back. He is an existential character, like the Panthers, in that he chose a new name and a new god to live by.

Garry was an independent Marxist for many years, and a pioneer in several fields. His work on the concept of "diminished responsibility" and in the field of forensic medicine anticipated the innovative research and argument that he was to bring to minimizing racism in his later political cases.

So he was tailoring by day and leading his law class by night; holding press conferences, calling pickets out on strike; thinking about running for Congress. He was a born advocate; in fact, he said, "I was born objecting and pleading." Garabedian was becoming Garry through the stormy law-schooling where the audacious fledgling was rehearsing the act of rebellion that we understand in today's students, but was then a sign of madness and genius.

There are men like Bertrand Russell and Jean Paul Sartre and Erik Erikson who retain all their life the qualities and motives of adolescence: loyalty and rebellion. Garry is like that. He loves young people and most of them love him, forgiving him everything—from, what is called, "male chauvinism" to his terrible energy that is a judgment on their youth.

In the 1950s, Garry worked on the West Coast Smith Act cases involving the Communist Party and behind the scenes at one late and particularly frustrating phase of the Rosenberg-Sobell appeal.

His instinct for political defense could not find an outlet until the mid-1960s. Breaking every rule of the "old Left," he joined in calling for thousands of people in the street on the first day of the Newton trial. In the street, Panthers stood at a tense parade rest, in the jammed courtroom a controlled crowd watched Garry fight in single combat. This same dialectic of street passion and court-room lucidity has marked all the subsequent contests. The Bobby Seale in New Haven would be a different man from the Bobby Seale in Chicago. The chairman of the Black Panther Party with Charles R. Garry at his side is not the shackled fugitive slave that called out for basic Constitutional protections in Chicago. In a sense the 1950s ended in 1967, with the inception of the Garry-Newton strategy of a political, dialectical defense.

As Charles Garry left San Francisco for New Haven, a bench warrant for his arrest was being issued by a Bay Area judge, and a citywide police demonstration was being organized to denounce him. When he returned to the West Coast to defend Huey Newton again, a motion to disbar him had started. His language to the judge in the trial known as "Los Siete de la Raza" was the pretext.

Of the few major political victories for the Left in recent years, Garry has engineered two. Both the "Oakland Seven" and "Los Siete de la Raza" were declared not guilty by California juries. The Oakland Seven were Berkeley activists prominent in the huge antiwar demonstrations that closed down the big Oakland induction center in 1968. After seven weeks of films and tapes and famous witnesses, the defendants were cleared of all the usual conspiracy charges. The Huey P. Newton trial had been a painful compromise to Garry, but it had infuriated law-enforcement circles, and several cars of police shot into the main Panther office, empty of Panthers, thanks to a far-seeing order from Newton. The cases surrounding the battle that erupted when the Panthers claimed that police forced Eldridge Cleaver, Li'l Bobby Hutton and other Panthers into a shoot-out after the assassination of Martin Luther King, Jr., are still going on. Hung jury follows hung jury in the "Cleaver cases" but each time the state moves for a retrial. It was one of these retrials scheduled to begin at the same time as the trial of Bobby Seale and Ericka Huggins that led to the bench warrant for Garry. At the same time the San Francisco court had scheduled the David Hilliard case (for "threatening the life of the

President" in a speech to a hundred thousand people—"We will kill any motherfucker that stands in the way of our freedom"), and the retrial of Huey P. Newton to fall on the calendar while the New Haven case was in progress. It was the Siete case that brought the issue to a head.

Seven young men from Salvador, living in San Francisco's mission slum district, were arrested and accused of fighting with two well-known undercover police and of killing one of them with his partner's gun, and then, of running away from the scene of the crime. Los Siete de la Raza were represented by Charles Garry and three outstanding young lawyers whom he attracted to the case, and the Panthers took up their cause in newspapers and rallies.

Charles Garry rises at 6 A.M., works, stands on his head for five-minute periods, practices yoga, chews vitamins, and is ready at night, after court combat, to lecture or talk.

In his seven-hour closing oration to the Siete jury, Garry had given a modern version of Darrow's radical American logic.

"At the outset, I am going to tell you that I am ashamed to be in this courtroom under these circumstances. I am ashamed that I am representing clients who have had to spend seventeen or eighteen months in prison awaiting what is commonly called a fair trial and justice.

"I am ashamed to have to stand before you and have to take apart a human being like McGoran—you can call him a human being; well, other people have other names for him which aptly fit him. . . .

"I am going to sit down in a few minutes. I will not be able to talk again because the closing argument is going to be given by the Prosecution. Why he gets the chance to make a closing argument, I've never understood. They use the law-school theory that they have the burden of proving their case against the defendants beyond a reasonable doubt and to a moral certainty.

"I haven't talked to you about any law. I have been talking to you about the facts. The rest of the attorneys will probably talk to you about some law in relationship to this. But I have come to the conclusion that the law be damned. I have come to the conclusion that it's about time we start talking about the events of society, and we start talking about human beings and their relationship to the contemporary society that we're living in. I have come to the conclusion that it is about time that men are not taken out of their daily lives and thrown into dungeons and prisons and segregation and to live in the mire and the crap upstairs while they are awaiting trial, under the theory that they are presumed to be innocent, and yet they have to pay for the penalty before they are ever tried or convicted.

"And I am getting mighty tired of the judges calling the law narrowly so that they can get a conviction, and they don't give a damn whether some Appellate Court at some subsequent time will reverse the conviction. They say, 'Well, you have protected your record.' Big deal, that you have protected your record after you put in months and months in prison. This is the kind of a system that I don't like, I don't respect, and I have something to say about it, because I have been at this for thirty-two years, and I have got to the point now that I am going to call the shots as I see it, and I don't care whether I practice law another hour or not.

"I am going to say these things because, for one thing, I have the ability. The second thing, I have the experience. And the third thing, I know where the bodies are buried, and the bodies are buried right here under the guise of due process of law, and when the day comes, and when the day comes, as William Shirer said at one time in a public address—and I was present—he made the statement that what is happening in America today is analogous to what happened two years before Adolf Hitler in the dying days of the Weimar Republic, where the lawyers capitulated and gave up their rights and their dignity under the guise of law and order. In those days it was a fight against communism—that is what Hitler was fighting—and then they brought Nazism into Germany. Lawyers and judges began to say, 'Heil Hitler.' And I, for one, will not do that; and I know my colleagues will not do that; and I hope you will not fall into that pattern."

The style is deceptive. The prose is proletarian and muscular, not lyrical like Darrow or Kunstler. Big-muscled, beautifully tailored, he is still the common man, the fierce and vital Armenian who never quite melted in, who makes standard grammar sound like idiom or argot. But when, during the New Haven trial, he met to talk with small groups of Yale law students he was fluent and hypnotic, with a flowing syntax until suddenly the bitter profanity would shoot out to jolt the children of affluence. Unlike his friends who are used to his passion, the students had been lulled by his graceful plea to them to become "brave advocates for the unrepresented."

"I've lost confidence in the system," he told students all over the country. "But our job is to get political leaders freedom, if it's an hour, a day or a year; get them 'back on the brick.' But the system can't be saved; an abrupt change with as little violence as is humanly possible—an abrupt change is needed." When the students praise him for his victories he tells them sharply that "Los Siete were locked up for seventeen months, and Huey P. Newton was locked up in solitary confinement for thirty-four months, and Huey is out on $50,000 *cash* bail, and they won't change it over to property, and they want me to be back in San Francisco on January 11th, for a retrial! They have *not* had fair trials. What have I won?" Then he warns them that hyperbole and rhetoric are not enough and that they must become "good technicians." New Haven is not San Francisco, he concludes, and each case must be fought specifically; he will not talk about the New Haven case since the judge had banned comment by counsel *after* the scare headlines following the arrests and later the indictments.

Speaking at the conservative University of Pennsylvania about the Chicago Conspiracy trial, Garry stirred his audience deeply with a combination of tirade and idealism.

"I don't care who the lawyers were in that case. That judge, that senile old son-of-a-bitch had made up his mind from the day we walked in there on April 4, 1969, that he intended to get a conviction, that he intended to put the lawyers and the defendants in jail no matter what the hell happened. . . .

Then warming to the subject:

"It's about time that in the federal judiciary system this lifetime-appointment bullshit stops. They pick the judges from the political trough; some accidently have some talents in some human equation, but most of them are part of the political hack system who'll die to represent the establishment. . . . Oh, I know, some of you will say they can be impeached; when is the last time a mother-fucker was ever impeached? . . .

"But remember the goal of America. . . . The America that we have always dreamt about is the kind of America which belongs to all of us, not just a few. We must bring America back to the people!"

Charles Garry and Bill Kunstler were shaking up students all over the country as the courts and the nation headed into the 1970s. During the long trial of Los Siete, Garry flew thousands of miles every weekend to keep speaking engagements; these were his only source of income.

What inspires this almost atavistic but immensely coherent energy in the lean, gray-haired advocate? It must be that in the legal intercession, as in the religious, at some point empathy passes over into ecstasy. Only a secular ecstasy, under the tough demeanor, could so piece out the man's finite capacities for combat and tenderness into a career of advocacy, jeopardy and radical solidarity with the despised who claw at the entrances to history.

He had been spawned in that generation of immigrant poverty whose brightest sons grew up to be gangsters, labor leaders and Communists. Garry was a vibrant populist, as good an organizer as any labor boss, and as tough as the gangster he might have been so easily were it not for that tragic imagination and grace of spirit that set him apart from his generation.

Allowing for nineteenth-century style, what was said of Captain Dreyfus' advocate could be said for Garry:

But Maitre Labori, the advocate of Zola, is the most attractive figure in court. He is fair-haired, fair-bearded, with something of the look of a Viking, and all of the build. He tops his colleagues by the head; his chest is vast both in breadth and depth; in every movement is that of a good-humored giant overflowing with energy and force.

Most first-magnitude political trials have a dead body, but only, on occasion, a great or truly living lawyer for a champion. John Brown did not; Big Bill Haywood did; Julius and Ethel Rosenberg and Morton Sobell did not; Bobby Seale and Ericka Huggins did.

And when the fit is on him and Garabedian breaks out, he surges through the courtroom brushing aside objections and opposition, overriding everything, including his own defense table, and there are flashes from the big Byzantine eyes. The eyes are Armenian, black, huge and long, wraparound, peering everywhere, looking to turn up Justice.

The defense asks that a middle-aged white man be "excused for cause." The judge denies. Now the defense must use up one of its precious sixty challenges, or probe further to convince the Bench of the man's unfitness. Miss Roraback concludes on an ambiguous note:

Q: Do you have any objection to people who apply for welfare?
THE STATE: Objection.
THE COURT: Sustained.
Q: Do you feel people ought to support themselves?
THE STATE: Objection.
THE COURT: Sustained.
Q: Do you feel that Mr. Seale and Mrs. Huggins might be somewhat dangerous?
A: To whom?
Q: To the public.
A (long pause): No.

It is Charles R. Garry's turn. The audience stirs; with neither vanity nor modesty he begins. "How do you do? My name is Charles R. Garry. I'm from San Francisco and I'm representing Mr. Bobby G. Seale, one of the founders and the Chairman of the Black Panther Party. Now, I don't want to intrude on your private life in any way, do you understand? But I must find out if you can be what we call a fair and impartial juror, do you understand?" Looking like a well-tailored American version of Julius Caesar, Garry stands with his arms out, pantomiming the scales of justice for the round-eyed "witness." He begins the clear-voiced search:

Q: Have you heard the words "All power to the people"?
A: Not that I recall.
Q: Have you heard the phrase "black power"?
A: Yes.

Q: What does that mean to you?
A: I never heard it defined.
THE STATE: Objection.
Q: Do you know who used that phrase, Black power?
A: I believe the Black Panthers.
Q: Do you know any of the other slogans the Black Panthers use?
A: No.
Q: Do you have any friends or know any people that belong to groups known as "law-and-order"?
THE STATE: I object.
THE COURT: Sustained.

Bobby Seale is smiling. In Chicago, he had bitterly denounced the court for referring to the clenched-fist symbol as synonymous with "black power":

MR. SCHULTZ: That's the number, your Honor. We would like to offer it at this time so that before the next witness takes the stand—
JUDGE HOFFMAN: Show it to counsel.
BOBBY: That's not a black-power sign. Somebody correct the court on that. It's not the black-power sign. It's the "power to the people" sign.
JUDGE HOFFMAN: Mr. Marshal, will you stop the talking, please.
BOBBY: Yes, but that is still wrong, Judge Hoffman. It's not a black-power sign. It's a "power to the people" sign, and he is deliberately distorting that, and that's a racist technique.
MR. SCHULTZ: If the Court please, this man has repeatedly called me a racist. . . .
BOBBY: Yes, you are, Dick Schultz.
MR. SCHULTZ: And called Mr. Foran a racist. . . .
JUDGE HOFFMAN: Ladies and gentlemen of the jury, I will ask you to leave the court. Mr. Marshal, remove the ladies and gentlemen of the jury.

The Panthers were the enemy of black power if it meant, as it had come to mean to many, "black capitalism." Black people had to choose sides just like whites. Seale had said many times, "A pig is a pig is a pig." He meant whether white or black, police or panther. There were "nigger pigs." The believers in black culture, or Africanism, like Ron Karenga and Stokely Carmichael, were merely "pork-chop nationalists," he said. But how would the court—leaving aside the jury and the public—ever understand that the Panthers based their decisions on a world view that was revolutionary and political, not racial or cultural? To white America, all the "colored people" now calling themselves "black" looked the same.

Charles R. Garry of San Francisco goes on without letup. How to bring it out? The next technique will be used again and again, the District Attorney always objecting, the court sometimes sustaining, sometimes denying, always uncomfortable:

Q: If you were in that place instead of Mr. Seale, and you were a black man, would you feel satisfied that there were twelve jurors sitting in judgment on your cause. . . .
(A long pause)
Q: Your life is at stake.
A: I think I'm a fair man.

More pressure now:

Q: Have you ever had a bad or uncomfortable relationship with anyone in the black community?
A (A long pause): Just once. It was just business. I don't recall it now, but . . .
Q: Because the defendants have been indicted by a grand jury, do you feel there is some element of guilt?
A: It's not what I say, it's what the judge says. . . .
Q: Do you think there's an element of guilt there or he wouldn't have been indicted?
A: Yes.
Q: I think this is the time for a challenge for cause. On two or three different occasions the prospective juror has said there is some element of guilt or they wouldn't be here.
THE COURT: No.
Q: In your mind, do you associate the Black Panther Party with violence?
A (after a long pause): Yes . . . in this case right here . . . what I read in the papers several months ago.
Q: As you think about it?

A: You're making me think about it. I normally don't.

Q: Do you believe there is such a thing as white racism?

THE STATE: I object.

THE COURT: The charge here involves all black people. Racism has nothing to do with it.

Bobby Seale smiles and glances back toward the one row of spectators he can see. The pitting of black against black is considered by black people to be the cruelest and most insidious tactic of the racist power structure. Malcolm X had summed it up when he lamented the use of black agents to disrupt the growing liberation movement. "Niggers ruined it," he said. In New York, at the same time, a half dozen black agents are testifying against the "Twenty-one" (Panthers on trial for conspiracy to blow up public buildings and murder police).

Garry is through; the defense will have to use another one of its own challenges.

Q: Do you believe in the death penalty?

A: If I had the power to abolish capital punishment I would do it, but if the courts say it's the law then I will go along with it.

He sits; the man is excused; the court announces an hour for lunch. Ericka Huggins stares ahead; Bobby Seale looks disgusted.

The contest with Arnold Markle had begun months before.

After flying all night from San Francisco and the Los Siete pretrial, Charles Garry forced the High Sheriff to physically take the stand and account for the New Haven Grand Jury system. The agon began with this intervention. It was the first of many and the State was not used to such early and sharp resistance.

In a day-long session that was at once hilarious and sobering Garry exposed the caprice of the 73-year-old High Sheriff that was called a Grand Jury.

Q: How did you go about selecting these Grand Jurors?

A: I go to the various towns, the twenty-six towns of my county. I talk to people and try to find out who would like to come on the Grand Jury.

Q: In other words, what you are saying, Sheriff, is that you are picking men and women that you have known yourself?

A: Not exactly. If they are recommended. I find out if they are electors, decent people, as far as I know. I pick them from all classes, and colorwise. I never ask them their religion, and so forth.

Q: What standard do you have to follow to see whether a person is decent or not?

A: The same standard we have on all juries.

The Grand Jury concept grew up in order to *protect the individual from the power of the State.* Like so much else it has been turned around and the very words chill the political and the poor when they hear them.

Q: By the way, are you an Elk?

A: Yes.

Q: It is true, is it not, sir, that the Elks Club excludes by its own constitution any member who is of the black race?

Originally the Grand Jury was a group of neighbors. The structure roots back to the pre-literate *Gemeinschaft* of early man and the trial by oath.

Q: Let's talk about Mrs. Abbie Creem.

A: Yes.

Q: How did you get ahold of her?

A: I know Mrs. Creem. I knew her husband for several years before he died. I know who she is.

Q: You have known her for several years?

A: I know who she is.

Q: How many years have you known her or her husband?

A: For quite a few.

Q: About thirty?

A: It is kind of hard to place this . . .

Q: What ethnic group does she belong to, if you know?

A: I don't know what church she goes to.

Q: I am not interested in their church. Religion is immaterial, whether they believe in God or don't. I am more interested in the color of their skin.

A: She is white.

Q: Now, Mrs. Creem is a person whom you have had personal relationships with, and I am not implying anything improper now, Sheriff.

A: The only experiences I have had is having her on the Grand Jury.

Q: How many times?

A: Over the years, many times I have had her on the Grand Jury . . . Surely I am not going to pick someone or put someone on the Grand Jury that you can tear apart on their respectability.

Q: What do you mean by "their respectability"?

A: A person that is considered a nice, decent person. A law-abiding person that lives in the community.

Q: By whose standards, yours?

A: Not alone mine.

Q: Whom else's?

A: In this one, it is my standard because I am picking the jury.

Q: In other words, you decided who is respectable and who isn't?

A: Right.

It went on all day. New Haven had never seen the likes of this irreverence. Garry danced around the old institution.

Q: Let's talk about Mr. Joseph Phalen. How did you find him?

A: He was recommended by one of my deputy sheriffs.

Q: What type of work does Mr. Phalen do?

A: He might be a retired fireman or something like that; I don't know. He is retired.

Q: Would you say he is over seventy?

A: Over sixty-five.

Q: White?

A: I don't recall.

Q: You don't know whether he is a white man or not?

A: He is white. I thought you said, "wife." Excuse me.

Garry in his vulgar elegance and the High Sheriff were like some outrageous politicized agon out of Faulkner's Mississippi.

Q: Let's talk about John Pakacimas. How did you get ahold of him?

A: He was recommended to me by my deputy.

Q: Which one?

A: Deputy Demapolis recommended him to me.

Q: Who?
A: A sheriff named Demapolis in Waterbury.
Q: I see you went back to Waterbury for this man, again?
A: No. He is Lithuanian.
Q: You mean he is a Lithuanian?
A: Yes.
Q: It sounds more like Greek to me.
A: No. He is a "Lith."
Q: What did you want a Lithuanian for?
A: I wanted to mix it up.
Q: Did you think Mr. Seale was a Lithuanian?
A: Who? We didn't even know Mr. Seale was going to be before the Grand Jury when we picked this. Do you know that? I never asked who's coming up.

It is all in the record, but the motions were, of course, denied. But the court and the culture were on notice that the actual fight for the life of Seale and Huggins had begun, and that from the High Sheriff on down no one would be spared.

The long road that leads to the New Haven arena began for Bobby Seale in crushing poverty in Texas in 1936. The elder Seale was a stern father to Bobby and to his brother John, an important member, too, of the Black Panther Party. Bobby Seale learned carpentry and later drafting and design. Apolitical, he had obvious talent as a drummer, comedian, actor, even before he joined the Air Force in the late 1950s and quit for ambiguous but race-related reasons in 1958.

While trying to choose between the stage and engineering, his two highly developed skills, Seale ran into Huey P. Newton at Merritt Junior College in Oakland during the Cuban blockade, and it was not long after that his mordant wit and blueprint-planning talent were being dedicated to the revolution.

"Huey and Bobby" began by talking about bank robbery and politics, and their synthesis was revolution and the Black Panther Party. Bobby Seale would be the chairman and Huey the minister of defense, and someday they would say to the state, "Put 'em up, motherfucker, this is a holdup, we come for what's ours."

Then Huey P. Newton was convicted, and only Bobby Seale remained. Under the Panther Chief of Staff David Hilliard's tireless organizing the Black Panther Party spread to more than thirty cities. Seale spread the good news of Huey P. Newton across the country, and then "they" came for him, and the myth of the old Panthers began to bog down; but that would not be apparent until the jury had been almost picked.

Seale and Newton began humbly in what they saw as their corner of Babylon, the Oakland ghetto in 1966. They talked to everyone who would talk, and they came up with a ten-point program. Huey carried a law book and a gun, Bobby was a nonstop preacher of the good news of guns and food, pigs and education, housing, health care, niggers and socialism. The phenomenon came upon the fisher of souls, Eldridge Cleaver at the *Ramparts* building, and he was to write:

The most beautiful sight I had ever seen. Four black men wearing black berets, powder-blue shirts, black leather jackets, black trousers, shiny black shoes—and each with a gun! In front was Huey P. Newton (later shot in the stomach while unarmed, framed on the charge of murdering a policeman, and kept chained to his hospital bed during surgery) . . . Beside him was Bobby Seale (later bound, gagged and beaten in open court while on trial for "conspiracy" in what was subsequently declared a mistrial, and now sentenced to four years for contempt of court in protesting that mistrial). . . .

Now the first "five-year plan," if anyone would later call it that, was coming to an end. Before the trial's end Eldridge Cleaver and Huey P. Newton would be pitted against each other in a revolutionary life-and-death struggle, and Bobby Seale, watching from New Haven, would keep his counsel until after the testimony had begun.

The long weary increment since the days of the Alien and Sedition Acts continued. William D. Haywood and Clarence Darrow in 1907, Bobby G. Seale and Charles R. Garry in 1970—one second in historical time.

Q: Do you feel that Mr. Seale and the Black Panther Party threaten you because of their philosophy, even though you say you don't know what their philosophy is?
A: All I know is it has something to do with overcoming the government.

Yet, in the McLucas trial as in the Haywood case, the state will object that "this case has nothing to do with politics," and the court will sustain. Seale glances around the cramped and confining tiny room. He and Huggins had run up against the modern recension of the "Fundamental Agreement."

The people who "bought" the New Haven territory from the Indians for some knives and cloth in the 1630s were wealthy people who had rebelled against Charles I's policy of taxation without representation. That was their last rebellion. The Indian country, Quinnipiac, was a "fair haven" for those first families of New World aristocracy, and when 1776 came, the leader of the militants in New Haven was Benedict Arnold.

Their form of government was a clever blend of mercantilism and theocracy: the New Haven First Church of Christ was also the first ruling council, and only those who owned stock in the New Haven Company could belong to the church, and only those who belonged to the church could vote; this was called the Fundamental Agreement.

The new "Fundamental Agreement" is different. It is tacit, "unconscious," subjective, covert, but it manages to more or less exclude ex-convicts, nonvoters, youth, nonwhite, and pro–life, or anti–death-penalty, people. All the people that Ericka and Bobby see as their peers.

Garry stands again to make a mordant comment about the crackling clock. "The whole system has something wrong with it," the judge says vaguely. "Right On!" explodes the rear gallery. "Order!" pounds a sheriff. All laugh, and the prisoners are led out separately, for the afternoon recess, to eat a snack provided by the New Haven Panthers.

Arnold Markle, the State's Attorney, had introduced the death-penalty theme for the first time. He insisted, and the judge upheld him, that opposition to the death penalty constituted automatic exclusion. The room was silent, it was out in the open. Unlike the previous trial, the State was suggesting that it was going to go to the limits of the conspiracy statute. Garry rose to argue the theory of the conviction-prone, "death-oriented" jury.

The ghetto man in the street was watching:

I feel the trial is unfair. I feel that the white man is gonna really do it to him. I also feel the way the jury thing is hooked up, he's automatically gonna be convicted. Everybody reads the paper! You know the people are lying when they ask that. You know everybody reads the paper, and the white man is known to get his paper.

This split in the party between Huey Newton and Eldridge Cleaver? I think that's the white man tryin to break the party up because the party's gettin' too strong, and you know how whitey is—he don't wanta see no black man git too powerful.

Can't get a fair trial because the white man got everything hooked up his own way. Like in a dope trial they go for "cop-outs." The courts and shit is falling—they don't have enough judges so they ask for cop-outs just to push the brothers out. You can't get a fair trial. Shit. I could get a job, but I want to get in the white man's union and then get my own business before I get twenty-five years old. Shit, I have a trade. I'm gonna have what I want! I'm gonna take it from whitey. I'm gonna play his little game, you know, go to school. "Yeah, yeah, Mr. Charlie, sure!"

The *voir dire* begins again. Catherine Roraback delves into the alienation of each new candidate.

Q: Do you know any black people?
A: At work.
Q: At work?
A: One.
Q: Any black neighbors?
A: No.
Q: Do any black people come to your home?
A: No [or] I'm so tired after work I don't have anyone over [or] A Puerto Rican was over once.

Q: Do your children have any black friends?
A: No.
Q: Are there any black people in your church [or] lodge [or] P.T.A.?
A: No.

The striking loneliness of the middle-aged American working class. The isolation and sadness of these Great Depression survivors who live walled in by their white skin. These aging bundles of secrets at bay in the witness box. "I am sorry to have to invade your sacred privacy," Charles Garry tells each one.

The only young person is excused to return to graduate school. Miss Roraback asks the next if the fact that her client must return to jail each day will be held against her. The judge winces and asks, "Why did you have to bring that out?" The jury is not to know, they do not see the sheriffs bring the prisoners in or out. Seale and Huggins, dressed in civilian clothes, are to play the role of innocent people until proven guilty while they are closely bound by the State and refused bail. This presumption of innocence is a shadow play, a transaction meant to mystify and pacify the super-ego of the State. But everyone knew before Katie Roraback broke the rules of the game. On pain of contempt the roles must be acted out to the end.

A Mr. Marvin comes in. Garry, the "old" Armenian, and Marvin, the old Jew, hit it off at once. They chat about the professions of the juror's children, of how proud he is of them. Mr. Marvin handles the probes for racism in a human way: "There's good and bad of all kinds." The heads at the defense table come together, the chairman nods.

DEFENSE: Accepted!
THE STATE: Excused.
THE COURT: Thank you, Mr. Marvin, you're excused.

The old man alights from the box, walks out slowly.

The last venireman enters. He knows no blacks; he knows "only what I read in the papers"; he "never discussed, never wondered,

is not interested" in the "struggle for black liberation." At last—
"Excused."

The average age of these first fifty prospective jurors is over
fifty. There is one older black man. Ericka Huggins has a baby
daughter, Mai; there are no young mothers in the venire.

Number 23, a spare man with the body image and clothes of an
insurance salesman in the 1930s, and a heavy-set blondined
woman (Number 24) are called out and then excused by the
judge. They walk in a creeping way—like figures on an old match-
book cover—from sheriff to sheriff to the door.

The last rap, the twenty-odd remaining came, pale white, into
the courtroom as if from the dark into blinding light. The sheriffs
try to round them up to leave by a back door. These older citizens
wander quietly, a frail woman says, "Goodbye, judge," and waves.
They finally file out; a man with a cane is last.

Bobby Seale rises and begins to leave, his plainclothes men
come alert and quickly form the escort. Ericka Huggins is gone by
another door.

THE SECOND DAY (NOVEMBER 18, 1970)

don,

rose has a composition book with some of my poems in it. use the ones
you want. i have some at niantic will bring them tomorrow. as far as a
one-page biography: let's just say that i was born in d.c.—5 february
'48.

my family was relatively poor. we lived between the housing projects
and the petit-bourgeoisie. i have a sister, ryra, who'll be 20 in february,
and a brother, gervaze, who is 18. the three of us shared a normal
childhood full of the bullshit black people survive through—

the only difference being that i was a little more pensive than most
kids. i left high school a sort of existential rebel—went to cheyney
state college in pennsylvania (outside of philly) to become a teacher. i
had this dream that i would one day be able to open a school for
retarded and birth defective children (maybe i will, after we *fanshen**

* Fanshen means literally the turn-around (or revolution).

[smile]). i left there because it offered no challenge educationally, politically or spiritually. where i went after cheyney however was no better. i went to lincoln university in pennsylvania, near baltimore, md.—to be exact near rising sun, md. which used to be the state headquarters of the KKK! the school was a political challenge. this was 1966. the era of black students awakening to malcolm. i met jon the winter of '67. we were just fellow black student congress members then. we, among others, were very disillusioned with the *nothing* that students were doing. i was disillusioned with me. i wanted to struggle in practice, not theory. the whole armchair revolutionary nationalist thing stunk. i was looking for something real. so was jon. in september, 1967, we both returned there, became friends, then lovers—we decided to go to california.

i remember reading an article in *ramparts* about huey's arrest and the newly formed black panther party. had to go and do something. amerika was destroying the people—we felt desperately the need to help.

in november, 1967, after leaving lincoln for new york to pick up a friend, we left for phoney city—l.a. we existed on nothing much except bare necessities until we moved to harcourt ave. and washington blvd.—where, by the way, mai was conceived. . . .

jon met a brother selling our newspapers and the next wednesday we went to a meeting at the old black congress building. this was late february, 1968. we joined and worked there until we moved to 4115 so. central. you know it from there, i guess. if you have any specific questions, ask. ok?

it's good to see you. haven't quite finished 'inquest' yet. i know how ethel r.* must have felt. . . .

> venceremos!
> love power strength
> ericka

> before a woman becomes grown
> if she's black and poor
> she learns that the world
> is cold   ready to rape you
> of everything

* Ethel Rosenberg.

if a blackgirlchild wants to ever
become free she has to really
    struggle like we did
    shouts of hatred
    and screams of amerikan misunderstanding
prison can make you look back on a lifetime
    of bitterness. . . .
        handed-down clothes—
        cold winter nights,
        —for whites only,
        colored served here
           etc.
memories only other blackwomen cd understand
        fully of
    trying to be what aint / of trying to see what's
    not   of trying to rid ourselves what never
        was
    of men crying
    of children dying
    of abortions—just because. . . .
memories that harsh and cruel of alley ways
    where people live
of 'police' who not only attack with weapons
    but with words (which you cannot combat)
      —if you're black and poor and female
      like my mama
      like me and my sisters

                  Ericka

This tall, angular twenty-two-year-old black woman revolutionary seems to materialize from the shadows of America, suddenly in 1967. She carries the last name Huggins; that is all anyone will ever know her by. The name, Huggins, belonged first to her husband Jon. The identities of the two young people are merged in the Panther legend.

Jon, soft and sensitive-looking, was the son of a well-known family in the New Haven "colored" establishment; the father, John Huggins, Sr., is still listed on a gold building sign as the "Permittee" of one of the town's exclusive clubs. Well educated and therefore enraged, Jon and Ericka traveled to Los Angeles and became prime movers in the new Black Panther chapter there. There Ericka had her baby, Mai, and lost her husband in a political assassination. Now she returned to New Haven, a Panther newspaper legend, and in less than six months was arrested on capital charges. The night Jon was killed, Los Angeles police arrested her and put a gun to the baby's head, laughed and said, "You're next."

REFLECTIONS ON MYJON . . .

i was inside
i was thrust out of warmth
into cold, into reality
   i was born (from fleshwomb)
I grew a little
   talked a little
   walked a little
   learned a little
and in 6th grade
   learned a little
      left
and in 9th grade
   learned a little
      left
and in 12th grade
   knew a little
   learned nuthin' (but luv)
      left
and at cheyney
   learned a lot about people and shit
      left
and at lincoln
   learned (about mind things)
      left
and in l.a.
   learned life and people things
   and man things and woman things
   learned a little 'bout hunger
   and i watched you lose weight, but not strength
and i watched my childbelly grow

and you heard it and said DANCE—it's life in there
(but hunger in a land of plenty hurts)
i watched you grow (not sizewise)
and learned a little, we both learned—
a little 'bout world things
money things
war things
ackshally 'bout america things REVOLUTION things
and at 806 w. century
learned a lot
loved a little (like our girlchild) and elaine bunchy franko gee and all
and they told me you were gone
spine severed and i learned a little 'bout brother things and sister things
'bout r e v o l u t i o n things 'bout death things
and i lost a lot
i was inside
i was thrust out of warmth
into cold, into reality
i was born (from lovewomb)
i grew a little
i died a little
and in jail
i learned a little
left
and in here
i learn a lot
hate a little
cry a little (for our girlchild)
and i am inside . . .

Ericka

She came, then, to trial a firstling of that existential generation
that had seen enough by the age of twenty-two to last a lifetime.

when i was little my mama used to let
us walk on days like this just walk in
the cold air
it's sunday / on days like this mama
would always have lots of food (and love)
for us
it wd be quiet i remember my sister
and brother and just the feeling of peace

i guess lotsa families are like this on
sunday . . .
    after 5 days of struggle and a saturday
    of cleaning and shit—sunday peace
my father always got paid on wednesday
never had anything by the next wednesday
but still we had peace on sunday
i wonder what it's like there now?—
    washington, d.c. 10 yrs. later
    with one a prisoner of war
    my sister hangin out
    my brother mourning life itself
    my father gone home to mama
        i wonder who mama has
        lots of food (and love) for now?
                                    Ericka

She existed most in the poems and diary that the matrons took
away from her because, they said, they were afraid they might be
either politically inflammatory or love letters to sister prisoners.

She did not exist in the state's melodrama of the twenty-one-
year-old witch who seduced the good Negroes of New Haven into
the crime against Alex Rackley.

                tall
                skinny
                plain i am
                ericka,
                fuzzy hair
                droopy eyes
                long feet
                        i love people
                        love nature
                        love love
                i am a revolutionary
                nothing special
                        one soul
                        one life   willing
                                to give it
                        ready to die. . . .
                                Ericka

The judge's clerk is a statistician. The average age of the first jury panel is 50.5! Charles Garry has been asked by the court not to use the term "S.O.B." in jury examination.

The second day, all the days pass like an endless loop of film. The people are old, nervous; they want out. Some cannot hear or see, the lawyers shout their questions, the court reporter, sitting three feet away from the witness box, must ask for the rejoinders to be repeated again and again as he tries to read their lips.

They read the New Haven *Register* or the *Journal-Courier* or the Waterbury *Republican*. They do not know, have never known, any black people, and their children will not know any. They cannot tell whether the defendants are innocent or guilty "until they know more." Time after time defense counsel remind the frightened people that the judge has instructed them that the state has the burden of *proving* guilt, that the defense need say nothing. Yes, they remember, but "they wouldn't have been indicted or arrested unless they did something." "Challenge for cause." The court: "Denied." On and on bringing out the poison; the judge complaining, "Mr. Garry, these are lay people and you have to help educate them."

Number 11A, a saleswoman—

A: That's the way they were meant to be.
Q: Do you think black people are different?
A: Not really.
Q: Will these defendants have to prove themselves innocent to you?
A: If they hadn't done something, they wouldn't be here.

"Challenge."

"Denied. Why don't you put the questions on the positive side?" It begins again.

They almost all lean on the newspaper as on holy writ for their opinions or bias. Reflexively, they will read about themselves that night in the evening papers—morning and evening newspapers in New Haven are owned by the same company—as those in the future panels will read about the difficulty of finding impartial jurors.

Like a Puritan's version of Falstaff's army, they wind in a chain out of the Naugatuck Valley: Derby, Ansonia, Shelton, Seymour, Thomaston. Most of these towns have enjoyed only occasional economic remission in the last forty years, when other sections of the nation put the Great Depression behind them.

The industrial giants of the last century ran away from the pursuing unions until the unions stopped at the approaches to the South and organized no further. There are abandoned mills everywhere. New aerospace complexes, of the age of atoms, took up the slack during the cold war. Defeats in the field in Asia, and a general demythologization of the military and its mind have started a momentum of cutbacks, now in the Northeastern section of the military-industrial complex. The day the trial began there was the news that the local Winchester gun factory was laying off seven hundred people.

The broken clock is now ten minutes fast, but the judge obviously intends to abide by it. "Luncheon recess."

The old woman who had waved at the judge transfers her tirade from the jury room to the court. "They're the same color, the same creed, they shouldn't have done it." The court interrupts the monologue to excuse her. She asks if she will get paid for today. "Yes, I know too much. So I'm out because I told the truth." Then to the laughing audience, "Drug addicts!"

Number 14A is questioned for ethnocentricity.

Q: Have you heard of the ghetto culture?
THE STATE: Object. That is not at issue here.
THE COURT: Sustained.
Q: Now, we may have a language problem here . . .
THE STATE: Object. There is no language problem.
THE COURT: Sustained.

The critical evidence will be a tape recording of the torture of Rackley with Ericka Huggins using the forbidden word *motherfucker.*

Number 16A will not be able to keep the Seale and Huggins cases or testimony separate in her mind. "How do you know?" the judge asks. The combat is starting to show now. The panel is dwindling, and each potential juror seems more alienated than the one before.

Three will give more credence to police officers or F.B.I. agents who testify. Excused. Number 22A cannot hear or talk; 24A is sick to her stomach; 25A will not admit she is hard of hearing, and the judge tests by turning his head away to question her; Mr. Markle shouts from the back, "Are you nervous!" Number 25A admits to high blood pressure and diabetes.

A Mr. Zahn and two others associate the Black Panthers with the "riots in Chicago." Why? "I don't know." (Or, "I read it in the newspapers.") To Garry's question of putting a loved one in Mr. Seale's place, "It's based on reason, not passion; love doesn't come into justice."

Q: Were you here on May Day?
A: I left town.

Echoing Yale President Kingman Brewster's statement of doubt that a black revolutionary "could get a fair trial anywhere in the United States," the Eastern section of the movement prepared to descend on New Haven on May Day to protest the "repression of Bobby Seale and the Black Panther Party." For his sentiments President Brewster earned the quick anger of a number of people, including the Vice-President of the United States, the Attorney General and Harold Mulvey, the Panther trial judge. The Attorney General, for his part, sent four thousand paratroopers and marines to Massachusetts and Rhode Island, while the governor of the state of Connecticut positioned twenty-five hundred National Guardsmen on the campuses of community colleges in the New Haven area, thereby angering many students into joining the May 1 demonstration. All police leaves were canceled, and the F.B.I.'s new New Left desk sent a task force of agents in to penetrate the events.

The split was classic. Vice-President Agnew denounced Kingman Brewster for his statement, Fannie Lou Hamer—who had watched Lyndon Baines Johnson and Hubert Humphrey smother the nonviolent civil-rights movement in Atlantic City in 1964—

came to New Haven to "thank God" for Brewster. At Harvard, the microbiologist, Jonathan Beckwith announced that he was turning over his $1,000 prize (for his work on the pure gene) to the Panthers, because they "are not only helping their own people to lose their feeling of powerlessness, but are also setting up free health clinics and free breakfast programs."

The Council of Churches circulated a pamphlet, *The Panther's Rights Are Your Rights, Too.*

> In Germany, they first came for the Communists
> and I didn't speak up because I wasn't a Communist.
>
> Then they came for the Jews
> and I didn't speak up because I wasn't a Jew.
>
> Then they came for the trade unionists
> and I didn't speak up because I wasn't a trade unionist.
>
> Then they came for the Catholics
> and I didn't speak up because I was a Protestant.
>
> Then they came for me—and by that time
> no one was left to speak up.
>
> —MARTIN NIEMOELLER

Liberal administrators were in constant touch with the Chief of Police. The media and the Justice Department predicted and insisted there would be violence—"GUNS ON WAY FROM BOSTON" was the headline in *The New York Times.*

But at the Panther headquarters "Big Man," from the Black Panther Ministry of Information, announced, "Not only do we need black support, but we need support from all the poor and oppressed people *and* the alienated children of the ruling class. This does not mean arbitrary confrontation, rampages through the streets and knocking old women—we can't be anarchistic and emotional, we have to be clear-headed and organized. An example of this type of clear-headedness is the fact that Yale students cut their hair and took the time to go into white middle-class communities to rally support for this trial and for the cause of justice in the United States. The people and the Party won't cause violence in the courts, the schools or the streets. . . ."

Agnew and his supporters, when they attacked Brewster were ranging themselves against powerful old elements of the Establishment. It was this same traditional power that Senator Joseph McCarthy had unsuccessfully assaulted in the 1950s.

The Black Panther Party measured its antagonist in its newspaper of December 5, 1970:

THE YALE CORPORATION
AND THE PRE-PLANNED MURDER
OF CHAIRMAN BOBBY SEALE
AND ERICKA HUGGINS

DESTROY THE FASCISTS AND
ALL THEIR INSTITUTIONS

ALL POWER TO THE PEOPLE

To the Panthers the Yale Corporation was a map in time and space of black people's deracination and nothingness. The Corporation was the grammar to the State's logic, its rhetoric.

It is clear that this Establishment was much more concerned with the power of the New Right than with the New Left or the Old Left.

In the courtroom, Chief of Staff David Hilliard and Minister of Culture Emory Douglas tried to receive a note from their chairman. Overreaction: six months in jail! Strike!

Bobby Seale was the common figure in the two courthouses of Chicago and New Haven, but it was the arrest of Panther leaders Hilliard and Douglas for reading a note in court that triggered Yale's moral dilemma. Hilliard and Douglas, surrounded, forced to the center of the courtroom, and handcuffed, were a physical tableau; and Yale students reacted in such a way as to leave no doubt that Black Panthers and white scholars share the same nervous system. Once again physical action had broken through the legal abstraction. At one point, at a tumultuous mass meeting on campus, a law student, beside himself, called for mass suicide until the Panthers had justice. Then came what some students called President Kingman Brewster's Ivy League *machismo*.

YALE CORPORATION

The Trustees of Yale University

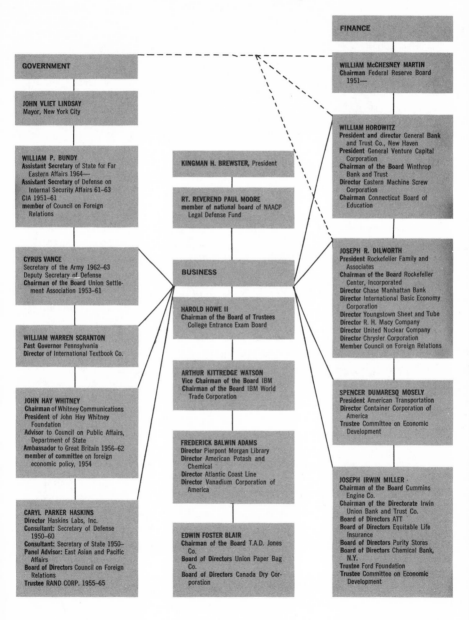

FINANCE

GOVERNMENT

WILLIAM McCHESNEY MARTIN
Chairman Federal Reserve Board 1951—

JOHN VLIET LINDSAY
Mayor, New York City

WILLIAM HOROWITZ
President and director General Bank and Trust Co., New Haven
President General Venture Capital Corporation
Chairman of the Board Winthrop Bank and Trust
Director Eastern Machine Screw Corporation
Chairman Connecticut Board of Education

WILLIAM P. BUNDY
Assistant Secretary of State for Far Eastern Affairs 1964—
Assistant Secretary of Defense on Internal Security Affairs 61–63
CIA 1951–61
member of Council on Foreign Relations

KINGMAN H. BREWSTER, President

RT. REVEREND PAUL MOORE
member of national board of NAACP Legal Defense Fund

JOSEPH R. DILWORTH
President Rockefeller Family and Associates
Chairman of the Board Rockefeller Center, Incorporated
Director Chase Manhattan Bank
Director International Basic Economy Corporation
Director Youngstown Sheet and Tube
Director R. H. Macy Company
Director United Nuclear Company
Director Chrysler Corporation
Member Council on Foreign Relations

CYRUS VANCE
Secretary of the Army 1962–63
Deputy Secretary of Defense
Chairman of the Board Union Settlement Association 1953–61

BUSINESS

WILLIAM WARREN SCRANTON
Past Governor Pennsylvania
Director of International Textbook Co.

HAROLD HOWE II
Chairman of the Board of Trustees College Entrance Exam Board

ARTHUR KITTREDGE WATSON
Vice Chairman of the Board IBM
Chairman of the Board IBM World Trade Corporation

SPENCER DUMARESQ MOSELY
President American Transportation
Director Container Corporation of America
Trustee Committee on Economic Development

JOHN HAY WHITNEY
Chairman of Whitney Communications
President of John Hay Whitney Foundation
Advisor to Council on Public Affairs, Department of State
Ambassador to Great Britain 1956–62
member of committee on foreign economic policy, 1954

FREDERICK BALWIN ADAMS
Director Pierpont Morgan Library
Director American Potash and Chemical
Director Atlantic Coast Line
Director Vanadium Corporation of America

JOSEPH IRWIN MILLER
Chairman of the Board Cummins Engine Co.
Chairman of the Directorate Irwin Union Bank and Trust Co.
Board of Directors ATT
Board of Directors Equitable Life Insurance
Board of Directors Purity Stores
Board of Directors Chemical Bank, N.Y.
Trustee Ford Foundation
Trustee Committee on Economic Development

CARYL PARKER HASKINS
Director Haskins Labs, Inc.
Consultant: Secretary of Defense 1950–60
Consultant: Secretary of State 1950—
Panel Advisor: East Asian and Pacific Affairs
Board of Directors Council on Foreign Relations
Trustee RAND CORP. 1955–65

EDWIN FOSTER BLAIR
Chairman of the Board T.A.D. Jones Co.
Board of Directors Union Paper Bag Co.
Board of Directors Canada Dry Corporation

The University cannot, however, contribute to the costs of the legal defense of any defendant. We could not use funds given to us for the tax-deductible purpose of education and turn them over for the benefit of a particular person where a gift would not qualify for a tax deduction. This is an absolute legal barrier to any use of university resources for a defense fund; the same, I am advised, would be true of bail funds for a particular person.

With a kind of Aristotelian dialectic the Reverend William Sloane Coffin summed up the conflict by saying that it was legally right and morally wrong to bring the Panthers to trial. The same phrase had been used by a juror after the Reverend Mr. Coffin's own trial with Dr. Spock in Boston.

One prospective juror is very hard of hearing and almost blind. Another is too nervous to listen to the news. (Another man has not read a newspaper since he was laid off two months ago; unemployment has doubled in the New Haven area in the past year.) That is a sign of mourning, for everyone else swears by the local press; it tells them that they exist and that others do not.

How many code words there are and how many associational complexes have been set in action by the media are hard to know. But in the first one hundred and fifty talesmen, only one did not say, "Just what I read in the newspapers," or something quite close to that reflexive sentiment of faith in print and abstraction.

The New Haven *Register,* in an editorial answering charges of unfair publicity, revealed that its treatment of the Black Panther Party is not accidental. After claiming that the paper had been merely reporting police charges, the editorial launched an attack on the Black Panther Party, describing Bobby Seale as "shouting profanely in Yale's Battell Chapel about the 'pig' police of a 'pig' society," and reporting an unidentified "defender's" statement that "sooner or later we are going to take up arms to smash this system." "With friends and spokesmen like these," the editorial concludes, "how can the Panther Party claim that anybody on the outside could possibly prejudice its position?"

Number 33A, a long-time Telegraphers Union member, who had never been on a picket line, is accepted reluctantly by the defense and challenged by the state. That is as close to a selection as there was to be after two days. The last man cannot see to drive at night. His wife, too, is at home sick. The judge, pensive, finds a sheriff to drive him home, with another car to follow.

"It's a bad night," the judge tells the few assembled survivors, "I'll let you go now. Don't talk to anyone."

The petite, heavily powdered woman who accompanies Ericka Huggins comes smiling for her; she is a head and a half shorter. Bobby Seale, in passing, reaches out to shake someone's hand; a sheriff steps easily into his path.

THE THIRD DAY (NOVEMBER 19, 1970)

Seale and Huggins have been up and traveling since 4 A.M. The men's prison, Monteville, is an hour from New Haven, as is the Niantic State Farm for Women. Ericka travels with her diminutive matron; Bobby rides in a car full of deputies, escorted by Connecticut Highway Police in unmarked cars. This is a rather bizarre example of male chauvinism; the man is dangerous or the woman is impotent.

Now and then the potential jurors can be heard laughing in the anteroom.

Mr. Seals, juror number 37A, is younger and black. He says he would "favor Bobby Seale" and that there can be "no fair trial," but he could "still be fair." The State's Attorney uses one of his challenges. Charles Garry is on his feet making the record that "a black man, the first so far, is being excused by the state." Mr. Markle will not forget this attack and will look all day for a way to even the score; in so doing he will begin to irritate the judge.

The parade of illness resumes with a spectacular case—an elderly man with ulcers and a hernia who is "under medication and tranquilizers." He stares into space; the judge shouts, "Excused!"

Number 44A is the first juror chosen! Reaction from everyone, sheriffs included. Franklin Dilger, a grammar-school graduate, forty-two years old, from the town of Wolcott, a mailman with four children. He wanted to get out—but "only the right way"—because he badly needs the Christmas overtime salary. The defense is impressed with his straightforwardness, and he holds up under the critical "innocent until proven guilty" series. Garry asks him, "Do you pack a rod?" No. Mr. Markle tests him on the death penalty and is satisfied. There is a long defense conference. Accepted. A sheriff rushes the prize upstairs to a big empty room.

The next batch read all the local papers, watch Channels 2, 3, 4 and 8, associate the Panthers with the 1968 "Chicago riots," but do not know why, feel Bobby Seale "is arrogant," but "can't say how," are "nervous" and "want to go home" and feel that the defendants must prove their innocence. The court lets them go. Recess.

The process of justice is commonly likened to "a game" where the state and the defense compete with chesslike tactics. But the metaphor of the game is too shallow.

The rhetorical or gamelike ritual of the courtroom is only a rather recent abstraction of a very old flesh-and-blood confrontation. The hidden reality of blood and power had begun to emerge in Bobby Seale's earlier Chicago case, and the country had not liked the look of it at all.

The process of justice, like Greek tragedy, is based squarely on physical combat between *antagonists,* who struggle to the death in the tragic *agon.* The *agony* of the defendants is not a sentimental battle of wits with the state; it is nothing less than an unequal struggle to the last. The death of one set of combatants is the birth of tragedy and, at the same time, the future. Thus, the Greeks equated tragedy with a strange joy, *eudaemonism;* Bobby and Ericka are *daemons* in the authentic sense of that term—not happy, euphoric, but joyful in their suffering and downgoing.

In our own law, until after the twelfth century, trial by ordeal stood side by side with trial by oath. Eventually this oath taking led on to the rudimentary trial by jury. But until recent times almost any infraction carried the death penalty. If it is a game at all, then, the stakes, in political trials of the first magnitude, are life and death.

When individuals are able to rise above motives and band together, then the state quickly takes their measure, for it fears combination and cooperation above all things, because the state knows from its own history that revolution is made by a relatively small number of people—Einstein said 2 percent—a vanguard who are willing to die for a future they may never see.

This is the setting for the Seale-Huggins "game." The state in its deep disappointment over the outcome of the McLucas trial will maneuver carefully to bring to a conclusion its conspiracy charge against Seale. The charge, in the first place, was considered a desperate gamble by many conservative observers, who feared such overreaching by power.

The lone fighters pitted against the armed state are not entirely alone, however. The gods of the past protect them, because the guarantees of equity and evidence and the "presumption of innocence" are a battle dress won through millennia of suffering and struggle. In our case, the Bill of Rights and the Constitution came after six thousand years of moral evolution *and revolution,* and therefore cannot be denied the poorest defendant upon pain of rebellion or new revolution. The legal counsel is the chorus who flourishes the abstractions of the past, won in blood, to protect the antagonist, who is otherwise at the mercy of power while he is closely bound in jail or prison. Out of this dialectic between the past and the state, comes the future as it walks into the court on long legs in the persons of the Chairman of the Black Panther Party and Ericka Huggins.

There are giants and dwarfs and beasts stirring in the half-light of the primitive shadow play behind the "political game."

The libido of the conspiracy scenario is "oral-sadistic." Under pressure the State acts out the fantasy—and stimulates it in the citizen—of an infant fixated in what Melanie Klein called the "paranoid position."

Everywhere there are hidden plots to invade the vulnerable openings of the prostrate body politic. The mother- or fatherland lies helpless, swaddled by a constricting legal binding, suffocating and unable to breathe in the poisonous *ambiance* generated by lurking and mysterious figures just out of reach.

The reaction is one of counterphobia. With a superhuman effort the helpless giant reaches out with its extremities to draw the shadowy figures into the light, to stare into what turns out to be an uncannily intimate and sinister face.

The dynamics are mindless and visceral. The atavism under the skin of the courtroom demands blood as the price of a return to the primal unity of the homogeneous body politic. Cannibalism begins. The insatiable old order now begins to eat its children.

There must be an incessant confession to drown out the silence. A litany of names must be recited to gorge the vasomotor madness and narcotize the twitching nervous system of the dying State. This is the phenomenon of the dying State regressively recapitulating the paranoid delusion of the infant.

The enemy is called by many euphemisms—stranger, heathen, devil, witch, Communist, Panther, to name a handful—but behind the masks the State always imagines the same implacable combatants: death, impotence, finitude.

The conspiracy strategy is doomed in advance because the future is a biological conspiracy that is inexorable, and death itself is a biological conspiracy so deeply imbedded inside the body that the State in its terrific throes can only speed up the mortal process. Put some gabbling informer on the stand to name the names of death and its fellow travelers, but in the end the State and its creatures choke on the endless list of finitude.

But the revenge of the old, dying order is a terrible thing. All that is left in the place of struggle when the agon has ended is the pitiless justice of the ubiquitous biology that outlasts all the verbal dragnets and the phobic formulas of magical name calling. The official chambers reek with blood, the ancient order stands for a moment in is formal and frozen narcissism and then drops dead; out of the entrails, half digested, crawls the hated future.

Combat is implied in the wording of the ideal in the administration of criminal justice—"A true deliverance between the State and the prisoner at the bar." The court—the legal arm of the State— acts as an arbiter mediating between adversaries even as the State itself is a grand referee between the nation's contending classes. This is the theory and the mystique of what critics call "bourgeois democracy." This "neutrality" of the State in word and symbol, if not in deed, is the result of a series of human-rights struggles, rebellions and revolutions since the ages of feudalism.

In the social scientist's vocabulary the philosophical concept of the stranger becomes the sociological one of the deviant. Kai T. Erikson says of the Puritan experiment in the New World that it proved extremely difficult . . .

to assemble all the different fragments of that "way" into a single blueprint.

It is quite natural, then, that they would seek new frames of reference to help them remember who they were; and it is just as natural that they would begin to look with increasing apprehension at the activities of the Devil. One of the surest ways to confirm an identity, for communities as well as for individuals, is to find some way of measuring what one is not. And as the settlers began to take stock of themselves in this new and uncertain land, they learned to study the shapes in which the Devil appeared to them with special care—for he had always loomed in Puritan imagery as a *dark* adversary against which people could test the edge of their own sainthood.

As old as night, the devil is almost always a black man, and the witches, even when they are men, always have breasts.

Number 59, an elderly black man in a neat threadbare suit enters, carrying an umbrella. Dennis Adams, retired, has lived in New Haven for forty years. He has two nephews on the police force, he cannot remember the name of one of them. The defense goes very carefully (they simply must have black jurors), while number 59 "signifies." Bobby Seale leans in to help, he is trying to interpret Mr. Adams to Miss Roraback:

Q: Could you give an impartial verdict in this case, Mr. Adams?
A: Well, I'm retired now. . . .

This, Mr. Seale was trying to signal, meant that Mr. Adams needed the ten dollars a day.

Q: Where did you work, Mr. Adams?
A: I was a floor man. . . . [It always seemed as if he had said "floor mop."]

Every answer trails off. The man is from the generations of "Uncle Tom," but the defendants and the black spectators are holding their breath; they "understand." So each answer is recondite, hanging in the air, and by a remarkable act of "physical" coordination the "answer" is thrown back to the interrogator to finish *any way he wants*. He could be deadly to the prisoners, but he has an unemployed son at home and the defense does not hesitate. Heads swivel, what will Mr. Markle do? They get through the death-penalty exchange, Mr. Adams says something about "the facts," thereby managing to convey at least three things at once; everyone thinks he has heard whatever he wishes. Arnold Markle is still stung by Garry's blunt baiting of the morning; he accepts! Number 59 is hurried off to join number 44A upstairs.

There the momentum ends, they will go to the end of the first week without even another close call. When nothing else works, Catherine Roraback swings into "If a law-enforcement officer testifies, do you tend to give him extra points over someone who is not in law enforcement?"

Katie Roraback is a fixture in New Haven and New England. Driving around the state between her two offices, collecting untouchable clients, excoriating almost everyone on the theme of male chauvinism and women's liberation, inspiring a flock of young lawyers to remember what is authentic in the New England tradition, always unarguably herself and fiercely loyal to her causes and her clients.

Before Katie there was the girl, Catherine Roraback. Her father was a well-known minister, her grandfather a member of the Supreme Court of Connecticut. There was a Roraback who was a public defender and another, J. Henry, a Republican party power broker of formidable political proportions. One of Katie's law offices, in Canaan, Connecticut, was founded in 1874. She knows, in Martin Buber's phrase, where she comes from in her New England of witches and Quakers, saints and sadists.

After graduation from Mount Holyoke, the young Miss Roraback went to Washington to work on war boards, then after that last popular war she went to Yale to study law. That Yale law degree went into courts up to the Supreme, into the Smith Act cases in the days when only the odd acquaintance was not afraid to talk to a familiar Katie suddenly made strange by the State. Speaking of those days at a testimonial evening for her, Thomas I. Emerson, Lines professor at Yale Law School said,

If one were to attempt a summary, there are two things, I think, that stand out. One is that Katie has upheld the great tradition of the law as an instrument for protecting individual rights, for facilitating social change, and generally for maintaining the ground rules of an open, democratic society. Secondly, she has brought the law much closer to the people, so that all members of the community, not only those financially privileged have an opportunity to share its benefits. The need for legal assistance to *all* people is finally coming to be recognized, and it is bringing significant changes into our society. But Katie has for years been New Haven's community lawyer.

There is a persistence of style through it all. From the 1874 small-town Canaan law office to the obligatory journeys into Mississippi, the pattern is consistent and the values rigorous. Charles Garry, the proletarian at the barricades of jurisprudence, could never quite understand Katie, the radical Christian socialist, aristocratic intercessor, who could never say the word "motherfucker" in the questions on language in the jury selection—or how much she loved the woods and lakes of the New England past, her compassion for the demoralized New Englanders themselves and always her awe for this country and what it might have been; the "gift outright," as Frost called it.

Music and skiing existed before the Panther trials. There was a little help from the various legal and civil-libertarian groups that she had helped to start over the lean bad years of the cold war. But how to pay the rent?

Now she was bringing into the defense a young twenty-seven-year-old Jewish aristocrat, David Rosen. He was the third lawyer. Beautiful, with long hair and rosy cheeks, with a lawyer for a wife, and a new baby.

So there was the Armenian street fighter, tough and elegant, Katie the unarguable New Englander, and the youth with flowing hair and worn-out expensive clothes—from Fieldston School, Harvard, London School of Economics and Yale Law School—the one whom Charles Garry always called "Boss" and whom he would assign to argue all the motions in a syntax, legal and literary, that none of them could match. They made an unlikely, but in the end indomitable, triptych of combat: the grand populist and the plain unvarnished aristocrat and David, the flower rabbi-lawyer.

Somehow Catherine Roraback and Ericka Huggins were destined to stand trial together. After Mississippi came the New England "riots" and the Martin Luther King, Jr., assassination aftermath with its wake of political cases. Rape in the ghetto, the naked Living Theatre at Yale, abortion suits—she defended them all. Her class-action case against the police, in the name of the black community, meant that the Panthers would not be far behind in time.

There is no wonder that Ericka and Katie came to love each other. Ericka's letters to her lawyer are rare missiles of trust and candor. They were not mother and daughter, they were sisters.

Catherine Roraback was in charge of the pretrial onslaught of motions and testimony against the State's case. She marshaled her experts and sources with such coherence that the State and Mr. Markle never quite regained the initiative that they had seized with the McLucas trial.

Armed with the Kerner Report and the Eisenhower Commission Report, Katie and the defense went for the heart of the jury-selection system. Building on the strategy pioneered in the Huey P. Newton case, they marshaled the experts and the statistics before a judge who they knew would deny their radical motions and a defensive State's Attorney who objected at every turn to American racism being put on trial. But the defense insisted on making a record for appeal and for history. Everyone knew that in the future this pretrial ground breaking would be of historic importance, and the representatives of the State banked on it to vindicate the system and their dedicated defense of it.

In summary the defense charged a statistical "sampling error" or distorted jury profile in violation of the Constitutional rights of Bobby Seale and Ericka Huggins. In other words, the jury population itself was fatally unrepresentative.

The biggest issues—racism and death-penalty scruples—were taken up separately and referred to throughout the jury selection. The premise from which the defense argued was stated by the first Mr. Justice Harlan.

The very idea of a jury is a body of men composed of the peers or equals of the person whose rights it is selected or summoned to determine; that is, of his neighbors, fellows, associates, persons having the same legal status in society that he holds.

The importance of this representation of the "masses" in the judicial process lies in the fact, tacitly recognized and assumed by the authorities quoted above, that judges, lawyers and other members of the judicial establishment do not belong to the masses but are representatives of an "upper class" far removed in many instances from the life and experience of those whose fate is placed in their hands.

This fact becomes especially important in a society which has only recently begun to recognize the existence of the great class and racial divisions existing within itself, and the implications which those divisions have for the institutions of that society. Thus it is that in such a society, the role of the jury as the leavening element in the judicial system becomes crucial and its composition and selection becomes a factor of key significance. This comes down to what the federal court has to say: "When the basic jury list was poisoned, the fruits of that list were also infected. To cure the infection, it is necessary to start the process anew." (*United States v. Rabinowitz*)

Using Department of Labor statistics, the defense startled the court with examples such as the fact that more than one third (or 27,683,000 out of 70,000,000) of women in the United States who are over sixteen years of age have children under age eighteen. Exemption from jury duty is granted to mothers with children under sixteen, *whether or not* the women are able to make satisfactory child-care arrangements. In fact, close to one half of all mothers with children under sixteen make arrangements for their children to be cared for on a regular basis. The stereotyped image of the full-time mother who spends all day in the home simply does not correspond to social and economic reality, particularly for black women and for poor women. Forty-nine percent of the women with children ages six to seventeen work. An even higher proportion of nonwhite mothers work—55.2 percent of the nonwhite mothers with children aged six to seventeen work; 42.1 percent of the nonwhite mothers of children younger than six years old work.

Thus, for nearly half the mothers the exemption provided will send them not back to their families but to their jobs. This creates the irrational result that men who work and who have children under sixteen are required to serve as jurors, but women, even if they work side by side with men, are excused if they have children.

The special statutory exemption for women, having no reasonable basis for its existence, constitutes a clear denial of equal protection and is thus Constitutionally invalid.

There was even an expert to tell how black children are taught to lower their eyes in front of teachers and other authorities and the sad implications of this survival tactic. The defense had piled up the long and shameful evidence, looking over the head of the judge, trying to catch the eye of the people and of history.

So cogent and serious was the defense's use of the often perfunctory pretrial machinery that the Connecticut Civil Liberties Union joined in an *amicus curiae* brief citing as its reasons:

I. White racism is a widespread and pervasive feature of American society which will be carried into the jury box by white jurors.
II. Racism has deep social and psychological roots in any given individual, and its presence will be most difficult to ascertain during the *voir dire* examination.
III. The differing life experiences and cultural behavior determinants of white people and black people make it extremely difficult for white persons to understand and evaluate the testimony of black defendants and witnesses.

The Union took an interdisciplinary approach leaving the strictly legal argument to Roraback, Garry and Rosen. First, they cited the black psychoanalysts Grier and Cobbs from their book *Black Rage:*

Americans characteristically are unwilling to think about the past. We are a future-oriented nation, and facing backwards is an impediment to progress. Although these attitudes may propel us to the moon, they are deficient when human conflict needs resolution. They bring white Americans to an impasse when they claim to "understand" black people.

Then on to the conclusion of the President's Commission on Civil Disorders:

This is our basic conclusion: Our nation is moving toward two societies, one black, one white—separate and unequal. . . . Certain fundamental matters are clear. Of these, the most fundamental is the racial attitudes and behavior of white Americans toward black Americans. Race prejudice has shaped our history decisively in the past: it now threatens to do so again.

The Union offered public-opinion analysis from the standard Harris Poll:

Question	% responding affirmatively
Negroes smell different	52
Negroes have looser morals	50
Negroes want to live off handouts	43
Object to having Negro child to supper	42
Object to trying clothes Negroes tried on	31

There is a growing feeling of inexorability. All the State has to do is use its peremptory challenges to throw off "liberal" jurors, should any surface, while the judge will exclude any who have scruples against the death penalty. After the defense has exhausted its sixty peremptories, the sampling error in the gathering of the venire will provide the prosecution with the "death-oriented" panel that it craves. No matter how frugal the defense is (sheer brilliance and determination have brought them this far having used only *three* of their peremptory challenges) the day must come when Bobby Seale and Ericka Huggins will put their lives in the hands of a "death-qualified" jury.

How is this? In 1305, after the early days of trial by jury, the Crown lost its right to unlimited peremptory challenge. It was *not* a part of common law prior to the American Revolution or when the Constitution of the United States was adopted. When the Bill of Rights was drawn the First Congress stated:

The trial of all crimes, except in cases of impeachment, and in cases arising in the land or naval forces, or in the militia when in actual service in time of war or public danger, shall be by impartial jury of the vicinage, with the right of challenge and other accustomed requisites. . . .

After the Huey P. Newton trial, the sociologist and legal historian Ann Fagan Ginger pointed out that the right of the accused to challenge was classically regarded as an "accustomed requisite" of an impartial jury, and that the later right of the prosecution to peremptory challenge is not such a requisite, nor is it an equal right with that of the accused.

The Supreme Court, in *People v. Smith,* found that the use of the peremptory by the state to systematically exclude black people or all of the peers of the accused was unconstitutional. But armed with the challenge the prosecution can zero in on the few "defense-oriented" jurors who get through the skewered, ethnocentric selection process while the judge excuses for cause those with death-penalty problems. For the defense this ensures a "conviction-prone" jury.

But Huey P. Newton will announce at his press conference at noon that "the people will free Bobby and Ericka," that there will be a people's trial on the Green and that if worse comes to worst, "there will be no light for days."

In New Haven, in the beginning, there was no trial by jury, just one man adjudicating everything. In the old court and meeting house the slaves and indentured servants were brought before the bar. In those days gossip against individuals was always listened to by the Bench—it was the media. "Speaking evil of dignitaries" was a prime offense in those days. Bobby Seale, in the words of the hour, would have blown their minds, but even so they were still scandalized by his profanity, which had reached them from Chicago, and by the tape they had read about, that contained Ericka's epithets.

In 1643 New Haven's Fundamental Agreement was expanded to include Branford, Milford, Guilford, Stamford. New Haven was the governing seat for these plantations, as they called them, and so it is today. From these and like towns the New Haven juries are drawn.

These panels, predominantly Irish and Italian, drive here to do the citizens' work that the more affluent professional people of

New Haven and Yale are excused from. They come now as their ancestors walked and rode to trade and petition. These working people do not attend the churches on the Green, Christ's or Trinity, or the United or the Center. On Sundays they trudge out to St. Anne's or Holy Name of the Virgin and then back to guard their thin slice of property.

The town fears and hates the Yalies almost as much as they do the Panthers. The townies and Yalies fought on Chapel Street with guns and knives over a century ago.

No wonder these working people have no love for the Yale Corporation or its town. All they have ever got from Yale is pollution and riots and jury duty. Now they have to come and look at the Chairman of the Black Panthers and that woman. Two strangers.

The State's rhetorical position is an abstraction of the traditions of the West—Judaeo-Christian, Greco-Roman, Anglo-Saxon. This tradition, morally and legally, is defined by the strategy it provides for dealing, in a boundary situation, with the *stranger*.

The stranger is the *other,* the alien, the outsider. They are the witches, the scapegoats. So powerful is the impulse to kill the vulnerable outsider that all moral systems begin with protection for the foreigner. In New Haven, 1971, the stranger could be politically and physically strange in the stereotypical sense of the Black Panthers, or existentially strange like the romantic students, or psychologically strange like the sad and terrified array of jurors that were waiting to be called. In each case the stranger—in the flesh or in the spirit—must be repressed to stave off choice (freedom) and hence disruption and change. The confrontation with the stranger—in the court, the street, the bedroom—is always and everywhere a "limit situation," as Sartre calls it.

In the oldest religion in our culture the Lord hides inside the beggar, the wanderer, the outsider. Inside the skin of the footsore traveler he lies vicariously in wait for the prideful householder. Christian *caritas* results from the *identity* of God through man, "when you do it unto the least . . ." The Greeks were simpler, of course. Theseus says to the exiled criminal, the old blind Oedipus,

"I am a man and know it. Tomorrow's good is no more mine than thine nor any man's." This is *aidos,* what we might call ruth, but it is much more than pity.

The secular, sentimental version of all this is the presumption of innocence and the due process with its manifold safeguards. The court's rhetoric—which clothes the defendants with inviolable Constitutional protection—is the structural transition from savagery to civilization and freedom (in the ideological sense). The rhetoric is the word magic which transforms the chained prisoner into the being presumed to be innocent. This is the apogee of a system of received "rights."

When Charles Garry and Bobby Seale objected furiously during the jury selection to the question, "Can you be fair to the state?" observers were always stunned. Because the question betrayed the fiction: if you think the prisoner guilty you must be excused from sitting in judgment; but if you think the prisoner innocent, then you must not be excused, for the law too presumes him so. But, of course, if you *really believe* the prisoner innocent then you will, as a matter of course, be rejected from duty. Garry and Seale, being revolutionary existentialists, challenged the paradoxes and metaphors that are the very image of the State. Predictably, the State moved armed sheriffs in force into the vacuum after its rhetoric had been demystified and desanctified.

The hundreds of potential jurors about to begin their long march through the halls of justice will display such bewilderment and disorientation because they are strangers to the rhetoric and the guns of power too. Already powerless in body and soul, they will do almost anything to put more distance between themselves and those who are presumed innocent and who are always surrounded by heavily armed guards.

The prosecution claims it wants justice for the dead man, Alex Rackley, not vengeance. As proof it offers its traditional rhetoric; the Panthers spit on the rodomontade of the past and answer with their own rhetoric tending toward the future. The State insists that time will tell who the stranger is and what his fate.

Finally, the State's only moral argument is its rhetoric; besides that there is only the *guns.* The "facts" of the *criminal* case are caught in the larger *political* argument that is predicated on the

State's protection of the citizen from the stranger. The right to be "strange," the right to be oneself—that would be one definition of a "good society," a definition, perhaps, with the future on its side.

The argument and the rhetoric of the stranger, on the other hand, are in a very different vocabulary, like that of George Jackson, the Soledad Brother and Panther Field Marshal:

This monster—the monster they've engendered in me—will return to torment its maker, from the grave, the pit, the profoundest pit. Hurl me into the next existence, the descent into hell won't turn me. I'll crawl back to dog his trail forever. They won't defeat my revenge, never, never. I'm part of a righteous people who anger slowly, but rage undammed. We'll gather at his door in such a number that the rumbling of our feet will make the earth tremble. I'm going to charge them for this, twenty-eight years without gratification. I'm going to charge them reparations in blood. I'm going to charge them like a maddened, wounded, rogue male elephant, ears flared, trunk raised, trumpet blaring. I'll do my dance in his chest and the only thing he'll ever see in my eyes is a dagger to pierce his cruel heart. This is one nigger who is positively displeased. I'll never forgive, I'll never forget, and if I'm guilty of anything at all it's of not leaning on them hard enough. War without terms.

It was his brother Jonathan who had lifted the stakes of the argument of the outcast beyond rhetoric when he entered the San Rafael, California, courtroom and announced coolly, "All right, gentlemen, I'm taking over now." The structured honorific phrase paying an ironic tribute to the received rhetorical argument of the old State, now passing away, as Jonathan Jackson entered the boundary situation with his mind "not on murder but on freedom," as Huey P. Newton preached at his funeral.

In a pre-revolutionary situation the legal argument always gives way to the physical *agon* of combat.

WHARTON: Friends, what is the cause and wherefore have I been fetched from my habitation, where I was following my honest calling, and here laid up as an evil-doer?

MAGISTRATE: Your hair is too long and you are disobedient to that commandment which saith, "Honor thy mother and father."

WHARTON: Wherein?

MAGISTRATE: In that you will not put off your hat before the magistrates.

Thus, New England in the eighteenth century.

The prosecution would argue in the future—to those who called attention to the ringing statement of our Declaration of Independence that was attached to the Panthers' ten-point survival program—that the evil the Panthers fomented among the good but poor Negro population was so often invisible, but yet so invidious, that when an opportunity for criminal prosecution presented itself, or could be found or "reconstructed," then the State must reach out with its power in order to protect the people.

Bobby and Ericka, as strangers, were, thus, in the boundary or extreme situation, where every word and gesture were heavily laden with finitude. At the same time they occupied physically and in every other way the boundary line of the community itself. It is, as Kai Erikson says, that morality and immorality meet at the public scaffold, and it is during this meeting that the line between them is drawn.

The State was torn between its fear of popular intervention in the trial and its old desire to make a public example of the alien criminal element, as it saw the Panthers. Public hangings and floggings were abandoned only after there was a medium—the newspapers—to carry the message of "limits" to the citizenry.

Alexis de Tocqueville had made certain predictions about how xenophobia would be acted out in a democratic republic.

You are free to think differently from me, and to keep your life, your property, and all that you possess; but if such be your determination, you are henceforth an alien among your own people. . . .You will remain among men, but you will be deprived of the rights of mankind. Your fellow creatures will shun you like a leper; and those who are most persuaded of your innocence will abandon you too, lest they should be shunned in turn.

Bobby Seale is led in. "Give me some," he says when he spies his beloved Huey and reaches to hug him. The sheriffs pause. Ericka is seated, she turns to look at Huey P. Newton. He and

David Hilliard lean forward to give the clenched fist to Ericka. She has seen Huey at last.

Only Jean Genet could describe the search of Huey P. Newton by the police at the courtroom door. Huey, his brown leather jacket draped over his powerful shoulders, answered the courtroom guard's question about weapons, "I've got a machine gun under each arm." The guard had to lightly pat down the whole length of the heroic torso; only Genet could have described the ambivalence, sexuality and astonishment of the police.

Newton is tired. He has been speaking to overflow crowds in Boston, Ann Arbor, New York and Detroit; organizing for the Washington, D.C., Revolutionary People's Constitutional Convention, and announcing his new philosophy of "intercommunalism," which takes as its basic metaphor the oneness of global technology, now in the hands of the oppressor, "Amerika." Now, he sits in the front row quietly watching the trial.

The bundles of complaints and phobias trip along the gantlet of sheriffs pausing at the witness stand just long enough to disqualify themselves. A very concerned judge has given up even arguing with the defense.

The judge will argue, quietly, with number 89C; they all will. The attractive, well-dressed, young black woman with rosy-tan skin and light-brown hair is struggled over for a half hour before an almost prayerful gallery. She can be impartial, she tells the State's Attorney, but she thought the Chicago binding and gagging "terrible." Markle is on a spot, there is no cosmetic method for expelling her and there must be no racism in this trial.

"Will you consider the death penalty, Mrs. Pope?"

"No."

When the judge finally told her that she was excused, Attorney Roraback rose to present another argument against dismissing people because they did not believe in the death penalty. She noted that they were picking a jury to decide a verdict and not to determine the sentence. She said that it would be possible to empanel another jury for sentencing if necessary and that it was unfair to continue to search for a conviction-prone jury because there was a possibility that they would have to consider sentencing. Her arguments were recorded, but made no immediate difference.

Some time later, a man said simply, "I don't believe in an eye for an eye . . ." and he was excused.

"Consider, just consider," the defense and the court are almost pleading.

She seems torn; does Mrs. Pope know that the man in the front row is Huey Newton? She hesitates a long time before reiterating her opposition to the death penalty.

Studies of other trials, including the Newton trial, reveal that fully half of those excused for opposition to capital punishment are "minority persons." The studies of Professor Hans Zeisel, of the University of Chicago Law School, have become classics in this field and constitute much of the evidence in a test case offered to the Supreme Court of the United States, *Witherspoon v. Illinois.*

For instance, those white people opposing capital punishment approve of integrated housing at the rate of 59 percent as against 28 percent for those favoring the death sentence. Again, pro–capital-punishment jurors are likely to vote guilty on the first ballot in criminal cases.

Professor R. Nevell Sanford, of Stanford University, translates these and like figures into the psychology of the jury.

In what is called the F (for fascism) test and in a related work, *The Authoritarian Personality,* Sanford talks about this juror:

. . . set of interrelated characteristics . . . being . . . primary over-submissiveness to authority and undercritical acceptance of authority . . . a rigid adherence to conventional values to the degree that the individual involved is easily outraged by violations of conventional standards; a special kind of aggressiveness. . . . a form of aggressiveness directed particularly to people who are believed to be violating conventional standards and characteristically carried out in the name of some authority; a disposition to dislike weakness in other people, to seem to be very sensitive to the presence of weakness in other people and to present one's self as extraordinarily powerful and tough; to be associated with or identified with, insofar as possible, what is strong and to be disidentified with whatever is perceived as weak; a readiness to—to believe in dangerous goings-on in the world; a kind of suspiciousness or a readiness to believe the worst about people; to take a somewhat cynical view of human nature. . . . [to be] punitive and judgmental [and to show] traits of hostile rejectiveness.

Dr. Sanford developed a research instrument that has since become standard in the social sciences, the F scale. The F scale measures characteristics of rigidity and punitiveness in the authoritarian personality. "Death-qualified" jurors score very high on the F scale.

Dr. W. Cody Wilson joins this argument in the Witherspoon case with an affidavit,

People who have scruples against capital punishment are less likely to say guilty than are people who believe in capital punishment. . . . People who believe in capital punishment are more likely to be in favor of the prosecution than are people who have scruples against capital punishment.

The conclusions of these and other social scientists were summed up in the Newton case in an affidavit from Dr. Robert Crosson, who was one of the team of Zeisel, Sanford, Wilson and Goldberg in that empirical research, at once science and moral evolution, now resting before the Supreme Court, Judge Mulvey, and everyone else charged with the adminstration of justice.

"Excused." A groan. Garry is up fighting. The judge knows about *Witherspoon,* but what about *Glasser v. United States?*

Tendencies, no matter how slight, toward the selection of jurors by any method other than a process which will insure a trial by a representative group are undermining processes, weakening the institution of jury trial, and should be sturdily resisted. That the motives influencing such tendencies may be of the best must not blind us to the dangers of allowing any encroachment whatsoever on this essential right.

That is what the court found, and whatever interest the prosecutor may have in retaining authoritarian or death-oriented personalities for the jury, he can have no valid motive for exploiting a process which insures the *exclusive retention of such types.* There can be no justification for the sampling error of the jury population when the process of excluding those opposed to death creates a death-oriented jury which is not only conviction-prone but at the same time excludes 50 percent of the already grossly underrepresented nonwhite population. That is what the evidence and the court seem to say.

Miss Roraback rises to join in the exception, and the "sister" walks out under the sad gaze of the gallery. Huey P. Newton's face is quiet, David Hilliard's is masked behind dark glasses.

Near the end, a number 62 comments knowingly about the "Chicago Five." For a moment the radicals pause to pick over their memory or conscience for some forgotten quintet of bombers or saints before sinking lower on their spines in mild disgust. Seale is accused of not "acting like a gentleman," and the man is excused.

The court is adjourning early, there are no more candidates to question. Judge Mulvey announces that Huey Newton and David Hilliard may stay to meet with Bobby Seale and Ericka Huggins and that everyone else should leave.

Arnold Markle asks if he may stay to say something after the court is cleared. Alone with the Panthers and lawyers, Markle asks the judge to search Newton and Hilliard once more. "Why?" asks Mulvey; "they're standing right in front of me." "I would feel better," says the prosecutor. "All right, if it makes Mr. Markle feel better," says the judge. It is done, and then the old friends are left alone in peace. Ericka, they say, was quite quiet. There was no report of what was discussed.

THE SIXTH DAY (NOVEMBER 25, 1970)

Over the long weekend, Charles Garry had been seen in a barbershop, in a health-food store, and delivering by hand, to the media, a statement from his client. A black policemen's organization in Hartford, the Guardians, had announced that it would physically intervene should there be continued police brutality toward black or Puerto Rican people. Later some of the Guardians visited the trial.

PRESS RELEASE

We, the Black Panther Party, support the Hartford Black Policemen (THE GUARDIANS) as beautiful humane brothers who have taken a peoples' community stand against fascist-racist police brutality and persecution. Their position is that "The time is at hand when black and other minority police officers and citizens cannot and should not stand by and permit white, and any others who are also bigoted police officers to *UNJUSTLY* assault and abuse the dignity of the black, the Puerto Rican, or for that matter, ANY HUMAN BEING."

This position is exactly what the Black Panther Party has been saying from the beginning of our Party in 1966.

Just as Chicago's Afro-American Patrolmen's League and the Black Panther Party are able to function in supporting unity for a people's constitutional COMMUNITY CONTROL OF POLICE, to end white racist-fascist police brutality, we the Black Panther Party come forth to support and salute THE GUARDIANS for the simple reason that a better society can begin to be constructed upon the now falling ruins of white racism here in Amerika.

> Bobby Seale
> Chairman
> Black Panther Party

At the same time, a leaflet was circulating through New Haven calling for mass support for the prisoners. The judge had not seen this leaflet, but the police had shown him an earlier one, wherein he and Markle were hanged like stuck pigs. Garry, in the name of the Panther leadership, denounced the first flier as provocative and counterrevolutionary. The judge was also studying a copy of the newspaper *Black Panther* with its screaming headlines about the "NEW HAVEN RAILROAD."

This is the newspaper being offered into evidence in courtrooms all over America as proof of the antisocial, nihilistic identity of the Panthers. It is set over against all the hot breakfasts, free health clinics, busing programs for the families of prisoners, liberation schools, and the new miniaturized shoe factories to be worked by ex-convicts. The "niggers under the mud" are learning to read from this revolutionary tabloid with its extraordinary mixture of Marx and street music; rhapsody, rhetoric and savage epithets from the bestiary. In these pages Eldridge Cleaver poured out his underground heart, and simple reports about the "pigs" and their doings were filed from around the country by "Michael D." and "Sioux" and "Little Masai" and "Malik" and a hundred other existential correspondents on the revolutionary wire service from Babylon.

Here the religious core of revolution is palpable. A *Lumpenproletariat* such as the world has never seen is coming into history on a bridge of symbols, and the *Black Panther* news is continuous with *The Autobiography of Malcolm X* and *Soul On Ice* and *Soledad Brother*.

Maoist man learns to read, learns that he exists and comes into history through the little *Red Book* as medieval man came through the vulgate into self-consciousness and citizenship. This epistemological process has a nonrational libido: the nonwhite school dropouts of America have gone to the University of the Penitentiary and the streets, and there they find their vulgate with the picture of Huey P. Newton on the masthead. The police and all the intelligence services search in vain for a translation of the damnable phenomena; they stare at it, hard-eyed, and look for the cartoons of the youngsters killing *attacking* "pigs."

And yet, in a way, the State is, as usual, correct about the threat of the brightly colored thing. Just as the translation of the Latin gospel into the vulgar language signaled the end of pope and king, so this primer signals an end and a beginning for the wretched of the American earth with its cartoons of pigs, its apocalyptic and utopian word pictures for the future of those who, otherwise, have no future.

But surely more frightening than the pictures of pigs were the pages given over to "Rules" and "Program." The program was from 1966 and considered temporary by the Panthers.

1. *We want freedom. We want power to determine the destiny of our Black Community.*

We believe that black people will not be free until we are able to determine our destiny.

2. *We want full employment for our people.*

We believe that the federal government is responsible and obligated to give every man employment or a guaranteed income. We believe that if the white American businessmen will not give full employment, then the means of production should be taken from the businessmen and placed in the community, so that the people of the community can organize and employ all of its people and give a high standard of living.

3. *We want an end to the robbery by the CAPITALIST of our Black Community.*

We believe that this racist government has robbed us and now we are demanding the overdue debt of forty acres and two mules. Forty acres and two mules was promised 100 years ago as restitution for slave labor and mass murder of black people. We will accept the payment in currency which will be distributed to our many communities. The Germans are now aiding the Jews in Israel for the genocide of the Jewish people. The Germans murdered six million Jews. The American racist has taken part in the slaughter of over fifty million black people; therefore, we feel that this is a modest demand that we make.

4. *We want decent housing, fit for shelter of human beings.*

We believe that if the white landlords will not give decent housing to our black community, then the housing and the land should be made into cooperatives so that our community, with government aid, can build and make decent housing for its people.

5. *We want education for our people that exposes the true nature of this decadent American society. We want education that teaches us our true history and our role in the present-day society.*

We believe in an educational system that will give to our people a knowledge of self. If a man does not have knowledge of himself and his position in society and the world, then he has little chance to relate to anything else.

6. *We want all black men to be exempt from military service.*

We believe that black people should not be forced to fight in the military service to defend a racist government that does not protect us. We will not fight and kill other people of color in the world who, like black people, are being victimized by the white racist government of America. We will protect ourselves from the force and violence of the racist police and the racist military by whatever means necessary.

7. *We want an immediate end to POLICE BRUTALITY and MURDER of black people.*

We believe we can end police brutality in our black community by organizing black self-defense groups that are dedicated to defending our black community from racist police oppression and brutality. The Second Amendment to the Constitution of the United States gives a right to bear arms. We therefore believe that all black people should arm themselves for self-defense.

8. *We want freedom for all black men held in federal, state, county and city prisons and jails.*

We believe that all black people should be released from the many jails and prisons because they have not received a fair and impartial trial.

9. *We want all black people when brought to trial to be tried in*

court by a jury of their peer group or people from their black communities, as defined by the Constitution of the United States.

We believe that the courts should follow the United States Constitution so that black people will receive fair trials. The 14th Amendment of the U.S. Constitution gives a man a right to be tried by his peer group. A peer is a person from a similar economic, social, religious, geographical, environmental, historical and racial background. To do this the court will be forced to select a jury from the black community from which the black defendant came. We have been, and are being tried by all-white juries that have no understanding of the "average reasoning man" of the black community.

10. *We want land, bread, housing, clothing, justice and peace. And as our major political objective, a United Nations-supervised plebiscite to be held throughout the black colony in which only black colonial subjects will be allowed to participate, for the purpose of determining the will of black people as to their national destiny.*

When, in the course of human events, it becomes necessary for one people to dissolve the political bands which have connected them with another, and to assume, among the powers of the earth, the separate and equal station to which the laws of nature and nature's God entitle them, a decent respect to the opinions of mankind requires that they should declare the causes which impel them to the separation.

We hold these truths to be self-evident, that all men are created equal; that they are endowed by their Creator with certain unalienable rights; that among these are life, liberty and the pursuit of happiness. *That, to secure these rights, governments are instituted among men, that, whenever any form of government becomes destructive of these ends, it is the right of the people to alter or to abolish it, and to institute a new government, laying its foundation on such principles, and organizing its powers in such form, as to them shall seem most likely to effect their safety and happiness.* Prudence, indeed, will dictate that governments long established should not be changed for light and transient causes; and, accordingly, all experience hath shown that mankind are more disposed to suffer, while evils are sufferable, than to right themselves by abolishing the forms to which they are accustomed. *But when a long train of abuses and usurpations, pursuing invariably the same object, evinces a design to reduce them under absolute despotism, it is their right, it is their duty, to throw off such government, and to provide new guards for their future security.*

Like the iconography of another age of faith, little Panthers and guns decorate the corners and crevices of the printed pages.

By the end of the trial, Huey P. Newton and artist Emory Douglas had attacked and changed their own newspaper. No more guns or pigs—in print.

The mean temperature had shifted lower but the crowd waiting to watch, in court, was considerably larger. Word circulated that an upsurge in trial agitation could be expected after the Thanksgiving Revolutionary Convention in the nation's capital.

It goes on as the day before, the people from the past, from West Haven, Cheshire, Guilford, North Haven, Wolcott, who attend church at St. Agnes and St. Mary's and St. Michael's. A revealing pattern is emerging: many of the venire have either two jobs or are recently unemployed; the economic tensions are as great as the racial. In the towns, too, the seasonal holiday business is proving a big disappointment. Not many musical organs are being purchased this year for Christmas by the threatened Italian and Irish middle-class.

Catherine Roraback goes on meticulously asking each if he knows James Ahern, Stephen Ahern, Nicolas Pastore, Vincent DeRosa, Warren Kimbro, Sylvia Kimbro, Ernest Osborne, and others who may testify.

People are reading the newspapers and selecting their reasons for not serving with a surer hand now. Opposition to the death penalty is becoming quite common, to Mr. Markle's surprise. But the judge does not give up easily, and he prolongs the inevitable challenge for cause. Fear is coming out; number 106 sets the tune when she says, "I live alone. If they did anything against me— that's the only thing."

In their memories of the "Chicago Eight" conspiracy trial, the Chicago jurors had admitted to being swayed by fear far more than by sympathy. They had made it clear that if they were to be convinced that there *was* a revolutionary movement sophisticated enough to conspire and eventually succeed to power, then they feared what judgment might await them; thus, if Bobby Seale had not been separated from the trial by Julius Hoffman, they said, they would not have convicted. The Connecticut jurors are talking about fear more openly each day even before the street demonstrations begin again.

The Waterbury *Republican* features a story on Huey P. Newton and quotes him as saying that if "the people of the world are bound up tight, then they will hold back the night!" Several prospectives refer to a Mr. Newton and, in the words of number 115, "his threats of retaliation." There is no question that *conspiracy* is the magic word of fear.

A jury trial is only the last step in a long series of events. Each step of the process affects a defendant's chances in court. In effect, a suspect's trial begins as soon as he is arrested, so that a jury can reach a fair verdict only if the defendant's pretrial treatment has been fair. To the Panthers and some others, the short haul of the state's systematic violence was plain—

Eight people arrested without warrants, at Black Panther Party headquarters in New Haven. Heavily armed police break down doors, enter bedrooms where women and children are sleeping, and ransack the office (without search warrants), seizing personal items as well as money for the children's breakfast program.

Suspects denied right to have attorneys present, then questioned for twenty-four hours. This clearly violates their constitutional rights.

Superior Court issues bench warrant, orders suspects held without bail solely on the basis of a police affidavit.

Meanwhile, in Media, Pennsylvania, in the F.B.I. field office, orders were being issued.

TO	:	ALL AGENTS
FROM	:	SAC JOE D. JAMIESON
DATE	:	10/12/70
SUBJECT	:	REVOLUTIONARY PEOPLES CONSTITUTIONAL CONVENTION ORGANIZED BY THE BLACK PANTHER PARTY

For the information of all receiving agents, the Black Panther Party (BPP) sponsored a planning session for the above convention which was held here in Philadelphia 9/4-7/70.

At the conclusion of the above convention, the BPP held a press conference and stated that the actual convention would be held in Washington, D.C., on 11/4/70.

On 10/7/70 the Bureau advised that the dates of the above had been changed to 11/6-9/70 and that about 15,000 are expected to attend; this group will comprise of white as well as black extremists.

The Bureau has issued instructions that all offices must report the following information on a weekly basis:

1. various organizations planning to participate
2. mode of travel and identities of persons planning to attend
3. identities of organizers and persons who are to head work shops
4. identities of the leading speakers at the convention
5. agenda of the convention
6. plans for violence or disruptive demonstrations
7. plans to carry weapons or explosive devices
8. convention security precautions to be observed
9. literature regarding the convention
10. details concerning available housing

In view of the above, all agents are requested to contact logical informants regularly to obtain current data as per Bureau instructions. All such information should be reported to SA PHILIP E. BROWN.

It is Kai Erikson's brilliant perception, presented in his *Wayward Puritans,* that at the height of the witchcraft hysteria in Massachusetts, the sociologist in Cotton Mather began to notice that the witches who terrorized the countryside were really very similar to the honest men who prosecuted them:

'Tis very remarkable to see what an impious and impudent imitation of divine things is apishly affected by the Devil, in several of those matters, whereof the confessions of our witches and the afflictions of our sufferers have informed us. . . . The witches do say, that they form themselves much after the manner of Congregational churches: abominably resembling those of our Lord. . . . What is their striking down with a fierce look? What is their making of the afflicted rise, with a touch of their hand? What is their transportation thro' the air? What is their travelling in spirit while their body is cast into a trance? What is their causing of cattle to run mad and perish? What is their entering their names in a book? What is their coming together from all parts, at the sound of a trumpet? What is their appearing sometimes clothed with light or fire upon them? What is their covering of themselves and their instruments with invisibility? But a blasphemous imitation of certain things recorded about our Savior or His Prophets, or the saints of the Kingdom of God.

Thus the State is literally forced to redress and give the entire range of race-class related phenomena the very first priority, or to see a conspiracy wherever the conspiracy of the State is rejected. How quickly does a revolutionary movement fulfill the state's prophecy? The Panthers were being inched little by little toward the underground. During the trial they opened the new schools for Panther children in order to establish a base line for the future beyond which they would not slide. The charge was, inevitably, conspiracy.

The Panthers charge that not they but the government and its regional and local agents are guilty of a conspiracy, that the State is guilty of a conspiracy when it uses the elusive witchcraft of the conspiracy law to implicate their Chairman in order to kill him.

Supreme Court Justice Jackson calls conspiracy "that elastic, sprawling and pervasive offense [that] defies definition." As in the case of the grand jury, the law in its first phase, around the time of Edward I, was meant to protect the individual from false and malicious prosecutions. Then as now it was the State, at whatever level, that was able to marshal police agents, prosecutors, judges, and an army of bureaucrats against the individual. The State itself is nothing but a gigantic conspiracy, the revolutionary Panther argues, forbidding and punishing violence or symbols of violence in the individual's case in order to monopolize aggression for itself. Plundering, murdering, polluting, corrupting: by November of 1970, America to the Panthers and growing numbers of disaffected white youth had become Babylon, a criminal conspiracy, and the case against Bobby Seale and Ericka Huggins outright fascism.

The individual's protection was perverted in the period of the Star Chamber. At that time, the early seventeenth century, conspiring (literally, "breathing together") became *thinking together*.

The prosecution, since then, has to prove only that planning, not action, took place. Here is where the *agent provocateur* comes in—he, the agent, in case after case suggests that the Statue of

Liberty be blown up, or marijuana be purchased, or Macy's be bombed; he is taught to provoke *probable* wrongdoers so that they may be immobilized before they act.

Clarence Darrow's example of this conspiracy charge—which in a political case demands an informer or agent or tool—was that of a boy who steals candy and is then punished for a misdemeanor whereas two boys who *plan* to steal the candy but don't are punished for a felony.

From early in the nineteenth century (the beginning, the Panthers claim, of the American counterrevolution) the conspiracy law was used against the labor movement. Until the New Deal it was a criminal conspiracy to strike. In the 1950s the Smith Act focused conspiracy charges on a generation of "fellow travelers" in various movements. The flood gates opened after Julius and Ethel Rosenberg and Morton Sobell were convicted of *conspiracy* to commit espionage. As the years passed, growing numbers decided that it was the government that had conspired in this case and during the entire McCarthy episode. More pointedly the Panther-led revolutionary movement—and millions of other people, saw the assassinations of John F. Kennedy, Malcolm X and Martin Luther King, Jr., as planned by the most reactionary element of the military-industrial complex and executed by its agents. The federal government, the Panthers insist, is deeply implicated in the New Haven charges.

Conspiracy, the last refuge of a desperate or bankrupt government, as its critics call it, is the weapon most used in recent times against dissent. The case of Big Bill Haywood, so like this case, with Darrow instead of Garry, Harry Orchard instead of George Sams, Big Bill Haywood in place of Bobby Seale, and the I.W.W. for the Panthers. Eugene Debs, Harry Bridges, Tom Mooney, Sacco and Vanzetti, Alger Hiss, Julius and Ethel Rosenberg and Morton Sobell, Dr. Spock, the Chicago Eight and the Chicago Seven, Daniel Berrigan, the Seattle Eight, the New Haven Nine, including Bobby Seale and Ericka Huggins—all products of the State's inherent paranoid organization and the existential rebellion against it. Rebellion that is born of the wedding of biology and history.

The use of the conspiracy net has rankled conservatives as well as liberals in America; in fact, the ultimate downfall of the reactionary Joseph McCarthy in the 1950s was brought about by the decisive action of conservative elements in the United States Senate. The State "tied Bobby Seale in," State's Attorney Markle would say later; and many conservative people, not included in the jury venire for some reason, were concerned. For good reason.

Judge Learned Hand called conspiracy "that darling of the modern prosecutor's nursery," because of the many advantages it affords the prosecution. Hearsay evidence inadmissable under ordinary rules can be used to implicate a defendant not only in the conspiracy, but also in the supposed substantive crimes of his codefendants, about which he may know nothing, but for which he may be held liable. The effect of evidence introduced against some defendants may act on the jury in such a way as to produce convictions for all. The mere fact of being tried together associates the defendants in the jury's mind, and it may have trouble remembering which evidence applies to which defendant. If there is a joint defense, the defendants may be identified together in the jury's thinking. However, if the defendants have separate counsel, the trial may be lengthened by a repetition of motions and countermotions. For these reasons the Conference of Senior Circuit Judges, presided over by Chief Justice William Howard Taft, warned that "the rules of evidence in conspiracy cases make them most difficult to try without prejudice to an innocent defendant."

Taft's contention is amply borne out. The crime originated in the Star Chamber, an inquisitorial court of seventeenth-century England, and was reborn in America in 1806 in the Philadelphia Cordwainers case, which ruled that a shoemakers' strike was a criminal conspiracy. More recently it has been used against anti-war and other radical groups—the Spock trial, the trial of the Oakland Seven, the Chicago Conspiracy Trial (in which one of the defendants was Bobby Seale). The evidence used by the prosecution in the Oakland Seven trial shows how all-inclusive a charge of conspiracy may be. Among the overt acts charged were opening a bank account entitled "Stop The Draft Week," hiring buses to carry people from Berkeley to Oakland, arranging a meeting, and transporting loudspeaker equipment to the Berkeley campus. In interrogating Dean of Students Jan Blais, of the University of

California, District Attorney Coakley recalled that he had warned the administration that the use of university facilities could be considered a part of a criminal conspiracy, so that university officials could be prosecuted. Such broad use of conspiracy, it was later held, makes a mockery of the First Amendment rights of speech and assembly.

The hardest blow the State can strike is the substitution of criminal for political charges. The United States has always been extremely sensitive about admitting that there are such things as class and political cases. In recent years the Miranda and Escabedo decisions have faced in some little measure the scandal of the poor and their right to a fair trial, but political cases are still spoken of only in the tongue of the criminal code. If, however, there is still a broad popular agitation around these cases and juries insist on treating the defendants as political prisoners, then government has no choice but to make it a crime to belong to a particular persuasion. Then it becomes a conspiracy to associate, to advocate or to think. But when power has to resort to these acts, by so much does it lose credibility; thus it must choose between which is the lesser evil:—the freeing of how many Huey Newtons or Sietes or changing the law to entrap political dissidents in the conspiracy net. Which will serve best the overriding purpose of the status quo, the maintenance of order, and predictability? That is the rhetorical question that power asks concerning the Panthers; it is, finally, not a matter of race at all.

Racism like anti-Communism will be left to the good people, holding down two jobs, from the little towns of the Naugatuck Valley; that is *their* ideology. To Yale goes the humanism and ratiocination; to the twenty-eight towns from which the jury is drawn goes the ideology of warfare and welfare and race; to the ghetto, where the Black Panther office is located, goes the madness and the howling, and out of these *casbahs* comes the Malcolm X or the Huey P. Newton or the Bobby Seale. Even now the Panthers believe, and history supports the belief, that somewhere in Babylon some adolescent black boys and girls have their eyes fixed on Bobby Seale and Ericka Huggins as they wriggle in the clutches of power. The battle is being memorized and internalized. And, perhaps suddenly—it always seems so to the authorities—the furious epigoni of the Panthers will appear with guns and Ph.D.'s and *plastique,* and the masses will, as the Panthers used to predict, "do the dog right here in Babylon."

So they have always been called "criminal cases," and the union or the eight-hour day or the war or the bomb has never had "anything to do with it." What is more, big political cases almost always have a dead body—from John Brown to Sacco-Vanzetti to the Haymarket to Tom Mooney. These trials of the underclass are a steady theme in the modern American tradition. The great Pullman Company, or eight-hour-day, strike in Chicago in the nineteenth century was referred to by the prosecution and the press as "The Haymarket Riots"; the strike against extortionate rent by black tenant farmers in Arkansas became, in history books, "The Elaine Riots." When Haywood, Moyer and Pettibone were refused extradition and so then kidnapped to stand trial for more than a dozen murders, Eugene V. Debs wrote:

Let every working man who has a heart in his breast make a mighty oath that not a wheel shall turn in this country from ocean to ocean until the verdict is set aside and every one of the accused is set free. Let our factories be closed; let our mills stop grinding flour and our bakeries stop baking bread. Let our coal mines close, and let us die of hunger and cold if necessary to make our protest heeded. Let us show the world that the workingmen of America are not so lost to shame, not so devoid of the red blood of courage, that they will allow one of their comrades to suffer death at the hands of their enemies. Hurrah for the Great National General Strike.

The radical pacifism and union ideals of Tom Mooney did not prevent him from being charged as a "dynamiter and German agent." Sacco and Vanzetti became *criminal* anarchists and *criminal* syndicalists. The Rosenbergs and Morton Sobell were guilty of "the greatest crime in the history of the world," according to their judge. Today, all the big Panther cases involve "murder" and conspiracy charges. Since the New England witch hunts it is the conspiracy charge that emerges as the chief symptom of the troubled State.

In the larger setting of the New Haven *agon,* beyond the foreshortened courtroom, there is a different suppressed mass violence.

The ruined mill towns of the Naugatuck Valley—their industry
fled south after cheap labor—feed their culturally wounded into
the fief of New Haven, which in turn spreads out from the fortress
Yale. These wasted surroundings to the Yale kingdom produce the
third-highest pollution in the nation! Here, where famous architects—Johnson, Kling, Rudolph, Roche, Kahn, Saarinen—display
their industrial paradigms, the streets are choked with auto-
mobiles, and the town's Mill River is *anaerobic*—no oxygen.
These were the streets boarded up agaisnt the May Day demonstration as a third of the student body hastened home and the
faculty fell furiously upon one another as the moment of what
some feared would be truth approached.

The Yale people do not venture out very far beyond their ivy-
and-stone world. In the barren valley there are Minute Men and a
bitter, tough citizenry. Here, in this New Haven area, the history of
capitalism has been acted out. In between the incredible wealth
and power of Yale and the failing middle-class mill-town population of resentment, the black and Puerto Rican enclaves are
dotted. The jury must come from the Valley; the selection process
will see to that. From the violent and fading remnant of the industrial revolution and the wreckage of New England immigration and
indenture will come the death-oriented talesmen—unless Charles
R. Garry has some desperate plan to throw into the war of nerves.

The conspiracy strategy gives rise to an economics of combat.
With the conspiracy orientation goes a proliferating intelligence
system; these self-fulfilling, self-perpetuating systems act as a
shortcut in outflanking a growing popular movement. The undercover agent is required to complete, or if necessary foment, the
"conspiracy."

While the wheels ground in New Haven and authorities smashed
into Panther offices looking for George Sams, here and there
people were expressing real unease. The Mayor of Seattle in turning
down a joint raid with federal agents said, "We are not going to
have any 1932 Gestapo-like raids against anyone." Ramsey Clark
and Arthur Goldberg called for an independent investigation of the
situation. The Reverend Ralph Abernathy, Martin Luther King's
successor in the nonviolent movement, spoke out—"From the
general attitude of the present military government in Washington,

one senses the stench of genocide. Not only against the Black Panther Party but against all black people and poor people in this country."

The domestic euphemisms of the fifties and sixties were giving way to the body-count vocabulary of the Asian war.

The prophetic forerunner to this struggle in New Haven is the *Amistad* ship rebellion in 1835. After 1820 it was illegal to import slaves from Africa, so traders would touch down with their contraband human cargo in the West Indies, where slave export was legal, and then come to North America. A formidable man, a slave, named Cinque, led a ship's rebellion and came ashore in New Haven.

What Muriel Rukeyser describes as New England's profound sky and the Green and the warm brick and wood encapsulated the Africans and so, at the same time, the memory of the sun of Sierra Leone. The figure of the black Africans against the white New England ground—Rukeyser paints it brilliantly:

This color that they saw, these flickering delicate elms, the wide sweep of the Green, the profound sky—nothing in the tropics, nothing on the sea, could have predicted this! But there was more; for past the avenues of feathers gleamed a whiteness never seen before, in soft round pillars rising as marble never seen before, a new and enchanting whiteness, fluted intricately, and rising to support great shapes that floated like white reefs over these pale and columned porches, whose steps rose up to them in the whiteness of astounding sand; and beyond this, a warm red never seen before, warm walls taller than they had dreamed, with shining squares, the gleaming windows in the warm brick. More feathers, feathery trees in double and triple arches, fell into green shadows, green brilliance, wherever they looked. And under these walked tall, pale men in black; and through all these crowds women passed, swathed at the shoulders and thighs, bound tight at the waist, in the most voluptuous bindings and cascade and swirl of clothes they yet had seen. This field, these temples, these ox-carts moving among such fantastically dressed white men and women, these deep wild bells sounding from the pinnacles of the white steeples—this was the softest, most luxurious, most surrealist scene possible to dream. Even the grass was softer here, the leaves cut and curled into softness. The smells of farm-wagons, the fruit, the early fall vegetables, the oyster-booths at the corner of the Green, mixed with grass-smells;

and the rich shadows fell among this light more softly, more graciously, than shadows ever fell.

Cinque was put in the jail on the Green. A linguist from Yale established communications with Cinque and was able then to establish the truth of the slaves' illegal passage. After twelve years, John Quincy Adams won the freedom of the fugitive. Now, again, Yale linguists were testifying and lawyers were intervening on behalf of the Black Panthers, the latest avatar in almost half a millennium of slave rebellions.

In the pretrial motions on linguistics the defense found themselves quoting from their own client, Bobby Seale.

Nigger: This term is not generally used derogatorily by black people to each other. There are a very few sensitive black people with self-hate still imbedded in them, who resent it when brothers and sisters are in a general conversation and in a very laughing atmosphere and say, "Ha, ha, man. You niggers is crazy," or, "Say, man, this nigger is outa sight." When we are disgusted with each other, we might say, "What's wrong with you niggers?" but we aren't offended by another brother's use in this context because the use is in the context of some criticism and the criticism specifically is what we'll focus upon. College people and intellectuals have more self-hate, and they resent it most.

A quartet of Panthers called The Lumpen have set up a stage and sound system on the cold Green, and as the luncheon recess begins they begin to sing their song "Free Bobby." Just behind the apocalyptic lyrics is the inimitable sound of the old spirituals of suffering. This is Panther art—not the culture of African aristocracy but, instead, the four-hundred-year nigger wail and roar of rage and hope and illimitable grief.

On this Green was the first church and schoolhouse, and the jail and the stocks and whipping post for the slaves. Now The Lumpen are chanting and dancing as if a black slave had never been lashed there.

The court empties for lunch; only the plainclothesmen are left on the steps. They shift from foot to foot in the biting cold and stare, take in the mad figure of the black Lumpen, opposite, against the equally old ground of the Green and the white Church of the Regicides in the cold middle distance behind.

The waiting veniremen no longer laugh as the first panels did. They have no reason to laugh, for—in Brecht's term—they "have read the papers." Some play cards quietly.

The citizens move through the afternoon *voir dire* like figures on a German clock as the second week of trial stutters to its end. There is one long interruption, but sixty-five veniremen in a row have been directed through the process, with the defense using only ten of its precious sixty peremptory challenges. The courtroom is silent, the Dickensian bailiff, whose job it is to rap for order, sits half asleep until Number 138 enters for his turn.

Mr. Woods is black, he could be forty or sixty. He has a totally bald head and a watchful manner. Charles Garry asks him one question—"Can you be fair?"—and sits down. Arnold Markle pursues the point of whether or not Mr. Woods knows officer Vincent DeRosa, who will testify for the state. "No." While Corporal Schultz goes out for Number 138's file, Markle underlines the fact that Mr. Woods is unemployed. Mr. Woods agrees only if he is allowed to mention that he *"has* been working." Schultz returns with the file, and Markle calls for a conference at the bench.

As all the lawyers gather at the bench the crowd begins to stir from the frozen attention that each prospective black juror inspires. They know that the State's Attorney has discovered an arrest record on Woods. The prosecutor is acting as if it is a serious crime, yet ex-convicts cannot vote or be on a jury, though to be a peer of Bobby Seale you *must have served time.* The crowd thinks of this.

Charles Garry is obviously uncooperative and Markle is forced to go on with his interrogation. He moves in on the witness stand for the first time in the two weeks. He forces Woods to clarify a section on the information sheet that all jurors must fill out. Markle bores in on whether or not Mr. Woods has ever been convicted of a misdemeanor. Woods has grown apprehensive during the long bench conference, then he is confronted with the reason for all the ominous whispering: a ten-dollar fine in 1970 and a suspended breach-of-the-peace charge in 1960. Woods stares down at his "past"; the judge asks, "Can you read?" But Woods's dialect, almost impenetrable now, is thrown up like armor, he slips and slides and admits nothing. Finally the "fact" that might have been uncovered easily enough in the first place emerges.

CHARLES GARRY: Stand back, give him a chance!
THE STATE: Did you know that the arresting officer in 1960 was Vincent DeRosa?
A: I didn't know.

The partisan audience is angry, the press is scribbling swiftly and Bobby Seale is furious; if Charles Garry had not been there and on his feet fighting, there is no telling what the Panther might have said.

CHARLES GARRY: Now, I move, your Honor, that the defense be given the "rap" sheets on all prospective jurors.
THE COURT: All right.
THE STATE: I can't make any promises, your Honor. How do I know what files the defense has?
CHARLES GARRY: He sends a detective out every time a black person is called, your Honor. He has access to all the files.
THE STATE: That's not true.

The crowd gives a barking laugh of incredulity. Markle whirls to stare at them with a wounded expression.

Catherine Roraback is up and joining the action. It is combat now and the Bench is forced to gavel it down. The sadism ends, Woods is excused, the audience is staring at Markle with a new fear and hostility. Number 138 had not been able to signify fast enough.

The question of language is becoming more prominent. Katie Roraback asks if "swear words" would bother people. A few say yes, especially a woman; the defense is thinking of Ericka Huggins' "motherfucker" tape and Bobby Seale's gorgeous idiom and mimicry and his enormous command of dialect. Markle and Mulvey reiterate that there is no "culture" in this criminal case. Bobby Seale gazes at the wall over the judge's head.

There is no way in this setting to talk about the tyranny of standard language on the deracinated black, poor street dwellers on whom the Panthers have their eye. The logic of "Progress" and "Tradition" and "History" is inherent and inextricable from the grammar of the mother tongue from the mother country, and the destruction and parody of this white-ruling-class vocabulary is one of the oldest acts of symbolic rebellion in the small arsenal of the half men of the American colony in the ghettos and the barrios, where the "King's English" is murdered every day of the year.

Some, like Malcolm X or Huey P. Newton, who does not use the word "pig" or even swear, become the masters of this syntax and then turn it like a gun against the canons of traditional value, controlling the syntax of the past with their revolutionary logic from below. Others, like Bobby Seale, adopt an amphibious attitude toward their oral tradition, now matching wits with middle-class intellectuals using a dazzling array of facts and parentheticals, now talking "shit" with the "street bloods" in the code that the "Man" can never decipher. What will the eventual jury, partially hard of hearing, do in this acoustical nightmare when Seale takes the stand to "run it down"? In what tongue will he be moved to speak? Or George Sams?

There is another black man, but he allows that "Otha Buffaloe is a friend of mine." A relationship with the "nigger pig" is enough for Bobby Seale. "Excused." Mr. Markle smiles.

Number 150, the last of three panels, comes in, announces his opposition to the death penalty "except for the murder of police or officials." His name is Coon, he wears a flag on his lapel and he answers that "if a person is innocent he wouldn't be arrested." Exhausted of jurors, the judge calls a week's recess in order to convene a new venire.

The lone two jurors, Dilger and Adams, are brought down and admonished again. Adams smiles this time, he has added a few touches to his costume; he seems prepared to wait forever.

Ericka drops two combs, bends from from her height to pick them up, straightens, smiles and "All Power to the People."

The bailiff: "This Honorable Superior Court now in session for the transaction of criminal business now stands adjourned. Until December 2nd at 10:00 A.M."

The audience hurries out; many of them are going to Washington, D.C., for the Revolutionary People's Constitutional Convention.

THE SEVENTH DAY (DECEMBER 2, 1970)

Over the long recess, while the judge tried to round up a new population of talesmen, Charles Garry went to New York for private meetings with Angela Davis, and almost everybody else in the New Haven "movement" went to the convention in the freezing nation's capital.

This convention, this new Declaration-Constitution, had begun without fanfare over the Labor Day weekend in Philadelphia following a week of serious ghetto eruptions. All together, it had been an amazing sight and sound.

The multitudes in Philadelphia at the Revolutionary People's Constitutional Convention were overwhelmingly poor and black and, most significant of all, typical; the singular events of September, 1970, in Philadelphia could have happened anywhere in America! There were no buses of white students and peace people from outside, as there would be later in Washington.

After a generation of media heroes the man—"Huey"—who had looked out at them from posters for so long spoke without any rhetoric at all. He seemed almost boyish, but powerfully built and wonderfully handsome.

"Friends and comrades throughout the United States and throughout the world, we gather here in peace and friendship to claim our inalienable rights, to claim the rights bestowed upon us by an unbroken train of abuses and usurpations, and to perform the duty which is thus required of us. Our sufferance has been long and patient, our prudence has stayed this final hour, but our human dignity and strength require that we still the voice of prudence with the cries of our sufferance. Thus we gather in the spirit of revolutionary love and friendship for all oppressed people of the world, regardless of their race or of the race and doctrine of their oppressors.

"The United States of America was born at a time when the nation covered relatively little land, a narrow strip of political divisions of the Eastern seaboard. The United States of America was born at a time when the population was small and fairly homogeneous both racially and culturally. Thus, the people called Americans were a different people in a different place. Furthermore, they had a different economic system. The small population and the fertile land available meant that with the agricultural emphasis . . ."

Malcolm X had hinted or "signified" at what was coming. Huey Newton was spelling it out: a new American Declaration-Constitution.

The security tightened around him. The short remarks were near an end, the mass bent into the love.

"The sacredness of man and of the human spirit require that human dignity and integrity ought to be always respected by every other man. We will settle for nothing less, for at this point, in history anything less is but a living death. *We will be free,* and we are here to ordain a new constitution which will ensure our freedom by enshrining the dignity of the human spirit."

Surrounded by guards, Huey P. Newton moved out quickly. Everyone knew there had been death threats all day, a final warning had been issued by the Panthers to *provocateurs,* and two grenades had been discovered before the meeting. As the guard, perhaps with a decoy now, flashed past the entrances, the crowd turned and cheered and wept. The last phrase had produced an uproar—"a slave who dies a natural death will not balance two flies on the scales of history."

Outside the little food trucks selling Soul Food made do for loaves and fishes, and the word "revolution" chattered through the cooling night like a bird or a machine gun.

The speech, on radio and tape recorder, was on an endless loop all night in the seething and terrific North Philadelphia streets. The light voice on every block saying that America must have some socialism; in the press next day readers instead of seeing "off the pig" horror stories saw their own life described and the headline, "Huey Newton Calls for Socialism in America."

The corners, afterward, were like the decks of small ships tilting under the weight of the standing thousands. As sensational as the St. Petersburg Haymarket an age ago, and the Panthers were everywhere talking the putative people's army out of a premature confrontation.

The street's enormous respect for the Panthers turned the tide, even though thousands had been kept standing for hours with no information and it had hurt deeply not to "see Huey." They went home, and they came back to work on the new constitution the next morning.

The next morning the heat wave had broken, breeze and blue sky and the people waiting patiently at all the churches to begin the workshops. The irony was enormous: the pre-literate black masses and some few saved post-literate anti-intellectual students were going to, finally, write the new constitution that the middle-class intellectuals had been calling for since their birth. The aristo-cratic students led by the women, and the street bloods, they were going to do the writing.

Somehow an old woman got the microphone, on the last day of the Philadelphia convention, and told a long, disjointed story of the death of her two-year-old grandchild. It was boring, embarrass-ing, appalling: that woman with her crazy aria of grief and remorse, standing by the altar of the huge church, was the final sign and significance of the plenary convention and the raw heart of the future constitution.

Philadelphia had been transformed for the second time. Now the call of the South would be answered, the Revolutionary People's Constitutional Convention, itself, would be held in Wash-ington, D.C., in November. From prison, campus, military base, barrio, ghetto, church, underground, Third World, factory, they would come to run it down in the Capitol—the "city of lies."

The Panthers, who worked through all the hot Philadelphia nights, handed out the plain-spoken position papers and it was over. People stood in knots to say goodbye; a breeze began to blow through the blasted streets. Would a wind be far behind?

The man known as Malcolm X had seen it all, had seen Huey P. Newton coming with his love and his gun, had seen Babylon and the chickens coming home to roost.

But the Washington plenary session had had to be postponed

from election day to the Thanksgiving Day weekend. Registration went on even after Howard University held out for an $11,000 rental fee right up to the eve of the conference. In Oakland, where he had gone from New Haven, Huey P. Newton announced that the responsibility for trouble would belong to Howard.

In Washington, Howard University—where Stokely Carmichael and cultural nationalism have a strong base—and the National Guard Armory had both been barred to some ten thousand people (more than half of them white this time). There were many who could not forgive the Panthers for not bringing off a triumph in Washington like the one in Philadelphia. They stood around on street corners, the radicals, and cursed the Black Panthers. However, the first national day of protest over the New Haven trial had been set for December, and Huey P. Newton had spoken at a Capitol church for three hours concerning the imminence of world communism, waiting only on the passing of the American Empire.

It was too bad about this fiasco in Washington that the Panthers were being blamed for. Radicals might profitably have spent their time visiting the *genus loci* of the black revolution, the vast and terrible ghettos of Washington and Baltimore. These ghettos are typical of the proving grounds where these troops of hell are massing *with or without the Black Panther Party,* for the genie of black liberation is, as the Panthers say, out of the bottle, and in Baltimore, on Huey P. Newton's birthday, there was a jail uprising.

The Black Panther Party is an American phenomenon, out of the American experience, an experience which whites can see only statistically. To help the blind the Panthers circulated the observations of a critic from abroad.

When a lynching was to take place or had taken place, the press seized upon it as a good occasion to increase sales. The affair would be reported with a wealth of detail. Not the slightest reproach to the criminals. Not a word of pity for the victims. Not a commentary.

The *New Orleans States* of June 26, 1919, published a headline running right across the front page in letters five inches high: "Today a Negro Will be Burnt by 3,000 Citizens." And immediately underneath, in very small print: "Under a strong escort, the Kaiser has taken flight with the Crown Prince."

The Jackson *Daily News* of the same date published across the first two columns of its front page in big letters:

NEGRO J. H. TO BE BURNT
BY THE CROWD AT ELLISTOWN
THIS AFTERNOON AT 5 P.M.

The newspaper only neglected to add, "The whole population is earnestly invited to attend." But the spirit was there.
A few details:

This evening at 7:40 P.M. J.H. was tortured with a red hot iron bar, then burnt. . . . A crowd of more than 2,000 people . . . many women and children, were present at the incineration. . . . After the Negro had been bound from behind, a fire was kindled. A little further away, another fire was kindled in which an iron bar was placed. When it was red hot, a man took it and applied it to the Black's body. The latter, terrified, seized the iron with his hands, and the air was immediately filled with the smell of burning flesh. . . . The red hot iron having been applied to several parts of his body, his shouts and groans were heard as far away as in the town. After several minutes of torture, masked men poured petrol on him and set fire to the stake. The flames rose and enveloped the Negro who implored to be finished off with a shot. His supplications provoked shouts of derision.
—Chattanooga *Times,* February 13, 1918

15,000 people, men, women and children, applauded when petrol was poured over the Negro and the fire lit. They struggled, shouted and pushed one another to get near the Black. . . . Two of them cut off his ears while the fire began to roast him.
Another tried to cut off his heels. . . . The crowd surged and changed places so that every one could see the Negro burn. When the flesh was entirely burnt, the bones laid bare and what had been a human being was but a smoking and deformed rag curling up in the flames, everyone was still there to look. . . .
—Memphis *Press,* May 22, 1917

. . . someone cut off his ears, another removed his sexual organ. . . . He tried to cling to the rope, his fingers were cut off. While he was being hoisted to a tree, a giant of a man stabbed his neck; he received at least 25 wounds . . . he was several times hoisted up, then pulled down into the brazier. Finally a man caught him in a lasso the end of which was attached to a horse which dragged the corpse through the streets of Waco. The tree on which the hanging took place, was right under a window of the mayor's house. The latter looked on while the crowd was in action. All along the way, everyone took part in the mutilation of the Negro. Some struck him with shovels, pickaxes, bricks, sticks. The body was covered with wounds from head to foot. A shout of joy escaped from thousands of throats when the fire was kindled. Some time after, the corpse was hoisted up in the air, so that everyone could look at it, which raised a storm of applause. . . .

—*The Crisis*, July 1916

That was what Ho Chi Minh saw in America in 1929, when he came looking for democracy (from the Greek "power to the people").

To the Panthers, Bobby Seale and Ericka Huggins were survivors of those thirty million Africans "lost" in the middle slave passage to America, alone, in the seventeenth century. The statistics that pour down from the body of American racism are their flesh and blood. The ghetto, the courtroom—"we're all Black Panthers in our hearts," one refused juror would say later—the black people, with or without the Panthers, were in a boundary situation from which they would shoot themselves out, if they had to, sooner or later.

Meanwhile, in Montville, Bobby Seale fought off the anxiety and depression of the long recess by inventing a new card game. Charles R. Garry returned from his meeting with Angela Davis, and the judge began his instructions to the fourth venire.

The new game was called "Revolution." The Ace of spades was Huey P. Newton, Bobby told the other prisoners, and the Queen of clubs was Ericka Huggins, the black nines and tens were *lumpen* revolutionaries, and the red nines and tens were white radicals.

At the end of each week, gambling winnings would be used to help out the prisoners who did not have commissary money.

There over the holidays they played cards and told tales about revolution as if they were God's spies.

Back at court the word circulates that Mr. Markle's mother-in-law has dropped dead during the lunch hour, and court will be adjourned until Monday morning. One of the younger sheriffs says, "Right on!" Bobby and Ericka must go back to their prisons that resemble rest homes from the outside, and Bobby must wait in isolation over another long recess.

Inside, Dilger, Adams and the third juror, Miss Sheila Pennix, are admonished and told when to return. As Ericka leaves, the crowd projects their "All power to the people." It has been another bad day, the judge's neck is red—"If you do that after we have a jury, I'll clear the courtroom. If you do that after we have a jury."

It is quiet after the lip service of the day. Katie was keeping her daily record: Comments of women:

"I work six days a week. I haven't time for more than the washing and ironing. My husband reads the paper."

"I don't know much of anything. I only like to work in the garden or around the house . . . I never get out to *do* anything. . . ."

"I think I'm pretty dumb."

"I feel so stupid."

"I couldn't stand to hear a woman use bad language. Yes, it would prejudice me."

"An opinion? Not really."

The male bias is severe in American juries. New Haven County has a population which is 49 percent male, while the jury array is 64 percent male. Naugatuck's jury list is 80 percent male, though its population is only 49 percent male. These results could be attributed to chance much less than one time in a thousand—that is, there is some systematic process at work which substantially overrepresents males and underrepresents females. (Katie Roraback never let any of the men, including the defense, forget it.)

THE EIGHTH DAY (DECEMBER 7, 1970)

> Have you ever stood
> In the darkness of night
> screaming silently you're a man

Have you ever hoped
That a time would come
When your voice could be heard
In the noonday sun?
Have you waited so long
Till your unheard song
Has stripped away your very soul
well then believe it my friends
That the silence will end
We'll just have to get guns and
be men.

The words and stabbing music of one of Elaine Brown's Panther songs on a portable tape recorder, of a waiting black girl. Elaine Brown, from the Panther Ministry of Information, is coming to Connecticut to see her closest friend Ericka and the child, Mai, who was the first Panther baby, mothered by all the women in the Los Angeles collective. The Panthers that constituted that commune are all dead, exiled or imprisoned now except Elaine Brown.

The session is late. The young black woman, Sheila Pennix, the third juror chosen, has been excused! The press cannot find out why. "Talk to her mother," Garry hints. She had received a threatening telephone call (the defense had urged that the jury be sequestered for just this reason). Now, Charles Garry stands to ask for a dismissal:

"Your Honor, I wish to ask for a mistrial at this time. There was a story in the November 27 New Haven *Register* about kidnapping and ransoms for Bobby Seale, but we let that pass. But in the *Register* for December 6, the following statements appeared:

. . . Hoover devoted nearly one fifth of his 27 page testimony to an updating of his verbal assault on the Black Panther Party, which he previously had branded as the country's "most dangerous and violence prone, of all extremist groups."

This time the FBI chief's statements were so specific that they could be viewed as prejudicial because they dealt with two men about to go on trial.

Hoover said that Bobby G. Seale, Black Panther national chairman, is typical of "top party leaders [who] almost without exception have been engaged in crimes of violence." A Connecticut court which is trying Seale for aiding and abetting the kidnap and murder of another

Panther has been laboring with scant success since mid-November to find jurors able to claim they are not prejudiced about the controversial Seale. Hoover's statement won't simplify that task.

Ericka is writing a furious, left-handed message to Catherine Roraback.

Markle was up and objecting. He read a story from the New Haven *Journal-Courier* about the Panther free Christmas dinner and food program for the hungry and he wondered "if the state can get a fair trial"; titters, and Markle glares and reads:

The People's FREE FOOD PROGRAM is being established by the People's Committee to help meet one of the most basic and immediate needs of the black community. The ever-increasing unemployment rate in the black community and the inflationary practices of the Nixon Administration demonstrate the government's unwillingness to meet the needs of the poor and oppressed people in general and black people in particular. The black community is reminded daily that the machinery of this government does not work in its interest.

Both Chairman Bobby and Ericka Huggins saw the necessity for meeting the basic needs of the people through the implementation of socialistic programs like the Free Hot Breakfast for Children, Free Clothing and Free Health Centers.

The incarceration of these servants of the people and others is clearly an attempt by the government to put a stop to the people's programs. But the people have shown that the spirit of Bobby and Ericka still prevails and that we the people will continue to move to feed, clothe and defend our communities.

So we are calling on *all human beings* to meet with People's Committee on Saturday, December 5th, at 1:00 P.M. at the First United Methodist Church, Elm and College Streets, to discuss our first actions:

1. Canvassing for immediate food commitments,
2. Planning our free Xmas dinner at Yale,
3. Organizing ongoing research and action committees.

David Rosen is heard, for the first time since the pretrial ended, to the effect that Mr. Hoover is repeating what he did in the McLucas trial with his prejudicial comments.

THE STATE: No one locally, for the state, has commented, your Honor.

GARRY: The Federal Government is involved in this case. George Sams is an FBI agent, FBI agents will be testifying here, the FBI is in this area, they are cooperating in the prosecution of this case. How can you separate the local and Federal police? For the Director of the Federal Bureau of Investigation to make this charge, to poison the atmosphere, when Bobby G. Seale has never even been charged or convicted of a crime of violence! And he makes these statements when these clients are on trial for their very lives!

THE COURT: Denied.

GARRY: My client would like a recess.

The wire-service reporters break for the phones. Everyone talks about Hoover. From the Palmer raids fifty years ago to this morning's *Time* magazine with Hoover's attack on Martin Luther King:

I got a wire from the Reverend Doctor King in New York. He was getting ready to get the Nobel Prize—he was the last one in the world who should ever have received it. He wired asking to see me.* I held him in complete contempt because of the things he said and because of his conduct. First I felt I shouldn't see him, but then I thought he might become a martyr if I didn't. King was very suave and smooth. He sat right there where you're sitting and said he never criticized the FBI. I said, "Mr. King"—I never called him reverend—"stop right there. You're lying." He then pulled out a press release that he said he intended to give to the press. I said, "Don't show it to me or read it to me." I couldn't understand how he could have prepared a press release even before we met. Then he asked if I'd go out to have a photograph taken with him. I said I certainly would mind. And I said, "If you ever say anything that's a lie again, I'll brand you a liar again." Strange to say, he never attacked the Bureau again for as long as he lived.

The last two weeks have been like a speeded-up film of Hoover's career: the Berrigan brothers and the Catholics, the radicals and the Black militants—faster and faster, like a time capsule.

* The celebrated meeting between the two men occurred December 1, 1964, after Hoover called King "the most notorious liar in the country" for advising civil-rights workers to avoid making complaints to FBI men because they were Southerners, and King then suggested that Hoover had "faltered" under the burdens of office.

In New Haven on that Sunday a black minister will tell his congregation that after the attack on Doctor King all progressive clergy would soon be under fire.

Back inside a new record: twelve jurors excused in less than an hour. Four in five minutes. Then the number mounts to three again; Number 169, Miss Goldson, black, quiet, wearing a lavender Indian-print scarf, an Avon saleswoman, no opinions. She wears a smart leather jacket, the kind popularized by the Panthers in their early days. What are the limits of style? Does Avon have a line of "black" cosmetics? But now the polarization is obvious. If a potential juror states that he has "not read too much in the papers" it means that he is *friendly*.

Number 194 found it "difficult to believe everything I read," and knew about the Black Panther Party's ten-point program. Excused by the state.

The next one had heard that they were "criminals—in the papers."

In San Francisco the Mayor, before a large audience, referred to the ten-point program that Newton and Seale had polled from the black community, "Have you read the ten commandments of the Black Panther Party? Did you like that section about robbing and raping?"

The Panthers have eight, not ten, points of attention:

1. Speak politely.
2. Pay fairly for what you buy.
3. Return everything you borrw.
4. Pay for anything you damage.
5. Do not hit or swear at people.
6. Do not damage property or crops of the poor, oppressed masses.
7. Do not take liberties with women.
8. If we ever have to take captives do not ill-treat them.

But Mayor Alioto was only in the tradition of the President, the Vice-President, the Attorney General, the Director of the Federal Bureau of Investigation.

There was, however, a "split in the ruling circle"—as Marxists like to describe overriding mass moral dilemmas—and a commission to analyze the causes of violence and the means of prevention, set up under the chairmanship of Milton S. Eisenhower at the Center for the Study of Law and Society in Berkeley, University of California, August 28, 1968, submitted its report March 21, 1969. In discussing black militancy its report said:

The Black Panther Party has been repeatedly harassed by police. After the conviction of the party's leader, Huey P. Newton, for manslaughter in the death of a white policeman, Oakland police fired into the Black Panther office with rifles and shotguns presumably because they felt that a conviction for first-degree murder would have been more appropriate. On September 4, a group of 150 whites, allegedly including a number of off-duty policemen, attacked a group of Panthers and their white supporters in the Brooklyn Criminal Court building. The confrontation between the Panthers and some elements of the police has become a feud verging on open warfare. This warfare highlights the fact that for the black citizen, the policeman has long since ceased to be—if indeed he ever was—a neutral symbol of law and order. Studies of the police emphasize that their attitudes and behavior toward blacks differ vastly from those taken toward whites. Similar studies show that blacks perceive the police as hostile, prejudiced, and corrupt. In the ghetto disorders of the past few years, blacks have often been exposed to indiscriminate police assaults and, not infrequently, to gratuitous brutality. Many ghetto blacks see the police as an occupying army; one of the Panthers' major demands is for stationing U.N. observers in the ghettoes to monitor police conduct.

In view of these facts, the adoption of the idea of self-defense is not surprising. Again, in America self-defense has always been considered an honorable principle, and the refusal to bow before police harassment strikes a responsive chord in ghetto communities, especially among the young.

On the first day of the trial of Lonnie McLucas, J. Edgar Hoover had called the Black Panther Party the "most dangerous group in America." As the trial of Bobby Seale and Ericka Huggins began, Hoover announced that that Panthers and a group of priests and nuns had planned, in their separate ways, to sabotage Washington, D.C. This is physical combat, not rhetorical device.

In the corridor, editors from Harvard and the Boston area crowd around Charles Garry and Katie Roraback. They explain that the movement is not relating to New Haven because it "is going through a period of introspection." Garry: "Bullshit!"

Liberation News Service (L.N.S.) has an appropriate quotation:

i began as a student and acquired at school the habits of a student; . . . i used to feel it undignified to do any manual labor such as shouldering my own luggage. at that time it seemed to me that the intellectuals were the only clean persons in the world, and the workers and peasants seemed rather dirty beside them. having become a revolutionary, i found myself in the same ranks as the workers, peasants, and soldiers of the revolutionary army . . . i came to feel that it was those unremolded intellectuals who were unclean as compared to the workers and peasants, while the workers and peasants are after all the cleanest persons—even though their hands are soiled and their feet are smeared with cow dung.

—MAO TSE-TUNG

Court begins with a new panel. Like the dead souls of a nineteenth-century Russian novel the endless names on paper are passed from lawyer to lawyer.

Meanwhile, the day has begun for the three jurors already selected (Adams, Dilger, Goldson). They sit day after day waiting in vain, unable to "talk or read or think about this case." It is more than Pinter or Beckett could ask for in that big dim waiting room as the white mailman, the old black floor sweeper and the young middle-aged Avon representative wait with something between patience and fatalism.

DILGER: Cold.
ADAMS: Surely is.
GOLDSON: This room is so drafty. I wish—
(Pause.)
ADAMS: Surely is cold.

In the corridor the "overall situation" and the "contradictions" are analyzed by the editors and the freaks. First is an advertisement in *The New York Times* of a citywide reissue of Gillo

Pontecorvo's *The Battle of Algiers*. In the trial of the New York Twenty-One the prosecution had shown the film as evidence or prophecy of a Panther conspiracy. The ad's headline reads:

THE PANTHERS HAVE SEEN IT.
HAVE YOU?

Inside, Garry quickly passes to Markle in the interrogation of a black woman in her thirties, Mrs. Coles.

THE STATE: Do you belong to any organizations?

A: Ladies auxiliary of the American Legion.

Q: Could you consider the death penalty?

A: I don't think so.

THE COURT: If it was your mother?

A: I don't see the good, it wouldn't bring her back.

THE COURT: But would you just consider it?

A: Maybe, if it was very gruesome.

THE STATE: I ask that she be excused for cause, your Honor.

THE COURT: Denied. She said if it was very gruesome.

THE STATE: Could you avoid pressure from the black community if you, as a black, sit on this jury?

A: I don't know.

At the New Haven Panther Headquarters, documentation goes on concerning J. Edgar Hoover's "oinking in the faces of the people" before a Congressional committee.

MR. ROONEY: Your reference to La Cosa Nostra prompts me to inquire if it is not the fact that the no-good Valachi was sentenced to Atlanta Penitentiary for 15 years by an Italian-American judge named Matthew T. Abruzzo in the Eastern District of New York?

MR. HOOVER: That is correct. The supervisor in charge of our investigations of La Cosa Nostra in the New York area happens to be of Italian extraction.

MR. ROONEY: During the course of his incarceration in Atlanta he murdered a fellow convict.

MR. HOOVER: That is correct.

MR. ROONEY: And is it not the fact that he was convicted in the case of a narcotics transaction which had nothing at all to do with Cosa Nostra or Mafia victims?

MR. HOOVER: I think that is correct.

MR. ROONEY: The case had to do with black people?

MR. HOOVER: Yes, essentially as to subjects and narcotics users.

MR. ROONEY: It was a black racket in narcotics which emanated from Harlem?

MR. HOOVER: That is correct, as I understand it.

MR. ROONEY: And there were no Italian-American people involved in the thing at all?

MR. HOOVER: That is quite correct, as I indicated.

In the corridor—someone reading from *The New York Times:*

INCA WHO LED 1780 REVOLT
NOW A LATIN FOLK HERO

In 1780, Tupac Amaru's badly armed Indian army of 80,000 conquered southern Peru, all of what is now Bolivia and part of Argentina. But the Spanish mustered reinforcements from Lima and Buenos Aires, and within six months had crushed the revolt.

Tupac Amaru was compelled to witness the execution of his wife, sons and military aides. His Spanish torturers then cut off his tongue before having him pulled to pieces by horses and displayed his dismembered body on pikes.

His death marked the beginning of widespread guerrilla actions on the part of the Indians throughout South America and was a factor in the destruction of Spanish rule four decades later.

Since then, Tupac Amaru's name, often in the contraction "Tupamaro," has been used by many groups of guerrillas, some of them political revolutionaries, others little more than bandits.

The best known contemporary Tupamaro organization is the Marxist Uruguayan group, which has caused trouble for the Montevideo government for the last three years. Earlier this year, Uruguayan Tupamaros kidnaped and murdered Dan A. Mitrione, a United States advisor to Uruguay's police.

Someone claims loudly that another man still being held by the Tupamaros is *not* a civilian advisor as claimed by the State Department, but is in reality the C.I.A. Chief of Operations for the area! Someone dares to ask the source. Perhaps the Brazilian press? Silence.

In the courtroom Katie discovers to everyone's dismay that Mrs. Cole's husband is a *volunteer* auxiliary policeman. Bobby Seale stops her from challenging for cause at once.

Q: How many nights a week does he serve?
A: Just one now.
Q: Does he get called?
A: On holidays when there's—tension.
Q: Does he wear a uniform?
A: Yes, but no gun.
Q: Do you own a gun?
A: No.
Q: Does he want to join the police force?
A: He's too old, forty-two.

At the Panther headquarters, Big Man reads the fables of the Congressional Record:

MR. HOOVER: The acceleration of violence is not limited to acts that can be attributed to the New Left. Black extremists have also been involved in terroristic activities.

A group of extremists was responsible in August, 1970, for the abortive escape attempt by Negro convicts on trial in San Rafael, California, courtroom. The judge, the prosecutor and three women jurors were taken as hostages. In the ensuing shootout, the judge and two convicts were killed and the prosecutor and one juror were wounded. Angela Davis, a communist, black extremist and former instructor at the University of California, was indicted on November 10, 1970, by a Marin County, California, grand jury for murder and kidnaping for her role in purchasing guns used in the bizarre incident.

In the corridor, the white radicals peer over one another's shoulders.

KILLING DESCRIBED AT CALLEY'S TRIAL

Charles A. West, a tall, lanky black from Chicago, testified that his company commander, Capt. Ernest L. Medina, exhorted the men to "leave nothing walking, crawling or growing" in MyLai 4.

At the Panther headquarters, the black revolutionaries curse quietly as they listen.

MR. HOOVER says in his annual report: . . . "The Black Panther" newspaper regularly contains cartoons depicting violent attacks on law-enforcement officers who are characterized as "pigs." Close to 150,000 copies of this paper are distributed each week to Black Panther Party sympathizers and supporters throughout the country.

This composite contains several cartoons which are typical to those appearing in "The Black Panther."

The cartoon depicting the release of Negro prisoners from jail appeared in the August 8, 1970, issue of "The Black Panther" which was actually distributed on August 7, 1970, the same day as the escape attempt was made at the San Rafael courtroom.

. . . In New Haven one Party member has been convicted and sentenced to serve 12 to 15 years in prison. Six have entered guilty pleas to lesser charges and have been sentenced. Black Panther Party Chairman Bobby Seale and Ericka Huggins, a top Party leader, are awaiting trial on charges of conspiracy to commit kidnaping and murder. Jury selections for this trial began November 17, 1970.

Seale was also one of eight individuals charged with conspiracy to cross state lines to incite riots during the 1968 Democratic National Convention disorders in Chicago, Ill. Because of his actions during the original trial of this group, he was severed from the trial and charged with 16 counts of contempt of court and sentenced to 4 years in jail. On October 19, 1970, Federal District Judge Julius J. Hoffman granted a motion for dismissal of the conspiracy indictment against Seale on the basis that the Federal Government considered it inappropriate to try Seale separately on the conspiracy charge since the jury acquitted the other defendants of that particular charge.

Top Black Panther Party leaders almost without exception have been involved in crimes of violence. Typical of these in addition to Bobby Seale, is Huey Newton, Black Panther Party Supreme Commander, whose conviction for the 1967 killing of an Oakland police officer was reversed and he is now awaiting retrial for voluntary manslaughter. This trial is scheduled to begin in Superior Court, Alameda County, Calif., January 11, 1971. Newton was released on bond August 5, 1970, with no travel restrictions of any kind imposed on him by the court. He is free to travel whenever and wherever he desires. In this connection Black Panther Party chapters across the Nation are contacting major universities within their areas in efforts to set up speaking engagements for Newton. Newton is demanding $2,500 plus expenses for any appearance on college campuses . . .

Panthers have substantial connections with hostile foreign elements, notably the communist regime in North Korea and Arab terrorists in Algeria. Arab guerrillas and other Arab elements reportedly are heavily subsidizing the Panthers and a new "international office" of the Black Panther Party was just opened in September 1970 in Algiers under the leadership of Eldridge Cleaver, another Black Panther Party fugitive.

Increasing ties between Arab terrorists and Panthers raise the ominous possibility that militants may seek to ape Arab tactics, including airplane hijackings, to gain release of jailed Panther members such as Seale. In this connection, two former Panther members returned to the United States in early September after a tour of Al Fatah training camps.

The Black Panther Party is organizing a mass meeting referred to as the Revolutionary People's Constitutional Convention (RPCC) in Washington, D.C., November 27–28, 1970. The Black Panther Party has been refused the use of the District of Columbia National Guard Armory. Current plans are for the use of three buildings at Howard University. The three buildings will be connected through a closed circuit television network.

The announced purpose of the RPCC is to rewrite the U.S. Constitution to make it more relevant to the "oppressed people." The Black Panther Party is inviting the participation of all "oppressed people," which it considers includes blacks, Mexican-Americans, Puerto Ricans, homosexuals, white radicals, "street people," women's liberation groups, and student groups.

In the corridor:

PRIESTS CONTEST PRISON'S CENSORS

Berrigan Brothers' Lawsuit
Says Rights Are Denied

At one point both priests contended that they lacked effective means of responding to widely publicized charges that J. Edgar Hoover made in his annual report, that the two were part of a movement to bomb underground power lines and kidnap a high-ranking Federal official.

PROSECUTORS SET IN BERRIGAN CASE

A 4-Man Team Is Chosen—
All Are Roman Catholics

At the Panther headquarters:

MR. HOOVER: . . . Willingness to employ any type of terrorist tactics is becoming increasingly apparent among extremist elements. One example has recently come to light involving an incipient plot on the part of an anarchist group on the east coast, the so-called "East Coast Conspiracy to Save Lives."

This is a militant group self-described as being composed of Catholic priests and nuns, teachers, students, and former students who have manifested opposition to the war in Vietnam by acts of violence against Government agencies and private corporations engaged in work relating to U.S. participation in the Vietnam conflict.

The principal leaders of this group are Philip and Daniel Berrigan, Catholic priests who are currently incarcerated in the Federal Correctional Institution at Danbury, Connecticut, for their participation in the destruction of Selective Service records in Baltimore, Maryland, in 1968.

This group plans to blow up underground electrical conduits and steam pipes serving the Washington, D.C., area in order to disrupt Federal Government operations. The plotters are also concocting a scheme to kidnap a highly placed Government official. The name of a White House staff member has been mentioned as a possible victim. If successful, the plotters would demand an end to U.S. bombing operations in Southeast Asia and the release of all political prisoners as ransom. Intensive investigation is being conducted concerning this matter.

MR. ROONEY: It is fantastic to think how far these sort of things have been permitted to go.

MR. HOOVER: Off the record.

(Discussion off the record.)

In the courtroom:

GARRY: I reluctantly must ask to challenge for cause.

THE COURT: Denied. Try again.

GARRY: Mrs. Coles, could your husband avoid pressure from the police if you sat in this case?
A: I don't know.

In the corridor:

MURTAGH FINDS PANTHER LAWYER
GUILTY OF CONTEMPT

Justice John M. Murtagh halted the State Supreme Court trial of 13 Black Panthers yesterday and held one of their lawyers in contempt.

At the Panther headquarters:

THIS MESSAGE IS FOR ALL THE PARTY MEMBERS, COMMUNITY WORKERS, PEOPLE'S COMMITTEE, NCCF AND REVOLUTIONARIES ALL WORKING AND FUNCTIONING HERE IN CONNECTICUT—NEW HAVEN, BRIDGEPORT, HARTFORD, BUT MAINLY NEW HAVEN. (THIS IS TO BE READ ALOUD AND EACH PERSON WITH A COPY IS TO FOLLOW ALONG.)

I know there is the People's Committee and they intend to start a "Food Program for the Hungry," and even if this is a program for the overall hungry people in this area, it also includes, without a doubt, the people's Free Breakfast for School Children and Free Lunch for Children.

It is *sad, sad, sad,* that we the real revolutionaries, Party members, community workers and People's Committee and/or what have you, NCCF, that the Breakfast for Children Program here in New Haven is almost a joke and that by now *there is no Free Health Clinic.* I know "man-woman" power is short, but any 5 people can get this going, hustle donations (in actual food and funds), obtain a church and/or church sponsor, whether the clergyman is White or Black, or even if the clergyman who will *sponsor* doesn't have his church in the Black community area. . . .

In the courtroom:

GARRY: Refused.

After lunch, in the corridor:

KLAN IS BLAMED FOR NIGHT RAID
ON CENTER AT DELAWARE CAMPUS

A lightning nighttime raid by a commando-style vigilante group on a controversial, ecumenical student church center at the University of Delaware has left this community of 18,000 persons in fear and political turmoil.

Bobby Seale's wife, Artie, has arrived in a stylish fur hat and an orange coat. A prospective slips and says, "The rules of our country are that you're guilty until proven innocent." An old German keeps repeating, "If my government disapproves so would I"; and, ". . . me, personally, I'm only one person, but the Government has the intelligence . . ."; Garry, angry, "Is the Government right on Vietnam?"; Markle and Mulvey in unison, "Don't answer that!" Then there was Mrs. Feces, who "had good days and bad days," and insisted over the judge's argument that "you don't get arrested for nothing." So it went on in the courtroom as the fourth week stuttered to an end.

At the Panther headquarters:

MR. HOOVER: I think we will always be plagued with statements made by pseudo-liberals on TV. Some of the commentators, I think, are way out in left field in their views and in their philosophies. I know they disagree with my position on many matters. They are entitled to their opinions and I am entitled to mine, and I am going to express them when I see fit.

In the corridor, the young woman from Liberation News Service reads:

ANOTHER GROUP OPPOSES RADICAL LEFT

Long a foe of the so-called radical right, the American Jewish Committee has turned its guns on the New Left and the extreme elements that have instituted violent attacks on the Establishment and who vow to destroy the social and governmental structure of the nation, not by constitutional means but by force.

Although, as its name implies, the committee is semitic-oriented, it has been a staunch defender of American democracy and the ideals upon which this country was founded. Since its inception in 1960, the committee has opposed extremism in any form.

The action of the committee in denouncing attacks on the democratic process is further evidence of the increasing sentiment against loud-mouthed, and all too frequently, lewd-mouthed, radicals who agitate against constitutional law and order, as well as those who sit back and influence others to wreck the system. More and more people are getting fed up with those who swing far to either side—right or left—and foment violence. There is no place for one or the other, for the biased or bigoted on the American scene. They serve only to incur the wrath of those citizens who enjoy our way of life, who accept dissent and are willing to make changes but only if achieved through normal processes.

The average citizen is slow to anger and reticent to become involved, but when he gets his dander up he is like a ferocious tiger. The radicals would do well to heed these indicators that the quiet American may be beginning to stir.

In court, Ericka is looking at *Love and Will,* Katie has thrown her coat around her client's high shoulders. The small courtroom that was chosen for its air conditioning is always cold these days.

The average age of this panel is 49.85 and there are *no* "black persons," Katie says for the record. Is this the longest jury selection in American and world history? Yale Law School says yes; several others say no. But it must be close. Someone will check, but do you measure by time consumed, by number of persons interrogated, or by length of individual interviews?

After eight panels a pattern is clear. At first, when the waiting room is jammed there is loud laughter, badinage and usually a card game; near the end, waiting, and silence. And their look is always the same, unblinking and invisibly wincing, when it comes: "My name is Charles R. Garry. I'm from San Francisco, and I represent Mr. Bobby G. Seale, who is the chairman and a co-founder of the Black Panther Party . . ."

The corridor:

PRIORITY FOR OPEN REVOLUTIONARY WORK IS THIS:

1) BREAKFAST FOR CHILDREN
2) FREE HEALTH CLINIC
3) PEOPLE'S "SHOWDOWN" DEMONSTRATIONS TO FREE ALL POLITICAL PRISONERS BY ANY AND ALL MEANS NECESSARY

THAT IS THE PEOPLE'S REVOLUTIONARY MOVEMENT'S WORK TO BE DONE. START RIGHT NOW! . . .

> BOBBY SEALE
> CHAIRMAN, B.P.P.

Bobby,

We can all internalize the quote by Jose Marti, "The best way of telling is doing." That is what you're saying, what we've both been saying for 18 months; set examples thru action . . . especially for the support of the poor and oppressed in the community. The message is beautiful, beautiful and right on time.

> ericka

At Panther headquarters a new reader has taken over:

MR. SMITH: With regard to these thousand new agents, how many are you estimating will be used on bombings?

MR. HOOVER: I would like to observe in connection with bombings on university and college campuses that until there are heads of these institutions with guts who will expel students for violation of campus rules and not interfere when the local district attorney wants to prosecute, that bombings on campuses will probably continue. I also feel that many members on the university and college faculties are far worse than the students who cause the disturbances and ultimately resort to bombings and arson.

There are rare exceptions concerning the heads of universities and colleges and such a one is Dr. S. I. Hayakawa, President of the San Francisco State College at San Francisco, Calif. There are several others who are just as firm and determined as he is, but the great bulk of them lack the backbone and the guts to expel disruptive students and those who engage in violent activities.

MR. CEDERBERG: Is there any objection to showing on the record that there is nothing the Congress or the FBI can do regarding the Cassius Clay matter—that is a matter for the courts?

MR. HOOVER: That is correct. It is due to the delays in the courts and to the constant filing of motions by defense counsel.

In the jury room, it is growing darker. Outside on the Green, the amber lights on the huge fir tree glow in the early evening dark; Mr. Adams, Mr. Dilger and Miss Goldson watch the dusk accomplish and wait for the sheriff to come for them and announce the end of another day.

In court, for the second time in a week, an entire panel is near exhaustion, but the judge saves a half dozen to be interrogated the next morning while a new venire is being prepared. The lawyers ask for the extra fifteen minutes to confer with Ericka and Bobby, and after an argument the bench overrides Mr. Markle and allows Artie Seale to join them.

On the Green the huge electrified Christmas tree is being set up. Two new flags, American and Connecticut, have been posted on either side of the Roman columns of the court. The Latin on the state flag is *"Qui Transtulit Sustinet,"* which means, "He who transplanted continues to sustain"—an adaptation of Psalms, Chapter 79, Verse 3, of the Vulgate. The vines on the state seal symbolize the colony brought over and planted here in the wilderness. We read in the Eightieth Psalm: "Thou has brought a vine out of Egypt: Thou hast cast out the heathen and planted it." On the grass is a Panther leaflet announcing a free food program.

The afternoon session is short. They have run out of jurors again. The Hoover quotes are a new theme in the *voir dire:*

RORABACK: Did you read the quotes of J. Edgar Hoover in yesterday's paper?
A: Yes.
Q: Did they impress you?
A: Yes.
THE STATE: Did you ever read any statements by Kingman Brewster, Jr.?
(The judge frowns.)
A: No.

They are all used up again. The judge had tried in vain to save one—"Could you consider the death penalty if someone killed your *mother?* The *President?*" "No. I could not execute another human being."

Long days. New panels of jurors are made ready. (Roraback's motion for a democratic jury selection process for the second five hundred venire denied.) An old Irishman claims he feels sorry for the defendants. "What about me?" asks the judge. The local reporters and the sheriff's men roar. The few left in the jury room must jump when the dull bark of laughter sneaks in from the arena.

Some sweet-voiced Panther girls are in the corridor, in line, every morning to greet the attorneys. Their voices are shy and penetrating, "Power to the People, Charles; Power to the People, Katie." Overwhelmed by the Roman architecture, standing there singing out forlornly like urchins in Pompeii, orphans in Babylon.

Now another fifty have to be impaneled. Two black people who knew the Huggins family must go off. One, from St. Luke's parish, had gone to Jon's funeral. So there are none again. (The previous panel had one.) The last panel had a high average age, 51.80; this one looks even older. The defense is in despair that these friends of the Hugginses speak up instead of getting on the jury. They want peers not judges.

They answer like school children who know how to manipulate the multiple-choice questions, or like their own children working their way through a lifetime of intelligence tests and civil-service forms. They creep like etchings across the old courtroom floor, the body tensions stand out in relief, this cuneiform of the silent minority is telegraphy to the prisoners. Ericka writes about it.

a whole chain reaction of thouts then. are prisons an extension of society? or is society an extension of the prisons?

i don't know if huey/bobby know the depth of the what they did? the idea of revolution here is so VAST!

depression is sneaking on . . . i can't understand how the collective can tolerate what they tolerate. my face must look awfully ugly right now. damn i wish that i cd do something to come out of this maybe fake a smile like i'm doing now or hold a straight face. maybe i'll just look ugly instead.

i think by looking at nothingness just plant my eyes and meditate—limbo again always the feeling of limbo—maybe when and if i leave the camp for the streets it will be the same. hope not. anyway that will be the future.

i know what fran meant now about crying alot i wd do the same but outside tears—like i said—have burnt *too* much! long for that quiet talk that will enable one to direct my energies. redirect them.

Ericka

Garry complained that the court reporter had a flag decal on his steno machine. The defendants were granted a half hour with counsel. Outside the cold had settled in, the evening paper carried two front-page headlines:

**PROSECUTION TO END
CASE AGAINST CALLEY**

HOLIDAY LAYOFFS STILL TO COME

10,000 in Area Without Jobs, Highest Since '58 Recession

The flags look frozen. . . . *QUI TRANSTULIT SUSTINET*.

It is a year this week since the killing of Fred Hampton and Mark Clark. Ericka's poem:

> This is the anniversary of their death
> > Fred and Mark
>
> Too soon a year appears again
> The officers of the law killed/slaughtered
> them—took them away from
> > family
> > comrades
> > the people
>
> I wonder how many more years will
> Go by before things will change
> —easy to be hard plays—it
> > is so easy to be hard
> > > to be cold

to say no
They have done this to us
for so long we must stop it
                end it all . . .
Stop the clocks
                Seize the time

                                        Ericka

The Thirteenth Day (December 14, 1970)

Outside Bridgeport, where the federal court is set, the pollution on the Housatonic River glints in the winter light. Here, before Judge Zampano, Bobby and Ericka are the plaintiffs, Markle and the state the defendants.

In the new Federal Building the courtroom is capacious and modern (modern in the way the "future" used to be pictured in the magazines of 1942). Mr. Markle, Charles Weeks, the F.B.I. field agent for New Haven, Janet York and Elizabeth Crouch of Niantic Prison and Ellis MacDougall of the Connecticut prison system are the targets of the Panther defense's injunction motion. Weeks never does appear. The charges are wide-ranging: Bobby Seale denied the visits of his young son Malik (Stagolee); Ericka denied all radical reading from *Ramparts* Magazine to the works of Lenin; Seale charges electronic eavesdropping.

The large press and crowd remind the state that they will have to fight Seale and his cadre step by step, from courtroom to courtroom, and always there will be "Charles R. Garry from San Francisco" with his legs planted wide apart and the powerful hands looking for an opening in the air.

The judge is dark and young-looking. Mr. MacDougall's assistant, Miss York of Niantic, is a big woman with a truly impressive bosom and massive shoulders; sitting next to her and dwarfed is Miss Crouch, the head matron. Mr. Markle is waiting in the witness room to testify. The counsel for the state is one Steven O'Neill, a man in his forties, who has the voice of a whining old man. Ericka looks lovely, lanky rather than thin, dressed in warm colors.

The moving parties are ready, and David Rosen introduces new counsel to the court: a white man, Stanley Bass, representing the National Association for the Advancement of Colored People; and Michael Avery for the Connecticut Civil Liberties Union. Roraback and Garry are ready for their client. Katie is not introduced, and O'Neill, for the state, is thrown off by her methodical style. The lawyers argue from behind a podium in the federal court. (In Chicago, Judge Hoffman constantly reminded William Kunstler not to lean on the podium designed by Mies van der Rohe, who "didn't design it that way.")

Ericka is first. Her voice is clear and intelligent as she lists her grievances: only female cousins can visit, and once Elaine Brown; her poems have been confiscated; her *Red Book* and Black Panther literature have been taken; her diary has been taken, because it is confused with "kites" (love letters to other prisoners); her clothing has been declared against regulations.

What are these "love" poems?

> i remember times when i had love
> to give and there was no one to love
> i remember times when i had truths
> to exchange and everyone regretted
> it
> i remember when i found that life
> is struggle and they told me that
> i wished it that way
> i remember times when i cried
> while everyone laughed hysterically
> i remember and now while i am
> calm everyone is screaming
> yelling
> pleading with me
> to tell them when/how/where/what we
> found out and i just remember
> times . . .
>
> Ericka

It takes the breath away to think of Crouch, York or MacDougall in their prurient exegesis, censoring a soul in hell whose love flaps like a rag in the wind. As if they, in their sad projections and nightmares, understood this ineluctable mixture of politics and simple loneliness. And the forbidden "kites" of the other women? To write to others you can lay eyes but not words or hands on? Does the state incarcerate, segregate and then think to call perverse or illegal what flows from imprisoned love abstracted from the world?

> i must give you something and so i want to give
> my total friendship the ungrasping, unchaining
>   yielding kind
>   i want to give you me
>   because you have given me you
>   i want to penetrate your soul i want you
>   to penetrate mine
>   i want but not the i that is ego
>   i want to stretch out my arms and grasp yours
>   extend my fingertips and feel the warmth flow
>   from me to you to me to you
>   mid-week will come and if you physically go
>   you shall take part of me spiritually and leave
>   part of you spiritually and give your
>   goodness to others you may meet . . .
>   Ericka

Q: Would you just tell me: Paragraph four is an accurate statement, is it not, that you had been denied the right to receive *The Black Panther* newspaper, the *Essays From The Minister of Defense,* and *The Genius of Huey P. Newton, Seize The Time* by Bobby Seale, *Post-Prison Speeches & Writings, Soul On Ice, Education & Revolution* by Eldridge Cleaver, *Ho Chi Minh's Essays* by Bernard Fall, and books by V. I. Lenin, including *State & Revolution,* and *Palm Wine Drinkard* by Tuotola, and *Mister Johnson* by Joyce Cary?
    Those books you have not been permitted to have?
A: Right, and there may have been others.

O'Neill cross-examines; he calls Ericka "Miss Hudgins" twice, the big audience is irritated. O'Neill paces over to consult with York and Crouch. (He had greeted them earlier, "Hi ya, girls.") Ericka brushes him aside:

Q: Mrs. Hudgins—
THE COURT: Huggins.

Q: Are you being treated any differently than any other residents of Thompson Hall?

A: What I am trying to tell you is that I don't have that kind of individuality that you're talking about, and so that whatever, you know, happens to another human being affects me in terms of the particular women in that house, so—

Q: It may not affect you, personally?

A: It doesn't affect me, personally.

Q: Except insofar as you have a feeling or an empathy for what happens to somebody else?

A: Yes, I guess you could say that, if you want to put it that way.

Q: I want you to say it. I do not want to testify.

A: Would you like me to give you an example of what I am talking about?

Q: Yes.

A: To me, little things are as important as big things, because little things amount to big things after a while. Sometimes I make things with my hands; you know, sometimes I make jewelry and sometimes I paint and I make posters, I make—And I see things in terms of people being free or people being not free. I think things in terms of the goal of freedom and people achieving it. And so that whatever I do, whatever I would be able to make with my hands, would express that.

And I have made headbands and I have made posters for people, you know, not for any special reason; I just gave them away. And I noticed that right after that the women were told that their rooms were too cluttered and there were certain things in their rooms that would create fire hazard.

That's what I mean.

Q: You are saying, then, that the posters and headbands that you made you could not give to other inmates? You could—

A: I don't know whether I could or not, you know. I am saying that I did and it wasn't—evidently it was wrong. I am saying it was unnecessary, because if I had—I am trying to tell you, the type of thing that I made—if I had made a poster with trees and ducks in the water and things like that, then that would have been all right, but it was a type of poster and what it happened to be saying—and I would like to add that it had nothing to do with hatred of anything, you know—

Q: What did the poster say?

A: They said things like revolutionary love would bring all people of the world together, you know, the kind of love that really comes from the soul, that all humanity needs, you know, and not only love but the kind of strength to endure the things that the oppressor has done to us. By "oppressor" I mean all parts of the system that is keeping us down, including prisons, basically—

december 1970
7 pm niantic

for who ran from the camp
and was eventually caught

hopes that render me speechless
fly through my soul
the reality of now is
too much to accept the
racism, fascism and oppression
we suffer/have suffered is
numbing my soul
if it is true that they
have stifled your attempt
to breathe air and see
life and be part of the
chaos that is the streets
then i cry inside
because no one will
    understand outside tears
    for you

personalities
sometimes
don't matter . . .

but that's good enough you are a
    part of me sister-love the part of me
that has been and will one day be . . .
    every door is not locked.

Ericka

Q: You referred to the oppressors, and by that term you mean who?
A: I mean the people who have made this society and others all over the world so one-sided that poor people and oppressed people, the people who have not, cannot exist fully, cannot create, you know, cannot be human. That's all I mean.

The judge is upset. The cross-examination has opened a wide door and it is getting late. The hearing is set to be continued the following Monday.

In the hall Markle and Corporal Schultz chat with some bearded plainclothesmen. As the session breaks up Ericka kisses one of the Panther babies—born in Niantic prison—and greets the big exhilarated crowd. She has given a powerful and unexpected preview of the New Haven trial. Now she and the crowd catch up on each other's news in the confused recess. This cannot happen in Judge Mulvey's orchestrated New Haven courtroom.

Before the close Garry demanded that Bobby Seale be allowed to talk with the well-known California psychoanalyst Dr. Philip Shapiro. "Mr. Seale is suffering from depression because of his prison treatment. I want the court to know that." Now the press has its headline, wiping out Ericka's quiet passion. Garry angrily rejects the offer of a state psychiatrist: "If I took that offer I should have my *own* head examined. I'm talking about a man Mr. Seale knows, who is exactly like a clergyman to him. You wouldn't deny a clergyman."

december 1970
6 pm
niantic prison

reflections on sunday:

sounds that come from the soul are always the
    same
        free
        open sounds
        giving
the kind that reach out and touch—
    that's what our sisters did/minimum
    touching maximum/showing oppression
        and the wish for its
      removal . . .
    feeling those sounds
    seeing them felt on others
    watching faces smile
    really smile for the first time in months—

getting high—on the natural power of the
people to resist/to laugh/to sing
            shout/love/give
                even here!!!!
wild hair, funky guitar
long hair funky voice (someone said
    bessie smith came to mind)
        hair—all lengths, legs, arms, smiles, music—
        and us . . .
        ragged peacoats, cotton dressed, rocking,
                                    swaying,
                                    screaming

    enjoying it—
    crying too—even if not too many
let the tears fall free
. . . us—black/brown/white/poor—SISTERS
and it was all a total exchange
        of energy
communication
even if we did not share words
we all knew their soul-sounds were
saying
we understand
we know
we can see what america is doing
to you—mother/daught/child/woman
    of oppression—
we can see, they sung
and our voices answered their guitar
horn. flute. voice de-
mand for freedom with an unspoken right on
. . . a feeling there that one day—soon—
    all people will be free . . . and
        we left
        stronger
able to smile (for a moment) . . .
til we returned to
rules that degrade
schedules that destroy sanity
racism that blinds us
sexism that rapes us of our womanhood . . .

and the locks, keys, windows, walls, doors,
  threats
  warnings
  bribes that harden our hearts and
chain our souls . . .
  the time
    must be
      seized

                                        Ericka

A group called "The Women's Liberation Band" had gone to
play for Ericka and the other prisoners. It had caused a stir. Did
Miss York and Miss Crouch listen from behind their office
windows?

At the New Haven Junior Chamber of Commerce monthly
dinner, Charles R. Garry took his first local public-speaking
engagement.

"William L. Shirer told me that he finds the conditions here in
America and especially in our courtrooms analogous to the condi-
tions two years before the rise of Hitler in the dying days of the
Weimar Republic. . . .

"The *Kerner Report* points out that two thirds of white Americans are racists, and the other third are latent racists. . . .

"*Time-Harris Report:* 63 percent of Negro Americans have lost
confidence in the system. In excess of 9 percent of Negro Americans consider themselves revolutionaries, which is in excess of two
million. The year before the report, the figure was less than one
million. . . .

"The despicable conditions in your own Whalley Ave. jail—
where you have to 'crap in a bucket'! . . .

"The term *motherfucker* has a thousand different meanings. If
you don't know the language—if they are separate and apart from
you, how are you going to judge them! . . .

"The Huey Newton case would have cost in excess of one million dollars; the Oakland Seven case in excess of one half million.
When the gag rule is imposed on the defense, how can we get out
and raise money?" . . .

He was not, he told the Jaycees, talking about New Haven or Judge Mulvey. The audience stared down at their place mats.

THE JAYCEE CREED

We believe:
That faith in God gives meaning and purpose to human life;
That the brotherhood of men transcends the sovereignty of nations;
That economic justice can best be won by free men through free enterprise;
That government should be of laws rather than of men;
That earth's great treasure lies in human personality;
And that service to humanity is the best work of life.

The Panthers, too, had their "literature," and Garry showed some of it to the head table.

SURVIVAL THROUGH SERVICE TO THE PEOPLE
VOLUNTEER SERVICE FORM

I HEREBY VOLUNTEER TO SERVE THE PEOPLE AS I MAY BE NEEDED (PLEASE PRINT)

NAME: _____

STREET ADDRESS _____

CITY _____ COUNTY _____ STATE _____

PHONE NUMBER_____.

I would like to work in the following activity:

1. Breakfast for Children Program _____
2. Health Clinics _____
3. Liberation School _____
4. Busses to Prisons Program _____
5. Welfare Loans _____
6. Free Clothing Program _____
7. Selling Papers _____
8. Fund Raising _____
9. Any Programs _____ 10. Transportation _____
   How many hours per week are you available? _____

Meanwhile the *Register* editorialized:

SHAKESPEARE VS. HUEY NEWTON

Earl I. Williams, local black attorney recently re-elected president of the New Haven Chapter of the NAACP . . . countered the catching, but rather meaningless, "Power to the People" slogan by pointing out that the true expression of power in this country is the voting booth. He advocated greater concentration upon voter registration and upon working "within the system." . . .

"My advice to black students is to study Shakespeare rather than Huey P. Newton," was his remark.

While Garry is at the Chamber of Commerce a few students not yet on Christmas holiday attend a showing, at Yale, of the Communist Chinese film, *The East Is Red*. Long, formal, and with stunning balletic energy. The Chinese students are more quiet than the white radicals, who take the occasion to politicize.

THE LAWS EXIST.

> . . . the President is authorized to make public proclamation of an "Internal Security Emergency" . . . and is . . . authorized to apprehend and . . . detain . . . each person as to whom there is reasonable ground to believe . . . probably will conspire with others to engage in acts . . . of sabotage . . . Persons apprehended . . . shall be confined in . . . places of detention . . .

THE CAMPS EXIST

AND JUST IN CASE YOU
DON'T THINK ANYBODY
PLANS TO USE THEM * * *

> "The Emergency Detention Act of 1950 provides for various detention centers to be operated throughout the country and these might well be utilized for the temporary imprisonment of warring guerrillas."
> —Report of the Committee on Un-American Activities United States House of Representatives, May 6, 1968

"Red China has been flooding the country with its propaganda and there are three hundred thousand Chinese in the U.S., some of whom could be susceptible to recruitment either through ethnic ties or hostage situations because of relatives in Communist China. In addition, up to 20,000 Chinese immigrants can come here each year and this provides a means to send agents into our nation * * *"

> —J. EDGAR HOOVER, Head of the F.B.I., testifying before the House Appropriations Subcommittee, April 17, 1969

But nothing on the local trial was being passed out. Why were the Yale students embarrassed by the trial?

The reality of *voir dire* is blurring into statistics and incomprehensible gestures. The court watchers now agree that this is the largest and longest jury selection in history. By cheating on time and reading the long instruction to the prospective jurors into the record twice, the questioning of each panel is stretched out over two court days. But for the stalling, *one panel per day could be exhausted.*

In the world the headlines accumulate. Bobby, but not Ericka, is allowed several major journals every day.

WHITE POLICEMAN FREED IN AUGUSTA

—He Was Accused in Death of Black Youth During Riot—

DALEY ANNOUNCES BID FOR 5TH TERM

5 RECALL 'IMPRESSION' MEDINA WANTED EVERYONE AT MYLAI KILLED

HOOVER STILL FIRMLY IN FBI SADDLE

Hoover said the FBI and the Secret Service do not worry about a president being shot by a Puerto Rican or Mexican because "they don't shoot very straight.

"But if they come at you with a knife," he added, "beware."

This last remark prompted Rep. Edward R. Roybal, D-Calif., to call for Hoover's resignation.

WITNESS REPORTS ORDER BY MEDINA

'The Party's Over' Reported
as Cease-Fire Command

ERVIN SAYS ARMY'S AGENTS SPIED
ON ILLINOIS POLITICIANS

In another part of the jungle, at the federal court in Bridgeport.

MR. O'NEILL: I believe, Mrs. Huggins, last week you testified that you made a headband which was taken from an inmate that you gave it to; is that right?

A: Yes.

Q: Is this the headband (indicating)?

A: It is.

Q: Are you sure?

A: Yes.

Q: Now, Mrs. Huggins, showing you defendants' Exhibit A, what does it say? (Handing exhibit to the witness.)

A: It says "Revolt."

MR. O'NEILL: I have no other questions, your Honor.

THE COURT: You have completed your examination?

MR. O'NEILL: Yes, sir.

THE COURT: Very well. Redirect?

MISS RORABACK: Thank you, your Honor.

Q: Since we were here in court a week ago Monday, Mrs. Huggins, did an incident occur concerning a birthday card or poster?

A: Yes.

Q: Would you tell me what occurred?

A: Well, I don't want to go on, you know, at any length, but if I have some time I can explain it. It's involved.

Q: For whom was it?

A: Well, it was for our little girl. I can't say she's my little girl, because she's not. My husband's. A poster was made of—

Q: You made a poster for her? And that was signed by you and some others; is that correct?

A: By all of my friends in Thompson Hall.

Q: And that was not permitted to be delivered to your daughter; is that correct?

A: Right.

Q: That was because other persons' names appeared on it—

A: Yes.

Q: —in addition to yours?

A: And the reason that it hurts is because it was a picture of her husband—I mean of my husband—who was killed, who was her father. And it was just a huge picture, with a poem that I had written surrounding it, and the translation to the poem was—well, not the translation—but the words were unreadable, so the words to the poem were written on the back.

And everybody just signed it because everybody loves her.

"for kani, a rollingstone"

if there is cosmic beauty
then your face holds it
if there is human understanding
then your soul is capable of it
if a mind ever thought of freedom
yours has flown to where freedom
lives and has drifted back
here to tell your body about it
and you long for it
            i can see it in your eyes
            aquarius sister-love
            i can see it . . . you
            must know that one
            day we will all
                be
            FREE

A young court reporter from Bridgeport is killing time in the front row while various Panthers and Puerto Ricans from the local Young Lords organization drift in. All the lawyers are in the judge's chambers.

The reporter and a Young Lord of about the same age begin a discussion about the "system." The reporter is a happy young man dressed in the outfit and hues of his class and world view. The Young Lord also has long sideburns, but the body image is lean and hungry, not like a well-fed and happy infant. The revolutionary's protest bursts through his frame into the beret, leather, buttons, verbal gestures of the new and hungry man.

"We don't need these psychiatrists. They go to school for ten years to tell us that we come from 'sociopathic' homes. It's capitalism, man. Capitalism fucks over the people, makes them crazy, turns us against each other. We know from history that there is progress—you know, capitalism was progressive then; it fit the technology, the ideas—now socialism fits the technology and the demands of the people."

Then the young reporter, who was cublike, began to worry about Poland and good cops, voting and violence, and the Young Lord blew him away.

"If they try to kill us it's like trying to kill the future. We are not violent. Money and capitalism is violence. We want to deal with the needs of the people. We believe in self-defense, if they . . ."

"But you won't have the—like if I want a certain kind of house—"

"The answer to that is struggle!"

"What kind of struggle?"

"Struggle, man. Constant revolution. Cultural revolution after the seize of . . ."

They all come in. A deputy tells the Young Lord to take off his beret. As MacDougall comes down the aisle, the Young Lords and the children with them start to sing, "Old MacDougall had a farm . . . With an oink oink here, oink oink there, here an oink . . ." Garry started right in on Bobby's right to grow a "neat goatee."

Direct examination by Mr. Garry:

Q: Would you tell us what your occupation is, Mr. MacDougall.
A: I'm the Commissioner of the Connecticut Department of Corrections.
Q: How much influence has Mr. Markle, the State's Attorney in New Haven, had with regard to my client, Mr. Bobby G. Seale, in his isolation?
A: None, sir.
Q: None whatsoever?

A: No, sir.

Q: You did not consult Mr. Markle or anybody in the State's Attorney's office in New Haven before you placed Mr. Seale in isolation?

A: Absolutely not. Mr. Seale was received as a single, individual prisoner, not with a group of prisoners.

Q: Then why did you put him in isolation immediately?

A: Mr. Seale put himself in isolation.

Q: In other words, Mr. MacDougall decided?

A: After consultation with the Department of Health, we did, yes.

Q: What Department of Health?

A: Connecticut Department of Health.

Q: May I see a directive of the Department?

A: I don't have it available here today.

Q: Whom did you consult with? Who are the persons you consulted with in the Department of Health?

A: I think we requested an opinion from Dr. Foote, who is Commissioner of the Department of Health.

Q: If Abraham Lincoln came and sat in your jail for a day or two waiting for trial, you would have him take his beard off, too?

A: Abe would get shaved.

Q: How about Ulysses Grant, one of the Presidents of the United States?

A: I'm afraid he'd be in the same category, including Ellis MacDougall or his brother.

Q: You kept him in jail, then, you kept him segregated, up until May, May 28, 1970, because of his beard. Is that right?

A: No, he kept himself in there, sir. All he had to do was shave it off.

The first press conference since the Seale arrest just happened. Garry, Ericka and Bobby sat at their table facing the press while everyone was waiting for Markle and MacDougall to emerge from the judge's chambers. The unused jury box was three-quarters filled with male and female plainclothes guards and deputies. As it goes on, everyone waits for someone to cut it off, but no one does. The police, immobilized, suddenly do not exist because they are not policing anyone, so the prisoners suddenly become "themselves," they exist because the authorities have sunk below the level of dominance.

"What do you want?"

"We advocate a twenty-hour week." Seale, making up for lost time, plunges into the reform program, forcing the guards to see and hear him as he talks about the parameters of their lives, the money and time and un-freedom.

Meanwhile Ericka chats with Rose, her old cellmate, about the children Che, Mai, and one named Bobby Jon Eldridge Huey Erick, but not in that order. Then Seale directs the reporters to Ericka for a definition of "intercommunalism."

"We don't see things in black and white, we see the world in technicolor."

"Right on!"

"We have boundaries of sex, geography, race, politics, class and we have to cut them off. The people of the world are only communities in the American Empire. And we are all tied up. We have to untie inside. . . ."

"Do you believe that individual love comes first, then?"

Seale: "Right on time! Revolutionary love is where it's at." He goes on about the "degenerate, demagogic oppressors" and "Hoover, the flattest foot in America."

"You feel that love—"

"I don't go for the Superman concept. All these years and he's never taken Lois Lane in that phone booth and kissed her—you see what I'm saying. But I like to do the 'bugaloo,' the 'dog' (in the streets). But I have time in jail to get into these vast analytical sets. . . ."

Then they discussed Rollo May and Erich Fromm; the bearded court clerk and the guards were being dragged after the reporters into the flesh and blood of the man with the neat black beard and the young woman when just then a guard in charge, with a flag in his lapel—who had not fallen out of existence in the snowbound, timeless courtroom—stalked in, unknowing, jerked his thumb at the prisoners and said, "Take 'em downstairs"—as if they were deaf or dead.

The few yards of light-blue carpet between the prisoners and the press and friends yawned open, the guards came back to life. The press was shocked, though the attitude was the daily, accepted mechanical method of relating that had become, by now, a second nature. But for a few minutes another nature had bled through the stereotypes of prisoners and guards and news people. As the clerk rose from his box he seemed to stagger, and his thick black beard, much bigger than Seale's, stood out like a plague spot on his pale and feverish face. The police broke up into laughing groups to remind themselves of their reality, and the clerk sat at his desk, staring like a Talmudic madman.

Ericka had drifted quickly out of the interview, back into her writing.

"for our lawyer (charlie . . .)"

sometimes i find the need to communicate
with people who i never talk to much
maybe because i want them to know
that cause i don't say too much
doesn't mean that i have nothing
to say
anyway—what could i say to you
except that watching you everyday
and getting to understand the
way you think is beautiful
even when you're angered by
the obvious farce the courts
of amerika are—your beauty
shines thru—i just have
to tell you that although
you are—confusing
sometimes i love you
in the way that servants
of the people love each other
in the way that victims
of a common enemy love
each other—
    not just because your
name carrys heavy vibrations
or because you have a nice smile
    but because
        your voice is gentle
        your whole being perceptive
        sometimes you give me
            strength

                Ericka

They all come in. The judge thanks all counsel for their co-operativeness. Each has made concessions, there are no "victors." Then he reads the complete capitulation of the state. It is all to be allowed, from Bobby's beard to Ericka's books. "You may have the *Black Panther* newspaper if it is kept in a sealed manila envelope in your room when you're not reading it." The psychiatrist is to be permitted, and urgent telephone calls and uncensored mail, and a state investigator to electronically check for state or federal eavesdropping!

"Papers are to be carried to the legal visiting room in a sealed manila envelope." The state stands to remind the judge, "We can shake the envelope." Garry is lounging in the jury box—"They may pat it, your Honor."

They had had enough of Charles R. Garry from San Francisco, representing Mr. Bobby G. Seale, the cofounder and chairman of the Black Panther Party. Mr. Markle had paid a very heavy price to escape the witness stand and the punishment meted out by Garabedian, who had been hiding in wait in the lawyer's well-cut suit.

The judge wished all a happy holiday, including the prisoners in their "difficult situation." He was so clearly mature and decent. Judge Zampano was, Seale confided to Garry, something else altogether from that other federal judge, the cunning old fury from Chicago. "Twenty times better, plus a hundred."

The preparation and these two days of suit for relief in federal court would have cost, for those who could pay, $10,000.

And MacDougall had given way, too. Was he, finally, a "pig"? He was a progressive criminologist who had not read the *Autobiography of Malcolm X,* the classic of modern rehabilitation, redemption by a method taught in no prison or state farm. His (MacDougall's) rules, what were they beyond reified reaction formations, guesses, superstitions, blind traditions and stubborn middle-class biases to be changed completely from one day to the next as had happened here in Bridgeport during the snowstorm that lasted two days? Garry had shown the official passivity toward institutionalized viciousness to him for a moment and the guards and staff had felt it too. No one with the state had anything to show for the whole experience except Ericka's headband that read

"REVOLT!" and was now filed away forever with the evidence, and the Chairman told the news people that after the revolution he would treat his jailers "better, much better than he had been treated."

They trudged out into the Christmas storm, these playthings of the reactive system that was not a system. Out they went, all of them overweight and red-faced, trying to push down, squelch the astonishment that had begun to rise in them when the judge had spoken softly to those who were in bonds, who had been presumed innocent.

As for the functionaries, perhaps it was as Chesterton said, "The horrible thing about public officials, even the best . . . is not that they are wicked . . . not that they are stupid . . . it is simply that they have got used to it."

THE TWENTY-THIRD DAY (DECEMBER 28, 1970)

Blacks	Women	Average Age per Panel
1	19	50.5
2	15	48.5
4	24	41.75
3	26	48.5
1	21	51.8
2	17	47.7
1	24	49.85
1	21	45.32
1	18	45.31
1	20	47.02
17	208	479.25
3.4%	41.6%	47.93

That is the invisible poetry of the courtroom, more than the numbers and the Latin. The death-oriented sampling errors, the last fifty of the first five hundred ended typically.

Excused:

—because of prejudice against the Party or the
defendants 8
—because of exposure to negative pretrial publicity 15
—because they did not understand the concept
of "presumption of innocence" 4
—because of opposition to the death penalty 3
—because of hardship 3
—by defense peremptory challenges 5

The defense has now used 33 challenges; the prosecution has used only 16. Each has a total of 60.

There was one black man, a churchgoer, who claimed the papers for his source, just like a white man.

The next venire would be convened after New Year's Day. They would be the same. The tics jumping in their faces, big lumps in their throats, the heads and hands shaking "no"—if you were to study them through a glass without knowing the occasion, you would guess they were accidental survivors of some illimitable tragedy. These talesmen are, Chekhov-like, in mourning for their lives. Each one separately announced proudly that their information is harvested "from the headlines"; television does not really count, it is still "the papers, you know." Then Garry in his pitiless kindness unburdens them of those terrible secrets that even the court reporter, in hiding at their feet, cannot understand.

There was a flicker of hope on the last court day of 1970, when a young woman named Anagnostakis seemed ready to qualify. Perhaps she had a face like Charles Garry's mother, like a Levantine Madonna, so Mr. Markle cranked up the death penalty. For half an hour the defense and the judge tried to soften her categorical refusals "to judge death for another person." The judge tried out her mother, the President, the Governor (as if this mechanical hierarchy would shake a moral evolution involving millions of years), but the judge and the defense could not save her. Garry, upset, began his objection while the young woman was still gathering up her coat. "Your Honor, we were going to accept this juror. I want the record to show that the State's Attorney only questions about the death penalty when a juror comes along who may have some human compassion." The press was scribbling, Markle looking down and his young adolescent son, on a Christmas-holiday visit in the press box, looking confused.

Garry, knowing that Markle will answer, refuses to give up the air waves. "I am saying that the prosecutor is not serious, is not in earnest about the death penalty. These questions are a ruse to eliminate sympathetic and humane jurors." Katie joined, saying, "This bears out Professor Zeisel's findings that we are losing the kind of person who might be extremely fair and sophisticated." At last Markle was able to talk—"They have no way of knowing . . ." In the puzzled silence the judge took over to talk the intervention down.

Garry slumps in his chair. In the silence the pipes knock and the jurors, off stage, yell. Ericka crosses her long, booted legs and writes as Bobby whispers in her ear.

Looking back on the first five hundred there was pity. The lower middle class hide their sympathy, the upper middle class their alienation.

The young people so far seem somehow worse. They do not go to Yale. One girl appears to read only *True Story* and looks exactly like one of their cover cartoons, palely erotic and ashamed and outdated. A young man, sideburned, "goes along with the others," he says, and is soon excused by the court.

Catherine Roraback is bitter that there are no young mothers.

It becomes harder and harder to find anyone to serve. Now the jurors move out swiftly from the jury room, half trotting toward the witness box to confess their bias. When there is a problem, Garry calls on his long career to talk to a C.P.A. or an insurance investigator or a nuclear-plant government employee concerning ther dependence on authority and law enforcement. In the half-empty courtroom the consummate legal performance goes on for five days without letup.

What stands out is the fear:

> "I just can't stand violence."

> "The Black Panthers are like the K.K.K."

"Every juror could be tagged for retaliatory action."

"Just the name scares me."

The pace of the *voir dire* is so fast by the end of the week, that the waiting talesmen are reassured—by the rhythm of short sheriff's knocks—that a modest confession of bigotry or fear, attributed to the newspapers, will be rewarded by a speedy refusal. The court becomes hypnotized at the choreography of the hustling middle-aged jurors pausing just long enough to demur, and the sheriffs stepping about to guide them out and the new veniremen *in,* to pass, in their turn, behind the jury box to the stand, their heads bobbing past the spaces between the jury seats that they will never occupy.

On occasion someone hesitates to "remember." An old man ruminates about Ericka Huggins, "Didn't she run into a court with a gun and kill a judge?" After the longest silence so far, the attorneys approached the bench; one woman ran in, with a letter, and out squealing and sobbing. On the Friday, Mr. Markle took to asking if the prospectives had been influenced by any statements of attorney William Kunstler of New York. More and more people are out of work or bankrupt. There was another poor white who said, "Some of my better friends are colored." The poor whites talk in frightened crazy circles like the older black people. The defense is divided over whether to fight for their inclusion and gamble on their racism. One poor Irishman delivered a frantic soliloquy—concerning what he had and had not read—directly into the upturned, lip-reading mouth and the unseeing eyes of the court reporter crouched at the foot of the witness stand, where that fashionably dressed young man plies his amazing feats of digital echolalia. The same man compared the Black Panther Party to the Knights of Columbus, and the judge, a member of the Knights, made a face like the old comedian Oliver Hardy. Kelly is thrown out. Some student "freaks" in the front row give him a small cheer as he searches desperately in the rack for his ancient overcoat.

Charles R. Garry's jury-selection strategy is stupefying. Even the other defense lawyers are taken aback. Three jurors after three hundred questioned! No one has ever seen anything like it. They had never seen anyone fight like this all day and then announce at a Yale meeting, at night, that the presumption of innocence is a fraud like the "rest of the system."

A few "quotes" hang in the air:

"I think they wear black jackets—like motorcycle riders."

"His [Bobby's] intentions might have been good from the beginning. Maybe somewhere along the way someone went astray."

"A lot of people don't like the Knights of Columbus; a lot of people don't like the Masons; a lot of people don't like the Black Panther Party."

"Some of my better friends are colored people."

"I'm very prejudiced against those people—all of them."

"I think they're Communist-inspired."

"They shouldn't have a party. They corrupt everything."

Everyone stands slowly, half waiting for the judge to wish Happy New Year. Seale is in a green sweater and holds a book about technology and power by Lewis Mumford; Huggins wears a long gold velour skirt she has made and a warm-looking purple sweater; Bobby embraces her. Then Garry hugs her, then he clasps Bobby; Bobby and Charles pound each other on the back. They are the center of all the watering, or alarmed authorities' male eyes.

This coming to life of stereotypes, of the dead, is all very hard on Mr. Markle. As the tableau breaks up, he blurts out his obligatory joke to the reporters, "I would have hugged Schultz, but he crushes."

THE TWENTY-SEVENTH DAY (JANUARY 7, 1971)

"Seale Outburst Mars Jury Selection," the bold headline read. More than black humor.

After a marathon of six hundred talesmen, who cannot say fast enough that they are incapable of rising above the headlines, the idea that there was anything left to "mar" was grounds for laughter and tears. Seale laughed later.

For the second time in two days the prosecution was grilling a black juror about the death penalty, and the defense was on its feet objecting every step of the way. "Who am I to judge? I don't give no life, why should I take one?" In the embarrassment (it is said that Markle is opposed, personally, to the death penalty), the judge tries to come to the rescue, "Is your mother living? What if your mother was brutally murdered?" "No." "Or the President?" (Why did he always leap from Mother to the President? What about the brutal killing of Father? Complexes within complexes.) The neatly dressed man was adamant, "I won't take no life." So he had to be rejected for cause. A lean middle-aged woman followed him in, and Mr. Markle began—"My name is Arnold Markle . . ." (He had taken to introducing himself in the wake of Garry's courtly style, but he left off the *l*'s as a child does and it sounded like "Arno Marko.") He asked the woman if she could give the state a fair trial, and Seale cracked down on the defense table with the flat of his hand.

"The defendants! Not the state, the defendants get a fair trial!"

The sheriffs stepped out from their corners into the combat zone, the judge leaned forward, the full courtroom was frozen, "Now, Mr. Seale, we haven't had any trouble . . ."

"I don't care about that. This pig is knocking off black people. We want fifty percent black people on this jury." "Cool it, Bobby." Garry half rises—"Can we have a recess, your Honor?" Bobby, quietly: "I need one, judge."

The wire-service people run self-consciously to telephones. The rest of the press crowds around the court reporter to get a verbatim instant replay for their stories. In the hall there are arguments everywhere over the state's selective use of the death-penalty question for black, young or "sympathetic" types. Garry had pounded away at "this ruse," but the State's Attorney and the judge insisted that the defense too was "selective in its questions."

It was not a matter of questions, partisans argued, the State could ask any question it liked, but it could not have it both ways: if opposition to capital punishment was grounds for exemption, then each and every juror should be asked, not just potentially defense-oriented ones. The discussion was heated, the press was personally getting involved, the death tactic was becoming an overriding issue.

Back in court Bobby Seale stood to address the bench. "I'm not emotional now. In Chicago my faith in the system of justice was destroyed by the violation of my Constitutional rights. But I am going to try my best, because I have my attorney here now, and see if Sister Ericka and I can get a hearing. You are not a Judge Hoffman. And I'm upset about what I read about Angela Davis last night, in her trial."

The judge caught the spirit. "You have your counsel from California who is very able. If you need a recess just tell him. But I have procedures, and I'm not going to permit outbursts from anyone. This woman could have had a heart attack."

It had been so short and heartfelt that everyone had been moved; Garry said later that if there were no more "outbursts," then the break had brought some reality into the cold courtroom. The seating arrangement was changed again—Garry, Bobby, Ericka, Katie, and David Rosen.

A half hour later Seale was laughing when a flag wearer named McGrath said, "The more I try to help the colored in my neighborhood the more thay hate me." And after a woman said that "they have to be proven innocent first," he began very discreetly to hold up a tablet that carried the bold message, "Help! Racism in America." The judge, embarrassed at the stampede of talesmen, joked, "They must have all had lunch together." Something else had happened to them.

They all know what they are doing to escape this trial. But theirs is a kind of innocence that makes them look startled when the judge throws them out. Some look stunned. They had taken on these biases and attitudes as protective coloration, as camouflage. Now, in public, they were being humiliated for not adapting to the State's rhetoric.

What can they do? Who and what is the majority? Everyone has guns and rhetoric except them? They are better, these sad people, than their answers and their pathetic little American secrets. They are much better, and the occasional liberal who turns up is not nearly as sound or loving as his clothes and his clichés promise.

What can the defense do? The ignorant, failing, dying lower-middle class is human but racist; the educated liberal class can afford not to be verbal racists, but they are mean as can be. Garry and Katie must keep searching those masks for a hand hold.

Despite everything, for the first time a full panel of fifty was exhausted in one day, and Charles Garry left for Boston to visit old relatives from his mother's day.

It was no good. The jury selection had become a rout, a panic, a stampede. A man threw up, and two more women broke down upon entering. Ten were excused in fifteen minutes; it was like the ultimate Gallup Poll. Three in ten minutes claimed diabetes. Records. The spring was wound up tight and all motions to stop the trial were denied, though once Markle said, "If you want a change of venue, I'll join you." What did that mean?

David Rosen had argued the motions after the New Year's recess.

MOTION TO DISMISS
RE PREJUDICIAL PUBLICITY

MOTION TO BAR EXERCISE OF
PEREMPTORY CHALLENGES BY THE STATE

MOTION TO DISMISS JURY PANEL

MOTION TO SUPPLEMENT JURY LISTS

He argued very well; it was good defense strategy. In his casual, aristocratic manner the young advocate showed flashes of what would one day be an authentic style.

Rosen's theme was simple: citizens were being denied their right to serve. The citations ranged from Blackstone to the Constitution of the State of Connecticut:

CONNECTICUT CONSTITUTION
Article First, Section Two:

All political power is inherent in the people, and all free governments are founded on their authority, and instituted for their benefit; and they have at all times an undeniable and indefeasible right to alter their form of government in such manner as they may think expedient.

The Panthers quoted it everywhere.

All motions denied. And it begins again, with Markle unable to refuse a black woman. Garry stands behind him and leads her reluctantly home.

Judge Mulvey sighs that a notorious case in London once chose a jury in twenty minutes. Some of the jurors seem to be identical with veniremen in the first five hundred. Regular observers and the press joke that they are sending people through twice. The sheriffs guide them without touching, the bodies in the box are contorted with an anxiety that an animal would smell at once.

The sheriffs are wearing bright, cheap Christmas ties and argyle socks, the gifts of the 1950s. "Bring Bobby in," one says; they too are getting used to this. Like a long-running play, the *voir dire* is being slowly economized until only the cue lines remain. The jurors, well coached by the newspapers, play their parts to the hilt. These are Tolstoy's masses "ruined by the government," and they have been in rehearsal all their lives.

All the while Charles R. Garry's long Byzantine eyes rake and scan the press and the crowd for their reactions to the occasional one who claims no opinion. For the rest he simply asks now, after the formal introduction, "Have you read about this case?" "Yes." "Have you formed an opinion?" "Yes." And that is it. "I join." "I join," the others say, and Garry moves for cause, and the next is called. Now and then it takes longer and we have vignettes— "Charles and the Engineer" discuss rhetoric versus action; "Charles and the old Pole" pretend not to understand each other; "Charles and the Christian Scientist" stare as if each thought the other insane.

One woman recalled the Lindbergh kidnaping case, and for those who remembered, nostalgia flooded the courtroom. Otherwise Garry hurried off most nights to Westport or New York to try to answer the charges of Panther anti-Semitism and secure some contributions to the defense. The defense expenses were all documented—$150,000!

In the last panel of the seventh week there were no black people and only twenty women. The audience had the wind up, they were all women. In the front row were Joan Bird and Afeni Shakur of the New York Twenty-One, and Artie Seale and Rose Mary Gross, the mothers of Bobby Seale's children, Malik Nkrumah Stagolee Seale and Huey Bunchy (Li'l) Bobby John Eric Eldridge Seale.

Mr. Dilger and the other jurors were let out into the falling snow. Miss Goldson stepped through the flakes under a pink umbrella, and Mr. Adams brought up the rear.

On the Green stood a contingent of women. They wore paper headbands with the word REVOLT! inscribed. This was an echo of that headband of Ericka's that had been confiscated at Niantic and was now entered forever into evidence in Bridgeport. Women from all over the Northeast had come to New Haven on Ericka's twenty-third birthday. (A lunchtine cake in court was denied.) The Liberation News Service collective and friends had lovingly produced a folder of Ericka's poems for the occasion. On the cover, a picture of her, snapped hurriedly in Bridgeport outside the federal court, smiling broadly in the driving snow.

> "don't let those silly
> fascists pluck at your
> nerves . . . smile and
> know that they are
> sad and completely
> void of the love that
> people like you possess."
>
> love, power, strength
> venceremos
> Ericka

The women march off to meet at the Bread and Roses Coffee House. Men are not invited. They hang around and argue with one another. A beautiful young writer, Elia Katz, who is passing through, provokes a correspondent from the Los Angeles *Free Press.* Katz says: "Manson is not insane. He is like Castro or Che. If Castro and Che had failed they would have been Manson; if Manson had succeeded he would have been Che." The young men are furious with the women (they must not be called girls) for not needing them.

As the death-penalty issue expanded, the New Haven Council of Churches called a press conference to express dismay over the jury selection and to announce a public meeting.

These men of God, with a woman, Vivian Noble, as their lay leader, could not rest because once the horror of the jail—Dostoevsky not Dickens—had been experienced, the sanctity of its antechamber, the court, was forever undermined. Like a house with a gorgeously appointed and immaculate drawing room above a ghastly, excrescent basement where a wild illegitimate child lay chained in his accumulated filth, the process of justice was defined for these good people by the Whalley Avenue jail.

It was beginning to dawn that someone besides the Panthers was using rhetoric. The Panthers took up the rhetoric of the powerless, but the State's rhetoric of power was something else—familiar, implicit, resonant. From the wall inscriptions of Justice and Democracy, to Judge Mulvey's endless enjoinder about the presumption of innocence, was there any basis in reality, or was it "just rhetoric," as people said of the Panthers?

Who are these "fools for Jesus Christ," as Paul called them, who challenge their own boards of directors and become involved in the hell of black liberation? Preaching to half-empty, aging congregations, standing alone under the waiting bare Anglo-Saxon crucifix, arguing for social action ahead of social service, these ministers and women of the Council are more timid than those businessmen in the market place who pay their bills, and yet they fear the undoing of the human spirit above any other thing. These are the kind who went to the concentration camps too. Their naked Evangel sometimes drives them from the established church into the revolution as they act on the Christian "socialism" of *their* rhetoric.

So while the "revolutionaries" were debating the question of "black nationalism," these fools for Christ were beginning once again to intercede for children and men, thereby scandalizing New Haven, that old "fair haven" and modern "model city," and violating its Fundamental Agreement.

The Nobel laureate, George Wald, consented to host a defense fund-raising party, and a popular rally in the black community was scheduled for January. Huey P. Newton would speak and then move to Yale for a student rally and a week in residence at Trumbull College. There, a dialogue between Huey and Erik Erikson would go on for three days. In charge of this philosophical coup would be the college's master, Kai Erikson, the son of the great man. The humanist community, too, was beginning to stir. Huey was just doing it for the money, the radicals said. But he was not.

On the Friday, Judge Mulvey held a whispered consultation at the bench. Garry went over to the gallery and quietly told them that demonstrations outside would bring arrests. This because, now that people were again being turned away from the courtroom, ripples of protest were beginning. Outside the bulletproof windows members of Youth Against War and Fascism chanted the slogans. The radicals had begun to trickle into town.

Inside the white heads of the potential jurors, under the white genetic envelopes, the metaphysics of the culture and its media abstractions enters through the skin. This is part of the dialectic and the symbiosis of justice, too. The oracular voice is *The New York Times* in this year of the courts:

ABOLITION OF DEATH PENALTY URGED BY U.S. LEGAL PANEL

At the time of the trial there were over 620 men on America's death rows. Should the Supreme Court reject the Constitutional test cases before it, another moral crisis, on top of all the others, would be added to the burden of the country that displayed outrage toward other nations who were still exacting capital punishment in 1970.

A professor of German at Yale, Tom Saine, was part of that fifty percent of America that rejects the death penalty. His wife's encouragement and his own anger at having been rejected from the Seale-Huggins jury for his beliefs sent him to Katie Roraback's office partner, Michael Avery, of the Connecticut Civil Liberties Union, who referred him to a Union lawyer not so close to the case.

"I am not a revolutionary," said the youngish, bearded Dr. Saine, "and it is not a matter of conscience, it's my rights I'm defending."

REJECTED JUROR SUES JUDGE
ON CAPITAL PUNISHMENT QUESTION

The furor over death sentences in Spain and the Soviet Union and in America was emerging in New Haven. Because of Garry's attack, the State's Attorney was beginning to question more jurors on their death-penalty scruples and, predictably, seemingly indifferent prospective jurors were showing scruple and ambivalence on the subject. This meant that Markle, who had used less than half the number of challenges used by the defense, would have to use more of his own peremptory challenges. On the day of Seale's outburst he used two, as many as in the two weeks before.

All the while, the conspiracy strategy snaked through the mind of the man in the street. Manson and Medina filtered through the New Haven *Register:*

TO CALLEY, THE ARMY'S
A FRANKENSTEIN MONSTER

WASHINGTON—In a published recollection of killing and torture in the Vietnam War, Lt. William L. Calley concludes "that the Army's nothing but a Frankenstein monster and I was a little part of it."

"But people still ask me, 'What do you have against women and children?' Damn, I haven't a thing! I love women, I love children, too. I love people. I haven't a thing against them, but people say, 'Why did you kill, then?'

"Well damn! why did I go to Vietnam? I didn't buy a plane ticket for it. Someone in Hawaii gave it to me. People say, 'Well then, why did you go? Why didn't you go to jail instead?' Dumb ass: If I had known it would turn out this way, I would have!"

"We went there to save those people, but God!" Calley laments. "We didn't give the scraps from the dinner table to them. We didn't have the common courtesy to talk their language or learn of their customs: We scorned them, and killed them. A real disgrace."

From the *Times,* the echo of the Bridgeport appeal:

JAIL CENSUS FINDS 52% NOT CONVICTED

WASHINGTON, Jan. 6—A pioneering Federal census of city and county jails showed today that 52 percent of their inmates had not been convicted of a crime and that many inmates, whether convicted or not, endured "less than human conditions."

Four jails still in daily use, including one in Fulton County, N.Y. were built before George Washington's inauguration, the study showed, A quarter of the 97,500 local jail cells in the country are more than 50 years old.

And from the *Register:*

CONVICT SAYS HE'S BEEN IN SOLITARY 10 MONTHS BECAUSE HIS HAIR IS LONG

At the same time Lonnie McLucas was following in the footsteps of Bobby and Ericka.

COURT SUIT CLAIMS McLUCAS' RIGHTS VIOLATED

While he was in New York Garry was meeting with the "Panther Twenty-One" lawyers. On the West Coast his office was cooperating in the pretrial motions for Angela Davis.

MISS DAVIS SEES A 'POLITICAL FRAMEUP'

SAN RAFAEL, Calif., Jan. 5—Angela Davis accused of murder, kidnapping and criminal conspiracy declared her innocence at her arraignment today, and said she was "the target of a political frameup."

Her request to speak came as a surprise, and often her words were lost in the shouted objections of Albert W. Harris, Assistant State's Attorney General.

Miss Davis, a black militant and professed communist, also asked that she be granted permission to act as co-counsel in her own defense.

She said that "a system of justice which virtually condemns to silence the one person who stands to lose most would seem to be self-defeating."

What were the radicals reading, the ones who were staying away from New Haven? They heard that an anti-Castro militant who had confessed to conspiracy to commit murder and who had blown up property was released by a New York judge. There were little things,

ACTOR CLEARED OF CHARGE

LOS ANGELES—Audie Murphy, America's most decorated soldier during World War II, was cleared today of charges of illegally possessing blackjacks. Mr. Murphy, now an actor, testified he was authorized to possess them because he is a special officer with the Port Hueneme, Calif., police force and a deputy with the Dallas County, Tex. sheriff's department.

and big,

FEDERAL JUDGE DISMISSES A SUIT ON ARMY SPYING ON CIVILIANS

MAYOR OF SAN DIEGO IS FOUND NOT GUILTY AT HIS BRIBERY TRIAL

ARMY DROPS CHARGES AGAINST FOUR IN ALLEGED MYLAI COVER-UP

GREEN BERET DEPLORES MYLAI; IS EXCUSED FROM TRIAL PANEL

NEIGHBORHOOD SPY PLAN DRAWS HEAVY CRITICISM

COLUMBIA KILLS LOAN TO HARLEM
NO PROBE OF KILLINGS AT KENT

Seale trusted only Jan von Flatern, of Liberation News Service. He kept demanding the "real facts."

2/17/71

BOBBY:

These are the figures I have. They may not be *precise* (my arithmetic rarely is), but they are close enough to make reasonably accurate percentages—

* defense challenge	59
* prosecution challenge	31
* hardship	143
* opposition to capital punishment	15
* failure to understand/accept the "presumption of innocence" idea	33
* association with cops (usually, wd believe one more)	57
* opinions formed by pre-trial publicity	411
* prejudice against the Party/black people in general	152
* miscellaneous (knew attorney, changed residence, felt incapable of judging anyone)	9
* felt defendants innocent, or that they could not get a fair trial	6
	916

The figures show that the people who had formed opinions on this case plus the people with general prejudices against the Party number 563 —or 60% of the total number questioned. I did not keep a record of the breakdown of hardships, so I can't tell you how many were hard of hearing, etc. (since none of 'em understand a fuckin' thing, its pretty hard to tell anyway . . .)

Be strong, brother—
Power and love,
Jan

The establishment newspapers were at all these endless trials. Only imagine if reason prevailed and technology, television and radio were permitted to take the public into these closed courtrooms. The nation would be plunged into a continental Theatre of Cruelty, switching from channel to channel in the stations of their lives. This would be the national therapy. The public would choose quickly as they did during the Kefauver and McCarthy dramas.

Soon, if the country was to retain sanity, there would be cameras in court and Congress and grand jury. Name one objection that was not made when the press, under the First Amendment, began its coverage of our judicial process. The ladies and gentlemen of the press are there to assure us of our eighteenth-century rights while our twentieth-century technology goes into wiretapping and weapons systems instead of bringing the convulsions of Chicago and New Haven and Los Angeles and Fort Benning to the people sitting at home—huddled around their consoles for warmth—waiting for the end.

In New Haven, Garry passed the bad news around personally.

GARRY—YOU SYPHILLITIC, NIGGER LOVING
MOTHER FUCKER—YOUR DAYS ARE NUMBERED,
BASTARD YOU & ALL YOUR COCKSUCKING BLACK
RUGHEAD DOGS ARE GOING TO DIE VERY, VERY
SLOWLY AT THE HANDS OF WHITE MEN, MAYBE
IF YOUR YELLOW BALLS WERE CUT OFF & PUT
IN YOUR VILE JEW—COMMIE—NIGGER SUCKING
MOUTH—YOU MIGHT LEARN—
DEATH TO NIGGER DOGS
AND WHITE PUSSYS LIKE YOU

But what got shoved down the throats of the veniremen slated to come to court that morning was

**JOBLESS ROLLS AGAIN
CLIMB IN CITY, STATE**

and

CHILE RECOGNIZES COMMUNIST CHINA

Gulping now before rushing to court,

VITAL FIGURES SHOW
MORE BLACK BIRTHS

One in every 12 white live births was illegitimate, and more than two in every five non-white births were out of wedlock.

More than one half (54.8 per cent) of the teen-age mothers were unwed. Nearly three in 10 white teen-age births (27.3 per cent) were illegitimate, while more than seven in 10 non-white teen-age births (70.8 per cent) were out of wedlock.

The second highest illegitimacy ratio, almost one in five, occurred among women aged 20–24 years.

At the courthouse waiting for them, waiting to break down the old Poles and the big blondes was Charles R. Garry, with forty of his sixty peremptories exhausted.

The Fifty-First Day (March 11, 1971)

It is over.

After eighteen weeks and thirty-one panels of fifty talesmen the world's longest *voir dire* is over. The defense ran out of peremptory challenges with only ten jurors chosen, the rest were forced on them. The state had spent over two million dollars so far on the trials alone.

The final motions had to be acted out. David Rosen was as good as his research this time. His voice resonated as he argued them one by one.

No. 15681	:	SUPERIOR COURT
STATE OF CONNECTICUT	:	
V.	:	
ERICKA HUGGINS	:	
No. 15844	:	AT NEW HAVEN
STATE OF CONNECTICUT	:	
V.	:	
BOBBY G. SEALE	:	FEBRUARY 22, 1971

MOTION TO DISMISS
RE PREJUDICIAL PUBLICITY

MEMORANDUM OF LAW IN SUPPORT
OF MOTION TO DISMISS

MOTION TO GRANT THE DEFENDANTS
THIRTY ADDITIONAL PEREMPTORY CHALLENGES

MEMORANDUM OF LAW
RE PEREMPTORY CHALLENGES

I. IF THE COURT REFUSES TO DISMISS THE PROSECUTION, IT SHOULD ALLOW THE DEFENDANTS 30 ADDITIONAL PEREMPTORY CHALLENGES EACH.

Later, after 1,400 jurors, there would be

MOTION TO PROCEED TO TRIAL
WITH JURORS ALREADY CHOSEN

Little by little the prisoners' reality was being established. Ericka had a handful of dried flowers, burnt umber in a cup and a flag pin from the National Liberation Front; the picture of Bobby's boy, Eric, leaned against the water pitcher.

Then Katie picked it up. Markle, who had returned deeply tanned from a holiday in Barbados, had angered her by scoffing at the defense petitions. For once the judge did not look out the window when she pleaded.

"Mr. Markle says this 'is absurd.' I have seldom heard such a callous remark. My client, a young black woman, is on trial for her life and after 1,400 jurors and four months of *voir dire*. . . ." There was no hesitation, Ericka and Bobby swung to look at her. She could not bear that Markle in his plump tanness had returned from the West Indies to call her loyalty and passion absurd. She could never forgive him for having severed the McLucas case from the others thus "polluting the atmosphere."

As for Garry, he shared the "state's diabolical scheme" with the world. Then suddenly after the denials, the judge bowed and granted the defense two more peremptories. He had stolen some of their thunder, since the defense had been going to take it all up to the Supreme Court, Garry said, never softening.

Then Mr. Markle, pale under his duskiness, rose to ask if the state would get any extras. No. Then he began again on how "Mr. Garry has violated your Honor's rule" forbidding discussion of the trial. Garry's strategy of protracted warfare had given the urgent shape of reality to the abstract motions which had been the same since the beginning; now he left early to go to another business-men's lunch leaving the State's Attorney to wail that the state was being slandered by Mr. Garry. In his fury after the motions, Markle splurged and rejected first a black woman and then a white man who had once belonged to the N.A.A.C.P. There was hissing.

With thirty-five percent of New Haven nonwhite, there should have been at least a dozen nonwhite veniremen on each panel. If that had been the case the state would have exhausted its challenges, too.

Garry's strategy of refusal to compromise on a jury had accomplished several points: (1) the judge, the State's Attorney and the public had been exquisitely sensitized to the validity of the pretrial motions concerning biased publicity, inability to find a jury of peers and impossibility of a fair trial; (2) by holding out, Garry had brought many more veniremen into the dock than normally would be seen, thus drastically affecting the probabilities of the number of black and young people who finally appeared on the jury: to have secured five black people on the jury when there were fewer than fifty called in all a statistical miracle, as are the three people under thirty out of a jury population whose average age was fifty; and (3) finally, the antiwar movement had had time to begin to get itself together and as the testimony began the winds of May were beginning to rise.

Here, at last was the abstraction of the fifteen hundred, the finding of which had reduced all but Garry to near-collapse and had forced the State's Attorney to go away for a ten-day vacation.

The regular jury:

Franklin Dilger, 42, white, of Wolcott, a mailman who has four children and whose wife is a factory worker. He stated that he has many black friends and "that as far as I am concerned, I'd be too good a juror."

Dennis Adams, 65, black, of New Haven, a retired floorman who has three sons, two of whom are unemployed and who says that he knows nothing about the Panthers.

Miss Dorothy Goldson, 41, black, of Waterbury, an Avon representative who reads the Waterbury *American* and says she knows nothing about the case.

Miss Marilyn Martino, 27, white, of Waterbury, a graduate student in sociology who has worked in child welfare in New Haven and plans to do so again when she finishes school.

Mrs. Jessie Wynne, 33, black, of New Haven, a factory worker who has two children.

Mrs. Jean Lowe, 57, black, of New Haven, a hospital worker. She has no fixed opinion and appeared to want to be on the jury.

Sivert B. Johnson, 67, white, of Hamden, a retired gunsmith who has three children and does not favor capital punishment, but would consider it in some cases.

Robert L. Gauthier, 30, white, of West Haven, who works as a telephone installer and is a scoutmaster. When asked about the Black Panther Party he said he thought that they were an organization founded to "help the black people."

William A. Fannucci, 33, white, of Seymour, an assistant bank manager. He said that he had no opinion and expressed a reluctance to consider capital punishment.

Miss Barbara Lanier, 31, black, of New Haven, an engineering assistant at the telephone company and teacher in Sunday school. She said of the Black Panther Party, "I don't believe anything is all good or all bad." She also mentioned the breakfast program.

Miss Barbara Foy, 42, white, of Ansonia, an office worker at B. F. Goodrich. She said that she felt that the Black Panther Party was both good and bad and stated repeatedly that they were trying to help their people, although "they might not always go about it in the right ways."

Miss Jennie Jesilavich, 61, white, of Prospect, a bank book-keeper, who called the events of last May "disturbing." She made frequent references to the Party's involvement in the case. When asked whether she would feel satisfied, if she were on trial with a jury of twelve people like herself that she would get a fair trial, she replied, "This is a court of law in the United States of America. I think I would." She was accepted under protest by the defense.

The alternates:

Mrs. Mary Armstrong, 42, black, of Waterbury, a former nurse who is now unemployed. She said that she has heard of the Black Panther Party although she doesn't know what it is about.

Anthony DeStefano, 51, white, of Cheshire, who belongs to the American Legion and the Italian-American Club. He owns a garage which derives forty percent of its business from towing provided by both the North Haven Police Department and the State Police. He repeatedly compared the Panthers to Weathermen. He also was seated against the wishes of the defense.

The countdown had seemed to begin on the twenty-ninth day, when the sixth juror was chosen and the defense had fifteen challenges remaining.

But this was the week of the anniversary of the death of Jon Huggins. On the date of the assassination of Patrice Lumumba, the guns were blazing at U.C.L.A. and killing Ericka's husband. Now, two years later, Ericka sat in her homemade clothes of gold, red, blue, African shawls, high boots, and wrote her steady left-handed message to the world. When she was not writing she was reading Lorca, and Pablo Neruda: "only the panther . . . declared her contempt . . ."

> barbarous
> queen
> in
> a box

midway
on the trash
of the street
Ericka

The real Ericka, in her unannealed hurt, was getting gaunt. Her baby, Mai, was brought to court one day by Jon's mother. (The mother and father of John, as they spelled his name, were quiet and very strong people.) The pretty two-year-old, in her navy coat with brass buttons, played quietly on the floor a stone's throw from the revolution that her mother had become. The tall, almost emaciated woman smiles at the child for a while and then resumes her writing.

don,
    you asked me to write you a note. well—that's impossible 'cause it seems when i start notes they continue on 'til they're letters and the letters seem to turn into rambling pages of disjointed thot. but i really feel like communicating with you, somehow just telling you about how i feel—especially about the ride back here tonight. the sky was lavender and there was the blueness there that only dusk creates everywhere. i looked above the speeding cars and chaotic cities. there were birds, small ones, large ones, gulls, sparrows, maybe a jay here and there / watching anything fly is so beautiful, so free—anything but airplanes. . . .
    but the lavender was so quiet it seemed as if i cd have detached myself from the handcuffs / state car / troopers and the reality that i was returning to this madhouse—full of women i can do nothing to help at this point. quiet lavender—i felt lonely and yet a part of something. soon it will be january 17 again two whole years since bunchy and jon left here physically—maybe that's why i'm getting the lonely feeling again or maybe it's just plain ol' oppression.
    i think about l.a. all the time. i'm always homesick for something if not for the near past then for the distant past when we were really free / part of the whole. i want to go home . . . back to real things, natural free things. the people want to go too. i feel so strange writing these particular thots because i'm aware that you may be looking for literary meaning. none here. just my thots—like my poems. that's why i asked you to tell me what you thot of them. you see i never wrote for people to read what i write / but just to help myself think. so if i don't

get the message across sometimes it's because i'm not really trying to / i'm just trying to get it all out of my head.

i'm writing now because for some reason i want you to understand me. maybe because sometimes when you smile you give me the feeling you comprehend—lots of things. sometimes i'm thinking of so many things at once until my mind is really a blank. does that make sense? like now—i'm sitting here with noise all around me and i'm thinking of jon / prison and what it does to people's souls / jan / my mother / bobby / how little boyish you look when you smile / mai and babies in general . . . and i find myself staring into space. i sometimes wonder if it's better to escape from it all and detach completely or to just put your whole self into it and become part of all the madness being a revolutionary means. i know the answer . . . see how i ramble on. when my mind evolves real fast i write like this sometimes for hours because if i try to talk it all comes out too garbled for 'sane' people to deal with.

i wish somebody were here that i cd talk to. all my spiritual comrades have been sentenced / gone home / or have deserted me tonight (maybe i've deserted them, i don't know) . . . anyway you're listening, aren't you?

katie says she'll be able to arrange for you to talk to me about 'the thing'—soon. i hope so. i always worry when i think of the money we need and how broke we are. we have to really plan a new system of value exchange rather than coin or paper money for the new society. this american shit is bad news, not just because it exploits everyone but it is such a negative symbol that we shd refuse to let it carry over in our future.

so what's there to talk about? nothing. Maybe i'll write more tomorrow. my head is tired. prospective jurors really exhaust me (smile).

revolutionary love power and strength,

me

The Black Panther that week carried

REVOLUTION IN OUR LIFETIME

by Ericka Huggins

This is just a message to all our brothers and sisters in the struggle and all freedom-loving people everywhere. . . .

Each day, as I sit in the alleged court of justice in New Haven, I am saddened by the dull, cold, narrow, often racist lives of the people who wish to try Bobby and me. I leave everyday angered at what Amerika has done to its people; angered at the apathy that is allowing Amerika to continue its oppression and brutality; angered at the truce Amerika calls on December 25th of every year so that its robotic, brainwashed population can Christmas shop and pretend to love one another. I get angered and saddened, and my thoughts are centered on the necessity for us to move swiftly and begin to change before it is too late, before too many of us ha e been ruled on, jailed, or sucked into the vacuum of apathy.

Communicate to Educate to Liberate

Venceremos!
Love, Power, Strength

Ericka, political prisoner

On the day of the anniversary of Jon's death Ericka wrote:

> waves of love spread out in a never ending flow
>   on and on
>   i give to you
>   to give to someone
>   to give to another
>   on and on. . . .
>   (and i think—wow:
>   it's good waves of hate don't spread that way)
> to think of you
>   always makes me send out vibrations of
>   peace / gentle loving vibrations
>   you are with me
>   i can feel it.
>   today i cried for marylou
>   i know you understand why
>   there were waves of hate then
>   coming from them to me
>   to give back to them
>   i did
>   i gave their hate back with my tears
>   they are so sad
>   her baby is not a prisoner—yet.

but i thot of you and somehow gained strength
   enough for me
          marylou
          and all of us—in here
   you represent sisterhood to me. . . .
                          Ericka

The days pass. In the waiting room sometimes there is the din of a pack of mad apes, sometimes dead silence. Inside Garry drives the defense on as the challenges disappear—14, 13, 12.

Like a great medieval chain of being smashed flat they come and go while the branches dance outside the tiny bulletproof window. Suddenly one will be chosen, surrounded by sheriffs, admonished by the judge, and hurried upstairs to join old Mr. Adams and the regulars. The challenges are wrenched out of Garry and Katie—11, 10, 9. The human rosary beads make the rounds (it does seem that people from the first five hundred are turning up again) while Bobby Seale digs the process with amazement. Even he of the rhetoric had not thought that death had claimed so many minds and souls. He and Garry are like Corsican brothers, continuous, a linguistic entity in the transition from blood to rhetoric and back again—7, 6, 5; an old Swede is chosen.

The world was turning. In the hall the sheriffs argued bitterly over the Berrigan case—"I'm not giving any more Sunday contributions if the Archdiocese is gonna pay for the legal defense."

Inside, Garry would say, "I want you to search the crevices of your mind for bias," and the heavyset women would cross their legs.

James Baldwin spoke out for his sister, Miss Angela Davis, in the *New York Review of Books.*

In considering you, and Huey, and George and (especially) Jonathan Jackson, I began to apprehend what you may have had in mind when you spoke of the uses to which we could put the experience of the slave. What has happened, it seems to me, and to put it far too simply, is that a whole new generation of people have assessed and absorbed their history, and, in that tremendous action, have freed themselves of it and will never be victims again. This may seem an odd, indefensibly impertinent and insensitive thing to say to a sister in prison, battling for her life—for all our lives. Yet, I dare to say, for I think that you will perhaps not misunderstand me, and I do not say it, after all, from the position of a spectator.

I am trying to suggest that you—for example—do not appear to be your father's daughter in the same way that I am my father's son. At bottom, my father's expectations of his generation and mine were the same; and neither the immense difference in our ages nor the move from the South to the North could alter these expectations or make our lives more viable. For, in fact, to use the brutal parlance of that hour, the interior language of that despair, he was just a nigger—a nigger laborer preacher, and so was I. I jumped the track but that's of no more importance here, in itself, than the fact that some poor Spaniards become rich bull fighters, or that some poor black boys become rich—boxers, for example. That's rarely, if ever, afforded the people more than a great emotional catharsis, though I don't mean to be condescending about that either. But when Cassius Clay became Muhammad Ali and refused to put on that uniform (and sacrificed all that money!) a very different impact was made on the people and a very different kind of instruction had begun.

He concluded as he had done, it seemed so long ago now, in *The New Yorker,* with a lament and a Jeremiad that neither that magazine nor the decade of the 1960s that lay ahead had understood at all.

So be it. We cannot awaken this sleeper, and God knows we have tried. We must do what we can do, and fortify and save each other— we are not drowning in an apathetic self-contempt, we do feel ourselves sufficiently worthwhile to contend even with inexorable forces in order to change our fate and the fate of our children and the condition of the world! We know that a man is a thing and is not to be placed at the mercy of things. We know that air and water belong to all mankind and not merely to industrialists. We know that a baby does not come into the world merely to be the instrument of someone else's profit. We know that democracy does not mean the coercion of all into a deadly—and, finally, wicked—mediocrity but the liberty for all to aspire to the best that is in him, or that has ever been. . . .

The enormous revolution in black consciousness which has occurred in your generation, my dear sister, means the beginning or the end of America. Some of us, white and black, know how great a price has already been paid to bring into existence a new consciousness, a new people, an unprecedented nation. If we know, and do nothing, we are worse than the murderers hired in our name.

If we know, then we must fight for your life as though it were our own—which it is—and render impassable with our bodies the corridor to the gas chamber. For, if they take you in the morning, they will be coming for us that night.

Therefore: peace.

Brother James

Who would write a *J'Accuse* for Bobby and Ericka? Instead, as the trial approached, "information" was being leaked to columnists and wire services of a nationwide "Panther burglary ring" that brought in great sums of illegal tender, some of which went to pay for Huey P. Newton's $650-a-month "sauna-bath luxury apartment." What had been police repression was now more finely tuned. There was no mention of the fact that four people shared the Newton apartment or that the rent was paid by a group of writers so that Huey could have the space, time and quiet necessary for his writing. The middle-class logistics of literacy cost money, and everybody seemed to want Huey Newton back in the street with his shotgun.

With Huey P. Newton out of prison, the tack seemed to be one of discouraging white financial support. Certain "journalists"— prominent in the government's defense of the *Warren Report* on the assassination of John F. Kennedy or the attack on its critics— were coming forward to question whether the fearsome Panther statistics were anything, after all, but a propagandistic nightmare dreamed up by Charles Garry. By a careful redefinition of the words "police forces" it was made to seem that only those Panthers who were killed, like Fred Hampton (Mark Clark, his companion, did not *quite* satisfy the new criteria either), qualified for public concern. Like the Asian wars (the foreign "police actions") the odd blunder—Hampton's murder—was a stupid accident, but hardly an element in a government conspiracy.

While this revision was unfolding, Garry's friend John Gerassi, in desperation, flew to Paris to consult Sartre and the state of health of the man in whom the French tradition now resided. France's saint, Jean Genet, had done his best, but could no longer get into the country.

For the white man, History, past and future, is very long, and his set of references is very imposing. For the black man, Time is short, for his history has been brutally interrupted and modified in such a way that the whites did everything to prevent him from having his own, original development. And in the U.S.A., we are still busy setting limits on black people's Time and Space. Not only is each and everyone of them more withdrawn within himself but he is also imprisoned by us. And when we have to, we assassinate him.

Because of his exceptional political stature, Chairman Bobby Seale's trial, which just started, is, in fact, a political trial of the Black Panther Party, and, on a more general basis, a race trial held against all of America's blacks.

Genet had his facts, too, when he remembered that,

There was a time in France when the guilty man was the Jew. Here, there was such a time, and there is still, when the guilty man is the Negro.

Naturally, this parallel with the Dreyfus Affair cannot be pursued point by point. And I must admit that up till now, in America, there has been no Clemenceau, no Jaurès, and especially, among the intellectuals, no Zola to write "J'Accuse." A "J'Accuse" which would bear witness against the courts of your country and against the majority of whites, who have remained racists.

When we speak of the Black Panther Party, we must also realize that in a year and a half, police repression has risen from 1 to 7. I mean that the number of police actions must be multiplied by seven.

This legendary *J'Accuse* was not written by a God, after all. It could be duplicated in America today by at least several people. Baldwin writing for Davis was in Paris; so were Genet and Sartre. What had Zola said?

I do not despair in the least of ultimate triumph. I repeat with more intense conviction: the truth is on the march and nothing will stop it! . . . When the truth is buried underground, it grows, it chokes, it gathers such an explosive force that on the day it bursts out, it blows everything up with it. We shall soon see whether or not we have laid the land mines for a most far-reaching disaster of the near future. . . .

After specific accusations in the highest quarters, he concluded, going past rhetoric:

The action I take here is simply a revolutionary step designed to hasten the explosion of truth and justice.

I have one passion only, for light, in the name of humanity which has borne so much and has a right to happiness. My burning protest is only the cry of my soul. Let them dare to carry me to the court of appeals, and let there be an inquest in the full light of day!

I am waiting.

Sartre might come or not, but in America there were no Pulitzer Prize winners en route to New Haven.

But Charles (as he was now called by the press and regulars) was speaking almost every night—and days too, at civic luncheons. The government was hearing or seeing Charles R. Garry wherever it turned. Markle took to asking jurors if they had "heard any radio shows."

In the famous old Center Church on the Green, Vivian Noble, the really aristocratic chairwoman of the New Haven Council of Churches' Task Force on Law and Justice, took that group to one of its finest hours. The old church of the Regicides was filled to capacity in the largest town meeting in memory. A carnal saint, the Reverend Phil Runner, had become a complete fool for Christ since May Day. He and the old atheist, Garry, beamed out at the audience.

The headlines and stories proliferated, maddening Markle.

JUDICIAL SYSTEM GEARED TO POWER CAN'T GIVE FAIR TRIAL, GARRY SAYS

NO JUSTICE IN U.S. COURTS, SEALE'S TRIAL LAWYER SAYS

Black Panther trial lawyer Charles R. Garry Wednesday night scoffed at the claim that justice could be obtained by minority groups in American courts and praised the alleged bomb conspiracy of the Revs. Philip and Daniel Berrigan.

He praised the Revs. Philip and Daniel Berrigan, Catholic priests who were charged Wednesday in connection with a bomb and kidnap conspiracy against the government.

Noting that the plot was allegedly designed to stop the Vietnam War, he said, "If what the Berrigan brothers were doing could stop the war, it would be a small price to pay."

Inside the church Garry was asking, "When Huey Newton was finally released, did anyone say they were sorry?" Outside, some men were passing out leaflets.

COMMUNIST LEGAL SUBVERSION
The Role Of The Communist Lawyer

REPORT

By The

COMMITTEE ON UN-AMERICAN ACTIVITIES
HOUSE OF REPRESENTATIVES

EIGHTY-SIXTH CONGRESS

First Session

February 16, 1959

This was the church where the news of John Brown was told New Haven; but Garry was speaking there now, syntax mangled by passion, never knowing or caring that the Center Church was modeled on the English St. Martin's-in-the-Fields and that the cornerstones were monuments to Goffe and Whalley, the King-killers of the Restoration—continuous with the Regicides, unaware of the buried revenants rising from beneath his feet into the *Gemeinschaft* of the old town hall.

New Haven had voted John Brown a thousand dollars, but had never raised it. After his death they held a martyr's service in Center Church. Garry was not interested in any martyrs.

So, Garry was the difference. In court it was

NEW CLASH ON PUBLICITY DELAYS
SEALE PROCEEDINGS

and to the Exchange Club it was—Garry cites,

STATE RATE ON JOBLESS HITS 10%

That was the main strategy now, to generate crowds large enough to force the court to reconsider and grant the use of one of the big, empty, bulletproof courtrooms that had not been available the preceding summer. The ideal would be something like the scene that had greeted Zola in 1898, as Nicholas Halasz described it in his "story of mass hysteria."

Small shopkeepers and artisans sat on the jury, attentive, bewildered by the parade of so many generals, celebrities and renowned speakers. They remained awe-struck to the end. The vast hall was packed with officers, journalists, lawyers, society women, aristocrats and rabble-rousers of the Anti-Semitic League. The building was surrounded by a mob. The garrison of Paris stood to arms at the ready in the barracks in the event the police needed assistance.

The President [the presiding judge] refused to give the public exceptional privileges, yet they invaded not only the places reserved for the audience, but took seats around the judges and jurors, sat on window sills. Some climbed on the stoves. The lawyers sat along the walls, and on the steps; some young men sat on the floor, their legs crossed like Turks, right in front of the jury. [The women's] beautiful flowery hats brought a gay note to this sea of tumult.

That was what Charles wanted now.

They said of Dreyfus' grand representative that "he came in alert and eager, conscious, like all orators, of the effect he made, frankly delighting in it—a spirit half electricity and half sunshine. Officers and sightseers and journalists alike leaped up and shook the roof with clapping. He moved toward his place breast-deep in handshakes."

The response to Garry was repressed in the American style—New England at that. But little by little he and the defense were beginning to set the rhythm and pitch of the *politics* of the trial. The falling-away of the peremptories was fated, but the Yale speeches, town meetings, radio talk shows, television interviews, popular rallies, and corridor exegesis were beginning to undermine the prosecution's orchestration, which since the first arrests had been unimpeded.

He told church groups that according to *The New York Times,* Chile plans to set up neighborhood people's tribunals to try minor crimes, and that the Reverend Ralph Abernathy had said, "We can't let them suppress the Black Panthers. If we do, we're next on the list. We can't let them get away with Angela Davis."

Mr. Markle fumed, but Charles was irrepressible:

GARRY HITS LACK OF BLACKS
ON POTENTIAL JUROR PANEL

GARRY UNDERLINES DANGERS
OF CURBING JURY PROCESS

POLITICAL UNION AT YALE
TO HOLD DINNER FOR GARRY

The meeting, which is open to the public, will begin at 7:45 P.M. and be preceded by a private dinner given by the Union in Garry's honor at one of Yale's residential colleges.

The dinner was originally scheduled to be held at Mory's, the University's private dining club, but was switched to a residential college when Garry protested against Mory's policy of barring women from joining its dining fraternity. Garry is representing Panther Chairman Bobby Seale in Superior Court here.

Garry literally screamed out at the inhuman prison conditions from the Tombs to Soledad, "See how yond justice rails upon yond simple thief. Hark in thine ear: change places and, handy-dandy, which is the justice, which is the thief?"—quoting from King Lear (whom he resembled in his primitive rage and "noble anger").

He stumbled only once, and that was on the David Frost show on nationwide television, and for that once he looked desperate. It had been a long day.

In the morning, Superior Court, in the afternoon, federal court to excoriate Mr. Manson, Mr. MacDougall's successor, for "reneging on the beard." He asked Manson if he had ever had crabs, saying that he, Garry, had and was an expert on them and that they did not come from beards.

A big black limousine took Garry and party to New York and the David Frost show. Frost and Edward Jay Epstein, who had written a *New Yorker* article attacking the Panther charge of genocide, were all over him. They demanded a body count before they would listen to the charge of genocide. Abernathy and the great black lawyer Haywood Burns and the black caucus in Congress—Epstein called them all "civil-rights leaders," using a phrase not heard in active circles since the middle '60s—had all been influenced or duped, he said, by the white Marxist from San Francisco.

Frost kept saying "but what about poor Nathanial what's-his-name," and they went on to dispute the identity of his killers.

Waiting backstage for Epstein was Gail Sheehy, who had written an article on the Panthers in *New York* magazine that had infuriated them and the parents of John Huggins.

Outside, some black people and some old Jews waited to squeeze Garry's hand. On the way back to New Haven, he and the chauffeur, James, and his secretary, Pat Gallyot, stopped at Manny Wolf's Steak House to blot out the humiliation of what the New York liberals can do to you in their Philistine and shameless cruelty. Manny Wolf's!

THE DEFENSE: Now, were you in the habit of going to high-class restaurants?

JULIUS ROSENBERG: I don't know what you mean by high class, Mr. Bloch.

THE DEFENSE: All right. Did you ever go to restaurants where the prices were expensive?

JULIUS ROSENBERG: Yes, I did.

THE DEFENSE: How many?

JULIUS ROSENBERG: Well, once when I was taking my wife out, to a place near Emerson Radio called Pappas, and on another occasion I have eaten at a place called Nicholaus on Second Avenue.

THE DEFENSE: Did you ever eat at Manny Wolf's?
JULIUS ROSENBERG: Yes. I remember eating there once.

Were the Panthers and the remaining core of supporters degenerating into paranoia and despair? The C.I.A.?

Was there a pattern, in the black liberation movement? The first modern "revolutionary" had been Robert Williams. He had returned after years in exile in China and other socialist countries. The movement had expected a Lenin at the Finland Station; instead *The New York Times* reported that "Robert F. Williams, indicted in North Carolina on charges of insurrection, fled the country and spent some years in Peking. He is now at the Center for Chinese Studies, University of Michigan." But who really ran the Center for Chinese Studies? Radical heads wagged from Detroit to Oakland until Williams subsequently quit to fight narcotics addiction in the ghetto.

The next revolutionary was Malcolm X. It is an article of faith to many black historians and many others that the Central Intelligence Agency was involved in that death as it was in John F. Kennedy's.

The next was Stokely Carmichael. Now in Conakry, Republic of Guinea, he told *The New York Times* that "the black man should no longer be thinking of transforming American society. We should be concerned with Mother Africa."

Martin Luther King, Jr., could not be destroyed by the allegations that J. Edgar Hoover leaked far and wide, so he had to be conspired against. James Earl Ray now says he wishes to offer proof of who hired him. "The same as the Bay of Pigs," his brother says he says.

The Panthers also took note of a story and photograph in *The New York Times:*

SECRET REPORTS KEEP AIR FORCE
INFORMED ON RADICALS

**Black Panther Party
Major Subject of
Intelligence Unit**

SECRET

SIGNIFICANT
COUNTERINTELLIGENCE
BRIEFS

OFFICE OF SPECIAL INVESTIGATIONS

Volume 20 No. 1   Date 6 Jan 71

* * * *

North America

Recent Air Force brief refers to Huey Newton, leader of the Black Panthers, on cover

While the Associated Press too carried stories:

ARMY CHANGES MIND AGAIN,
TO KEEP DATA ON CIVILIANS

GIs TELL OF SPYING ON
LIBERAL CAMPUS SPEAKERS

McGOVERN HITS HOOVER

Sen. George McGovern (D-SD) says FBI Director J. Edgar Hoover is "obsessed with protecting his own image" and should be forced to retire.

The New York Times again:

ARMY SPIED ON 18,000
IN 2 YEAR OPERATION

PASSPORT OFFICE HAS
SECRET FILE

243,135 Names in Computer-
Applications Screened

The country was mad, certainly:

I WAS A PORPOISE FOR THE CIA

And China was taking "careful note" of the Central Intelligence Agency element in Northern Laos.

One year before the Seale-Huggins trial *The New York Times* had published a partial list of Panther statistics:

1968

Jan. 16— San Francisco police, without warrant, raid the home of Eldridge Cleaver. No arrests are made.

Feb. 25— Bobby and Artie Seale are arrested in their home by Oakland police without warrant. Charges of "conspiracy to murder," made against Bobby Seale, are dropped. A year later the arrests for "conspiracy to riot" are ruled illegal and dropped on 1/29/69. Four other Panthers arrested near the Seale home on the same pretext are released. Charges against two are dropped. The other two had been killed by that time.

Apr. 6—
Cleaver, David Hilliard and six others are charged with the "attempted murder" of two Oakland policemen. Charges are dropped by the district attorney. Bobby Hutton is shot and killed by police after surrendering in an alleged "shoot-out."

Sept. 12–13—
Denver police arrest seven juveniles as "delinquent" and three Panthers as "contributing." Panthers are all released for lack of any testimony against them.

Sept. 12–13—
Denver police arrest one Panther and kill another for alleged sniping. No one else was injured.

Sept. 23—
Colorado chairman of the Black Panther Party is arrested for arson. No evidence is offered for the charge and it is finally dismissed.

Nov. 19—
Eight Panthers are arrested on charges of shooting at police. Charges are dropped against seven. One is charged with the robbery of a service station in San Francisco.

Dec. 28—
Panther Headquarters in Jersey City is fire-bombed by "2 white men wearing police-style uniforms."

1969

Apr. 2—
21 persons identified by police as Panthers are arrested in New York for conspiracy to blow up the botanical gardens, department stores, etc. No overt act is charged. No one had any recent or serious police record. Bail was set at over $2 million.

Apr. 28—
San Francisco police, using tear gas, raid Black Panther Party headquarters and arrest sixteen. Twelve are released with no charges filed. Four are finally charged with "illegal use of sound equipment."

May 1— Los Angeles police raid Los Angeles Black Panther Party headquarters, seize weapons and arrest eleven. All eleven released with no charges filed.

June 3— FBI in Chicago raid Black Panther Party headquarters and arrest eight present for "harboring a fugitive." No fugitive is found. Police confiscate money, membership lists, literature. All eight are released with no charges filed. Confiscated material is not returned. Chicago police had cordoned off area in advance. The fugitive is George Sams.

June 4— Denver police raid Black Panther headquarters and arrest three, charging office worker Anita Hartman with possession of stolen goods. All three released; Hartman indictment dropped.

June 5— Denver police raid Black Panther Party headquarters and arrest ten. Two are held on federal warrants charging flight to avoid New Haven prosecution. Eight released with no charges filed.

June 5— Black Panther Party lieutenant in Santa Ana is arrested by police, charged with shooting an officer and held for a month. Charge dropped 7/6/69.

June 6— Sacramento police using tear gas raid Black Panther Party headquarters "in search of alleged sniper." No sniper found. Headquarters wrecked. Mayor condemns wanton destruction of food, office equipment, etc.

July 31— Police raid Black Panther Party headquarters in Chicago. Headquarters is totally destroyed. Three wounded Panthers are arrested for "attempted murder, aggravated assault, resisting arrest" during the raid.

Sept. 4— San Diego police raid Black Panther Party headquarters "in search of murder suspect" who is not found. Seize weapons and ammunition.

Sept. 20— Black Panther member Walter Toure Pope is killed by two Los Angeles policemen, who claim he had fired on them.

Dec. 3—   David Hilliard, only Panther leader alive and free, arrested for threatening the life of President Nixon when Hilliard said (in the course of a public speech), "We will kill Richard Nixon—we will kill any mother-fucker that stands in the way of our freedom."

Dec. 4—   Illinois Black Panther Chairman Fred Hampton and Peoria leader Mark Clark are killed by massive shooting raid of police on Hampton's apartment. Four other Panthers are seriously wounded. Two police injured.

Dec. 8—   Police raid Black Panther Party headquarters in Los Angeles. Three Panthers are wounded. Twenty-one are arrested in coordinated raids on three different locations including arrest of pregnant woman, who suffers a miscarriage.

Yet to come was 1970—police raids in New Orleans, Indianapolis, Philadelphia, Cleveland, Detroit, Baltimore and New Haven equal almost a hundred new Panther prisoners and a million more dollars in bail.

At the same time the American Civil Liberties Union prepared an interim report:

The record of police actions across the country against the Black Panther Party forms a prima facie case for the conclusion that law enforcement officials are waging a drive against the black militant organization resulting in various civil liberties violations . . . in one New York case the arresting officer acknowledged that he had no evidence but had been instructed to "get on the books" the arrest of a particular Panther who was already on the books of an adjoining county. . . .

ACLU affiliates in New York and Indiana report infiltration by government informants into black groups thought to be Panthers for purposes of entrapment. The evidence indicates that government agents have attempted to induce black militants to burglarize, in one case offering automatic weapons, in another providing a map of the likely target, a getaway car and the offer of weapons. . . .

Other police actions which bear out charges of harassment are reported from Chicago where police and FBI agents undertook a June 4th dawn raid on Panther headquarters with an arrest warrant for George Sams, but no search warrant. Upon smashing down the door of the office and failing to find George Sams, enforcement officials broke up furniture, confiscated literature, lists of donors and petitions and arrested eight Panthers on charges so flimsy they were later dismissed. The following day a similar raid was made in Detroit, the door broken down, documents photographed, three Panthers arrested on specious charges and later released . . . high national officials, by their statements and actions, have helped to create the climate of oppression and have encouraged local police to institute the crackdown.

All this is before the major police attacks of 1970 and the jailing of *The Black Panther* newspaper staff for protecting their sources of information.

So when the Associated Press asked Garry, during a recess, about Epstein and why he thought *The New Yorker* had left out documented statements—about breaking up the Panthers—by Agnew, Mitchell, Hoover, Jerris Leonard, U.S. Attorney Cecil Poole, Ramsey Clark and the others, Garry snapped "it's Government all the way." And he returned to the central casting of the jury selection—4, 3, 2, another young woman, later to be the second to leave because of threats, is chosen.

The "conspiracy," if there was one, seemed to be working; the *New York Post* headlined its story:

PANTHER LAWYER BACKS DOWN ON 'GENOCIDE' BY POLICE

Epstein later told the *Harvard Crimson* that since he had never done anything for civil rights he did not know why Frost had praised his rights record. He also asserted that Garry had made a mistake in not choosing a "white middle-class jury."

A member of the Panther Free Food Committee was receiving telephone threats. John and Ann Froines lost their car, after four tire slashings and sugar in the locked gas tank, and all of the rented Panther vehicles at the Huey Newton New Haven rallies were damaged and slashed. The job was done expertly and swiftly, and there was obviously prior intelligence. It could only be the police, the Panthers decided, and stake-outs were set up. When

Huey Newton came to Yale for a dialogue with Erik Erikson, someone in the dining commons spat on his coat as it hung on the rack. That seemed to depress Huey slightly.

"When he is not here," said Erik K. Erikson of Huey P. Newton after their dialogue had ended, "the room goes dark." He lifted and dropped his arm and hand.

The great white-haired psychoanalyst sat opposite the bursting vitality of the young black revolutionary; between them they exhausted the corporeal and ideological axis of the twentieth century.

"I got away from the Nazis, and in America psychoanalysis was not the 'underground' of my youth, and I was rewarded for what I had brought with me. So I am not taking the risk that he is." Pause. "I love him. I tremble for him."

The setting was the conference room of the Yale University Press, the cortex of the University. Along the two sides of a long table sat fourteen students, while Erikson and Newton sat facing each other. The moderator was the social scientist's oldest son, sociologist Kai T. Erikson, Master of Yale's Trumbull College. He and Professor Elting Morison would edit the book that they hoped would come out of the dialogue. Most of Yale was furious at the closed sessions. Huey had brought the sociologist Herman Blake with him in his party of five from California, and once Garry slipped in.

The first day was Huey Newton's. Beginning with Kant he worked forward to a post-Marxist dialectical materialism and his new vision, intercommunalism. As capitalism was the industrial forerunner to socialism, so the imperialism of the American Empire was the predicate for revolutionary intercommunalism.

The hairy worm becomes a butterfly, Huey said, as he discussed qualitative and quantitative change and "the negation of the nega-tion." We're a long ways from home, he said, and we inherit the burden and the legacy of revolution because we come last. The two high-school dropouts understood each other, but the students sat like voyeurs at an act of creation. The old man made green and red "notes" on a drawing board; a board as coherent to his artistic youth as the baton Newton carried was to his. He looked for the "new Newton in the old Huey," and the young hero divined Erik son of Erik who with his drawing board was coming full circle.

It was "armed love."

An old black butler, from Yale, served luncheon.

On the second day, Erik—as Huey now called him after the first day's "Professor"—responded, in his vocabulary of the psycho-analytic autosphere, to Huey—as he called him—and the Panther leader's cosmic grammar of the twenty-first century. At the coffee break he called Huey an "authentic hero" and the "least violent man in the room."

For a moment they stood next to each other discussing "species and pseudo species." Huey held on to the baton that he had carried since emerging from prison. They stood there—the old man sipping a little brandy supplied by his son—the nineteenth and the twenty-first century; the baton in the powerful hand a transi-tional torch passed on by the old man from the past, the Oakland shotgun abstracted for the task of facing down the great pig of nothingness, the future.

The old genius understood the young one. He was aware of Telstar and the S.S.T. and media weapons systems; what Huey called the reactionary intercommunalism that must be replaced by revolutionary intercommunalism. He wanted to talk about "inner colonies" and identity as a prerequisite for existential choice. Huey had been generous, he said, to refer to Freud and psychoanalysis, and now he discoursed on it from the top of a lifetime.

He pointed out that Huey P. Newton had generated authentic imagery for the wretched of the West. He spoke of rebellion and discipline and he was always in touch with his own adolescence of "judicious indignation." This rebellion with limits was as far as he could go. Psychoanalysis had been the "revolution of my lifetime. It is enough." Finally, building on Marx instead of Freud he announced that until there was a revolution, of values and every-thing else, "it is impossible to become an adult." There was no court that morning, Garry was there, and he liked that very much, saying it explained many things. They stood talking: Huey, Erik son of Erik and Charles son of Charles.

Then Erik ranged over Gandhi's symbolism and life and back to Huey and "where you woke up in your part of history" and the original vision of "one man, one gun."

They were both depressed at the break; each was convinced that he was not getting through to the other. After three days Huey and Erik were both played out. It was a dialogue in the strict Buberian sense, but very few at Yale, where the "clerks" only talk, believed or understood that. And the students, who were the children of the most violent class in the history of the species, had found it all rather abstract and bloodless. They craved sexuality from the old man's unconscious palette and blood from the slave's baton, but they were denied. The students were not privy to the "I-Thou" of the old man and the Panther and the man from the *Yale Press* looked unhappy, too.

That night they talked about another dialogue between a psychologist and a revolutionary. Huey's pupil, Eldridge Cleaver, had just put Erik's, Timothy Leary, under temporary "house arrest." There were many ways to start a true dialogue, most of them desperate, but film stars and intellectuals would use this incident to flee the encircled Panthers. There was a cheerful note to the international gossip; it had been a bad week for metaphysics, even though Algiers was much more typical, by far, of the awful American race and class gap than New Haven, Connecticut. Huey and Erik knew that, too. But for a little while yet it was still gorgeous theater.

At the intervening dinner parties the principals discussed the vicissitudes of the Oedipus complex and certain topics, in quiet tones, to one side of the drawing rooms that were filled with some of Yale's most celebrated thinkers, many of them famous former students of Erikson.

In the end the students bootlegged out a photograph of the "confrontation"—both men despised that description of what had been a fleeting moment of recognition (identity is always a surprise, Erik said), disguised as a seminar at Yale—and some marginalia to *The New York Times*.

ERIKSON AND NEWTON DISCUSS ISSUES IN CONFERENCE AT YALE

When it was over and farewells had been made, Erikson and his wife, Joan, the author, visited the court and watched that arcane vaudeville for as long as they could tolerate it. Garry had become impressed when he learned that the great man had left Berkeley in the early '50s, during the loyalty-oath turmoil, and now he introduced him in pantomime, from across the room, to Bobby and Ericka. Three, two, the last challenges were coming up.

Ninety-nine percent were still being rejected; less than one per hundred could be expected. Garry will not compromise, and thus he ruins every liberal image of the process. Nothing works. The February sky through the bulletproof window is darker than January. One shepherd came through, but he too had read the papers. Ericka is as attenuated as a Giacometti; Bobby makes her laugh sometimes.

The false life of the two extra challenges coincides with a break in the weather. It is as Camus said: happiness is inevitable, too. You wake up, and the sky is blue. It is less blue through the window, and Bobby feigns sleep as a man describes the trouble he had with his lead man, who was a "colored boy," sleeping on the job; and another characterizes the Panthers as a "colored motor-cycle gang." Black after black is rejected out of hand and one remembers Rap Brown saying once, before he disappeared, that "white people hate black people worse than black people hate white people. They hate us worse than we hate them, and we ain't *done them nothing.*"

Garry has taken to asking them if they have read *Soul On Ice, The Autobiography of Malcolm X, Seize the Time, Wretched Of the Earth,* and a book about his defense of Huey P. Newton, *Free Huey.*

Meanwhile, Michael Tabor and his wife, Huey Newton's secretary, disappeared from the trial of the New York Twenty-one. What new thing was going to happen to the Panthers? Were Tabor and the others victims of some new plot?

The San Francisco Mime Troupe and Tom Hayden came to town.

The San Francisco
MIME TROUPE

Presents

An Agit-Prop Documentary
SEIZE THE TIME

A-N-D

TOM HAYDEN
Co-Defendant in the Chicago Trial

"They have for more than a century been regarded as beings of an inferior order; and altogether unfit to associate with the white race either in social or political relations; and so far inferior that they have no rights which the white man is bound to respect."

In a church they acted out the agony of Bobby Seale and Ericka Huggins. It was Theatre of Cruelty, alternating between a grinding slow motion, cold and didactic, and the hot, brutal, "natural" pace of Chicago.

All the old favorites were back: Judge Hoffman and the Chicago repertory. The actors wore huge papier-mâché heads and hands. A primitive Greek-tragedy drumbeat without letup and a horn was heard. Suddenly it was more real and painful than the trial itself; hardened court watchers cried. It ended with a make-shift electric chair and a sign saying "New Haven."

Then Tom Hayden and the troupe went into a rap session.

"We have to do something about this 'eerie tranquillity' that Kingman Brewster says is gripping Yale. Now it's *Love Story* and *The Greening of America* and 'Consciousness III.' It's like the '50s, with Sidney Hook and his bullshit about heresy versus conspiracy.

"And now there's a book about the Panthers and *The Liberal's Paradox*. And now *New York* publishes attacks ('Panther-mania') against the Panthers, and *The New Yorker* and Joseph Alsop, and where is Yale looking into *those* facts? And who paid for Bobby to come to New Haven to get framed up, who was Yale's liaison with the black community? C. Tracy Barnes of the Yale administration and the C.I.A.? Those are some more 'facts' that some of these Yale scholars could research. *And who is George Sams?"*

Hayden was maddened over *Love Story* and "Consciousness III." "We need the reddening of America. I suppose the 'Greening of America' is supposed to start just after the execution of Bobby and Ericka!"

Then everyone sang a song about loving Ericka and Bobby and Angela Davis and George Jackson and Charles Garry, who was there and who had wept over Ericka's peom about being "just a revolutionary" and ready to die.

In the atmosphere of conspiracy charge and countercharge the Mime Troupe was surrounded by scenarios. A verbal stewpot was handed down daily from the press. Manson, Calley and Seale were slowly being fashioned into one single nightmare. Manson and his girls, Calley and poor Meadlo, Seale and George Sams, Jr. The Mime Troupe did a lot to break this fast-hardening stereotype by reliving the anguish of Chicago and the glory of Oakland in the days of the Panther Camelot. But in the public's mind, the defense feared, Seale and Sams were still but one "nigger" with a multiple face.

The chain of command in conspiracy was insisted on in Los Angeles and New Haven, but not at Fort Benning. Some super mime troupe might seize upon these conversations at midnight to make a Theater of Litany and a Babylonian eschatology played out before a high, cruel court of pigs, goats and monkeys.

(DOCTORS TESTIFY CALLEY WAS SANE)

A VOICE: Medina was a very fine officer, and I respected him very much . . . I am now and always will be very proud to have served under his command.

A VOICE: Mr. and Mrs. America—you are wrong. I am not the king-of-the-Jews nor am I a hippie cult leader. I am what you have made of me and mad-dog–killer–field-leper is a reflection of your society. I sit in your torture chambers as I have always sat in your torture chambers. You have showed me no mercy, compassion or pity and in my mind's eye my thoughts light fires in your cities.

A VOICE: Someone asked if we were supposed to kill women and children and everything.

A VOICE: What was Capt. Medina's response to that question?

A VOICE: He replied to kill everything that moved.

A VOICE: I had a knife and Patricia had a knife. We just started stabbing and cutting up the lady. What can I feel. It's happened. She's gone. You can't undo something that's done.

A VOICE: That was my order, sir. That was the order of the day, sir. They were all the enemy. They were all to be destroyed.

A VOICE: I feel no guilt for what I've done. It was right then, and I still believe it was right.

A VOICE: But how can it be right to kill somebody.

A VOICE: How can it not be right when it's done with love.

A VOICE: What were the people doing when Calley left?

A VOICE: They were all squatting down.

A VOICE: What were the children doing?

A VOICE: Just squatting.

A VOICE: What were the babies doing?

A VOICE: They were held in their mothers' arms.

A VOICE: Did you think they were going to attack?

A VOICE: I assumed every minute they were going to attack. That was all that was on my mind. . . .

A VOICE: Why didn't you tell other members of the family about the killings?

A VOICE: It's no big thing.

A VOICE: Seven bodies are no big thing?

A VOICE: Are they? Are a million people all over this world dead because you dropped napalm on them a big thing? You all think it's right—and what I did was right.

A VOICE: I was obsessed with the knife . . . once it went in.

(FBI CHIEF WITHHELD INFORMATION ON BOBBY BAKER)

A VOICE: We are thirteen men and women who state with clear conscience that we are neither conspirators nor bombers nor kidnappers. In principle and in fact we have rejected all acts such s those of which we have been accused. We are a diverse group, united by a common goal: our opposition to the massive violence of our government in its war against Southeast Asia. It is because of this opposition that we have been branded a conspiracy.

("A Texas state legislator told Congress today he has lost faith in America, and his wife her health, because the military spied upon him over the past decade.")

A VOICE: Our anguish for the victims of the brutal war has led all of us to nonviolent resistance, some of us to the destruction of draft records. But, unlike our accuser, the Government of the United States, we have not advocated or engaged in violence against human beings. Unlike the Government, we have never lied to our fellow citizens about our actions. Unlike the Government, we have nothing to hide. We ask our fellow citizens to match our lives, our actions, against the actions of the President, his advisers, his chiefs of staff, and pose the question: Who has committed the crimes of violence?

("The Army, acting 'in the best interests of justice,' dropped all charges today against Maj. General Samuel W. Koster, former West Point superintendent, accused in the alleged cover-up of the massacre of South Vietnamese civilians at My Lai.")

A VOICE: How did the people get into the ditch?

A VOICE: They had been ordered to go into the ditch, sir.

A VOICE: Who ordered them into the ditch?

A VOICE: Indirectly, I did.

("Two key Government witnesses at Calley trial say their My Lai decorations were based on false citations.")

A VOICE: I have no desire to stand in contempt of this court, but I must obey my conscience and I have no desire to stand in contempt of a court which I belie e is higher than any court of the United States.

A VOICE: This is an attempt to paralyze the peace movement in general. We are being used as a political lever by the government.

(ARMY DROPS CHARGES AGAINST FOUR MY LAI GIs)

A VOICE: Think about what you would have if every time a private got an order he stopped to question it. Think about the other Charlie Huttos in the Army.

(CALLEY TRIAL SUSPENDED BECAUSE OF TORNADO ALERT)

If the question of war crimes is put at all, Sartre said, the process will have to continue forever.

In Los Angeles the prosecution insisted that a Beatles record, "Helter-Skelter," was the ideology for the Manson race war. The state made that trial political and in some millenarian *folie à deux* the girls had blood-smeared the Panther word "pig" on the victims' door. In New York, the state was showing *The Battle of Algiers*. All this was a very sophisticated advance over the Chicago trial, where an apoplectic United States Attorney had ravened about the "fag revolution" with a paranoid purity that helped make that show-trial news. The absence of that brutal clarity had made New Haven history rather than news. The trial of the music and film, of the media themselves, was slowly being integrated with the trial of its "agents" in communes and ghettos, in one gigantic conspiracy.

In the Rosenberg trial, in the 1950s, it was the new technology that lay behind the *agon,* the State's magic versus science. In New Haven the *Black Panther* newspaper, at least, would be used categorically by the state. Little by little, the "underground" media and music were moving in the direction of "guerrilla theater" which is the most ancient medium of all. And the first white bombers, in New York, had been "writers."

On the eve of the trial in November, unknown to the public, a showdown between the American leadership of the Black Panther Party and its self-styled "Left wing," led by Eldridge Cleaver, was beginning in earnest. Huey Newton was turning out to be more than the "baddest nigger" of Eldridge Cleaver's hopes and the student radicals' poster fantasies.

On all sides dire predictions were heard. The Panthers had ridden out the attack from the Right by Stokely Carmichael. Could they weather the far more serious onslaught from the Left? Yet the present New Haven trial was a residue from the Carmichael period, Garry argued, and outside forces, he said, were already at work exploiting the rupture.

All waited for *The Black Panther,* recently retitled *Intercommunal News Service.* When it came, the cover bore Kathleen Cleaver's picture and the amazing slogan "Free Kathleen Cleaver."

There would, clearly, be many chapters to come. The same newspaper asked three questions:

IS ELDRIDGE CLEAVER ATTEMPTING TO DIVIDE THE BLACK PANTHER PARTY???

He Denounces Chief of Staff, David Hilliard and Minister of Defense, Huey P. Newton

IS ELDRIDGE CLEAVER ATTEMPTING TO DIVIDE THE COMMUNITY???

He Denounces Angela Davis

IS ELDRIDGE CLEAVER ATTEMPTING TO DIVIDE THE SOCIALIST WORLD???

He Denounces Cuba

and carried a message of love from Kathleen Cleaver to Ericka Huggins.

After lunch, when the twelfth juror was forced on the defense, Bobby Seale had to be overpowered by a combination of sheriffs and state troopers. Nine of them.

Seale, unshaven, had entered in the morning wearing prison browns over a blue sweatshirt. He of the smooth sweaters and hip-hugging pants flapped in the humiliation of the browns. He whispered loudly to Garry that a trooper sitting in the corner had refused to let him go to the toilet. "Punk!"

I'm running a day of protest looking the way I look at the Jail, being isolated in solitary day in and day out for the last eight months. This solitary isolation was done by the recommendations of Arnold Markle, et al. So by coming to court this way I use the Jail harassment product to register my protest that a so-called "fair trial" is non-existent. The fact that adverse pre-trial publicity and distorted, misleading lies have been projected throughout this State, New Haven County, and the country, has allowed people to make up some false notion that I'm already guilty and that Sister Ericka is already guilty in the prospective jurors' minds.

We have been hamstrung into being subjected to an outright railroading operation by Markle and racist company, fascistly incorporated.

The racist run government and Courts of Connecticut refused to use the constitutional authority to see that Sister Ericka Huggins and I receive a "fair and impartial" trial so that we are set free from this legal lynching operation. We stand in this protest and I register it further by showing the real minds of Jail heads and Markle who keeps me in isolation deadlock on any pretext. And I protest the fact that a slick, lying, bigoted person will be placed on the jury by Arnold Markle.

Bobby Seale

To the accompaniment of continuous screams of laughter from the unknowing jury waiting room, Garry and Katie tried in vain to get a commitment from the penultimate woman, who had been waiting for them since the previous November 17. She appeared to be an abstraction of the entire white middle-aged array, an apotheosis. All the while, Markle was objecting with a new fierceness, and the judge was cooperating with the prosecution in the rush toward jury closure.

She wore galoshes, pearls, checkered suit, black blouse, black felt collar, glasses, a black turban hat over "red" hair, a rhinestone lapel pin; she was a bookkeeper, farm owner, lived alone. May Day had "terrified" her; the N.A.A.C.P. did things "the right way"; Yale buildings had been "defaced" with Panther slogans. The defense fumed to no avail. Only Markle had to say "Accepted" now. When he said it, Garry asked for the woman to leave the room so that he could make a motion. Never under any circumstances, he said, would they be caught dead with this juror.

Now Bobby Seale stood up, picked up his briefcase and made *his* motion. "I'm going to the lockup." He was demanding a recess as he stalked toward the door to the lockup. Then the plainclothesmen were all over him.

"Goin' to lockup!" (They close in.)

The Judge: "Mr. Garry."

"That lady is a racist."

"Mr. Garry. Mr. Garry." (They wrestle Seale to the chair.)

"I've spent nine months in solitary because that pig Markle recommended it to MacDougall and now to Manson. . . ."

"Mr. Garry!"

"Bobby. Bobby."

"And you, you motherfucker, you punk in the background. If you mess with me I'll beat your . . ."

"Mr. Garry!"

"Bobby!"

"A racist on the jury. A racist." Then, in hoarse disbelief and outrage, "A *racist,* judge!"

"Take this man out of the courtroom."

"I want my coat."

Those had been his last words in Chicago, too. The judge called a recess. In the sudden hiatus heads swung to Ericka. She sat tall, staring straight ahead. Her back was arched as if she had been lashed, tears rolled down her cheeks. Markle and Schultz smiled, so did the deputies in the hall. What choice had they anymore?

A reporter for *The Black Panther* newspaper tried to rise. Heavy-set, sobbing, she hand-wrestled her way out. On the verge of arrest, she was hustled into the women's toilet by Pat Gallyot, Garry's secretary. Some underground-press people and partisan onlookers stood around sobbing: the endless, appalling, infernal *voir dire* and the enthusiastic violence waiting for Bobby and Ericka were too much for the impotent court watchers. Only Garry, beyond sentiment, without fear and without hope, worked feverishly during the recess to hold his team together and maneuver out of the trap he saw the prosecution setting for them.

God, what was that? What is it? A yell, fierce and poignant, the bursting of furious passion tightly pent up! It ripped the calm to pieces and you half expected the hall to split asunder. Dreyfus was up on his feet, his body bent double, checked in mid-spring by the officer's gentle hand on his arm, his fist pommeling the air, his head and livid face craned forward at Mercier, his teeth bared as thirst for blood. He looked as if he would have leaped upon him like a panther, but for the touch on his arm. And the voice! "You should say that" were the words—but the voice! None of us who heard it will ever describe it—or forget it. Men heard it that night in their sleep. It was half shriek, half sob, half despair, half snatching hope, half a fire of consuming rage, and half an anguished scream for pity. Before us all Dreyfus tore his very heart out. He was no corpse. Henceforth all knew what he was and what he had endured—was still enduring. In six words he told us all the story of the man from the Devil's Island.

"reflections on 3 march 1971"

tears. everytime i see your faces   tears.
  eyes blurred or staring at nothing
tears. thinking
        crying/angry/ready to move
        —such pain—
        anger and fear for this america and
        unable to comprehend these robots who masquerade
        as men and
                    me—useless—
                and our chairman beauty full
                            beauty full
                    we love you bobby
                    we love you brother
                        man
                        comrade
tears. my own cloud this page as i think of
        riding back to this prison tonight
                            rain pouring onto the world
                my suppressed tears   pouring into my soul
                    tears   i see their face again
                            unable to look at either
of us and comrades in the front row unable to look at each other
                                    or the judge
                                    or anything
  i smile and more
tears.   enough of our tears (along with our blood) have been shed
        why 10 'men' to 1 man
                we are so tired of this madness—
then lots of judicial bullshit and recesses and stresses on the necessity
                        to have courtroom decorum
and we return/a smile from bobby
            and i smile back i want to kiss him
                            gently
                    (but they degrade our love)
        and i notice because bobby smiles there are more tears
        more pain joysorrow—at his strength i turn my head he
                            does not see—
tears.
        they are so small. so are my words—
                                    Ericka

The break-away elements of the Black Panther Party announced that Bobby Seale was heartbroken over the treason of "dope fiend, Huey Newton." But Seale would make no statement and was quite calm as the two alternates were chosen. He smiled as the prolegomena came to an end at 1:40 P.M. (The judge drove them into the lunch hour as everyone sensed that the end was at hand.) Even the last strategy of excusing those who had seen the David Frost Show petered out.

Stokely Carmichael, on a lecture tour, came to New Haven for a morning meeting in the black community and attacked Charles Garry as a "notorious Zionist." Garry snorted and allowed that "Malcolm is turning in his grave." He was still getting it from the Frost show anyway.

DEAR MR. GARRY:
Your rudeness overshadowed anything worthwhile. You owe Mr. Frost and Mr. Epstein an apology.
Are you some kind of racist against all whites?
How many policemen were killed?

T.V. VIEWER

Ericka had stopped eating lunch. She wrote her poetry and ate a steady stream of chocolate-chip cookies baked by a friend.

The other shoe dropped: Michael and Connie Matthews Tabor surfaced in Algeria. The New Haven defense shuddered.

But as for the great world, all Bobby and Ericka knew was what they read in the paper:

PUZZLING EPIDEMIC SUBSIDES AT Y
ALE PANTHER WAR GETS HOTTER OVER
KILLING HARLEM KILLING TRACED TO
BLACK PANTHER SPLIT GARRY SCARRED
IN BITTER TV DEBATE SPYING ON CIV
ILIANS 'SCARED ME' EX-GI SAYS SPY
TARGET DENOUNCES ARMY NETWORK CHI
EFS AS 'TRUESUBVERSIVES' RED CHIN
ESE EDGE TO BRINK OF ACTION CHILE

TO NATIONALIZE BETHLEHEM'S MINES
PEKING OUTLOOK BEST IN YEARS ROL
LS ROYCE GOES INTO RECEIVERSHIP BRI
TISH GOVERNMENT TAKES OVER POLICE
CHARGE MITCHELL WITCH HUNT 200,000
MORE JOINS WELFARE ROLLS MONTHLY 10,
000 AT LABOR RALLY DRINK TO 'DALEY
'S THE ONE' CITY AREA UNEMPLOYMENT
HITS HIGHEST PEAK SINCE DEPRESSION
CENSUS FINDS RISE IN NEGRO FAMIL
IES HEADED BY WOMEN CITY'S WHITE
POPULATION DOWN 30,000 BLACKS HERE
UP BY 53.4% CONSTRUCTION UNIONS VO
W TO FIGHT NONWHITE QUOTAS RECRUI
TING OF NEGRO POLICE IS A FAILURE
IN MOST CITIES NEWTON DENOUNCES MI
SSING PANTHERS OVERFLOW CROWD HEARS
NEWTON DEFEND PANTHERS

The man who equated the Panthers with the Beatles, and all the other potential jurors, funny and sad, had melted away, except for numbers 12 and 14, who stood out like sore thumbs, who the defense had fought so hard to keep off after their challenges had been used up. Katie gave her last statistics as they waited for the jury to come down for the last time before being sworn for the trial: "One black and sixteen women."

Before the trial would start, Katie and David Rosen's wife, Kathy, made two of a legal team who represented nine hundred women in an abortion class case against the State of Connecticut.

There had been a bit of false spring for a few days, but now it was raining outside.

Finally, Miss Marilyn Martino, the attractive young social worker that the defense was betting on, asked the judge if it would be all right if she wore a pantsuit when the trial started next week. The judge checked with the lawyers. Katie was enthusiastic, but Charles, who was lounging in the press section again, muttered, "Being a 'leg man' I disapprove."

A class from junior high school, that has been observing, files out. Three boys comment:

"I found that the judge, D.A., and clerk felt resentment towards the spectators."

—HANS WAGNER, 9th grade

"The impression that I got from the picking of the jury was that it is very hard to pick an impartial jury of piers. It is very time consuming and it would help a lot if they would be more choosy at picking the prospective jurors. I also noticed that there were only two black prospectives which isn't a group of piers."

—GREG LAPIN, age 14

"I think that this was a very unusual experience. I felt that the people in the court got disinterested and bored."

—MIKE MARIN, age 14, 9th grade

PART II

THE

TRIAL

"A test of faith, patience, or stamina by suffering or temptation"

THE FIRST DAY (MARCH 18, 1971)

From Mitchell On Down
PANTHER SUIT CHARGES HARASSMENT BY LAW

Would Trade Politicians for Seale
WHITE PANTHER KIDNAP PLOT CLAIMED

Says Mulvey Humane, Decent
GARRY SUGGESTS CURB ON UNFIT JUDGES

SIZE OF SEALE COURTROOM AGAIN CRITICIZED

Charles Garry's old adversary, the High Sheriff, was yelling: "We have to seat the legitimate press. No 'underground' today; we can't let in these crumbum operations, we got the *Daily News;* and no *Phantom Books.*" The alternative press and those turned away in the big overflow from the courtroom surged through the building looking for satisfaction. One of the papers that was not seated was the *Daily World.* Ron Stevenson was furious.

SHERIFF: The *Daily World* is a Communist paper.
RON STEVENSON: First I'm black. Then I am a Communist. That puts you in double jeopardy.

Inside, the defense had rearranged its seating for the trial: Ericka Huggins, Catherine Roraback, Charles Garry, Bobby Seale, David Rosen. The state's table now included a young assistant United States Attorney and several assistants and detectives.

The jury was called in. The names were called by the clerk. "Dilger" (the sheriff would then call out their number—"one"); "Adams—two"; "Goldson—three." The indictment was read— ". . . combine, conspire, confederate and agree . . . decide whether she is guilty or not guilty . . . say so and say no more." And then: "Do you solemnly swear by the name of the ever-living God . . . a true deliverance to make between the State of . . ." There are sixteen sheriffs today.

At last. The State's Attorney rises. "Call Margaret Hudgins to the stand."

Legal Dispute Results
PROSECUTION CALLS SURPRISE WITNESS AS PANTHER TRIAL TESTIMONY BEGINS

A defense witness from the trial of Lonnie McLucas was now being called as a witness for the *prosecution!*

Instead of the usual forensic witnesses to establish the commission of a crime, the State's Attorney had chosen to subpoena Margaret Hudgins at 9:45 as she stood in the courtroom line!

Peggy Hudgins was a Black Panther, a close friend of Ericka Huggins, and one of her former cellmates at the State Farm.

Young, bone-thin, in green suede, she rose from the audience and walked to the stand like an old woman. She was still ill from her incarceration, suffering from a crippling rheumatism. She smiled at Ericka as she painfully ascended the stand; so she was an involuntary *prosecution* witness this time.

Garry whispered furiously to Katie. He wanted it exposed that Margaret Hudgins had earlier pleaded guilty to aggravated assault only on the condition she would not have to testify against her friends. But it did not come out until later.

The jury was excused three times before the surprise witness could say a word. Katie, angrily: ". . . a grandstand play to grab headlines . . . *subpoenaed as she stood here in line!* . . ." Garry: ". . . as an officer of the court . . . Mrs. Hudgins has had her charges—the same charges as 'Ericka Huggins'—*nolle-ed* and these charges can be reactivated at any time . . ." Katie:

"When we asked for immunity, Mr. Markle refused; but now, in this jazzy maneuver, he wants Mrs. Hudgins to degrade herself, to become an involuntary informer, a witness against herself and her friend. . . ."

The little heartface under the huge Afro watches the contest. Bobby Seale is dressed in black and blue, Ericka in a long black, brown and beige dress; they watch, content that the "surprise move" has been blocked temporarily. Looking on gravely from the front row are Mr. and Mrs. John Huggins, Sr., Ericka Huggins' mother and sister, and, behind them, a sea of Afros nodded and waved as the jury was ordered in and out.

Finally, Margaret Hudgins claimed the protection of the Fifth and Fourteenth Amendments after the defense had gotten the message to her. Then Mr. Markle offered her immunity, which meant that if she did not testify she could be locked up. Everyone was confused by this time and the court was adjourned an hour early for lunch.

It was Garry's sixty-second birthday and, after lunch in the corridor, he proudly displayed vulgarly affectionate cards from all over the country—for the "vulgar Marxist," he said—and a copy of *The Sensuous Man,* wrapped in a scandal sheet. Behind the running humor was a careful defense against any revelation of which way he felt the first round with the state was tending. He was not really quite as open as he seemed. Instead of answering tactical questions he passed around a copy of the startling suit that the defense had launched against the authorities during the dead week between the end of jury selection and the trial.

IN THE
UNITED STATES DISTRICT COURT
DISTRICT OF CONNECTICUT

BOBBY SEALE and ERICKA HUGGINS
Plaintiffs,

Vs.

JOHN N. MITCHELL, Attorney General of
the United States; JOHN EDGAR HOOVER,

Director, Federal Bureau of Investiga-
tion; CHARLES E. WEEKS, Special Agent   :
in Charge of Federal Bureau of Investi-   CIVIL NO.
gation, New Haven Office; JOHN DOE,   :
Agent of the Federal Bureau of Inves-
tigation; ARNOLD MARKLE, State's Attor-   :
ney for New Haven County; JAMES F. AHERN,
former chief, New Haven Police Depart-   :
ment; STEPHEN P. AHERN, Chief Inspector,
New Haven Police Department;   :
VINCENT DEROSA, Detective Sergeant,
New Haven Police Department; NICHOLAS   :
PASTORE, former Sergeant Director,
Criminal Intelligence Division, New   :
Haven Police Department; RICHARD ROE,
Agent of the New Haven Police Depart-   :
ment; all individually and in their
official capacities,   :

                               Defendants.   :
                          COMPLAINT . . .   :

There was not time to read it; the sheriffs were tense as they
rounded up the lawyers to begin again.

MARKLE: Where were you on May 17, 1969?
A: Yale.
GARRY: We have a motion.

The jury was led out after being seated for thirty seconds. The
defense was conceding nothing.

The court had ruled in the state's favor concerning immunity,
but nothing could stop Garry from objecting continuously for the
rest of the day. Each time he reared himself to his feet the jurors'
heads swiveled from the witness stand. As the afternoon passed the
bright cold sunlight faded into the dull artificial glare until only the
witness box stood out in a ray of sun; like a spotlight, it hit the
frail, pained face.

Some of the jury slept. Number 12, in a fuzzy white Tyrolean
hat, sat with her arms folded.

From her *ambiance* Peggy Hudgins recalled some random events from May of 1969: a retreat at Yale, George Sams shouting at everyone, Alex Rackley's bound and swollen hands and his burned shoulder.

Mr. Markle's voice is growing hoarse. Why did he not call police witnesses first to show the color photographs of Rackley's ordeal? What had the jury learned during their short stays in the dim and echoing chamber? Mrs. Hudgins had ranged vaguely over a four-day period full of people whose names she did not remember, going to places she had not known. The coherent pattern demanded of a conspiracy theory was missing from her jumbled and elliptical recountal, and then there was Garry demanding that everything be "connected up."

What emerged from her soft remembering was George Sams. Sams shouting, hitting, always with a gun during that May. Sams in his underwear with a gun.

The first day had been played for the bulging press section, not the jury. The judge told the jury to have a nice evening and not to make up their mind until they had heard much more. The jury hung on his every word, the judge was their rock in the room full of dark rhetoric.

Panther watchers were impressed with a solidarity rally on the Green just before the beginning of testimony. The New Haven Panthers were singing, marching and leading a disciplined vigil around the 500-yard perimeter of the courthouse. But the media were producing an elaborate obituary for the Panthers. (Malcolm X had said, "The time will come when you will wish you had the Muslims back.")

The Black Panther told the story: Angela Davis on the cover and George Jackson writing inside; these two stood for the Right and Left of the Party, which had now jettisoned its extreme Left. (The Eldridge Cleaver contingent had received a hard blow when the San Quentin branch of the Party had denounced him. These were the "madmen" and "wolves" that he had apostrophized and that were now dashing his hopes.) And for the first time there was a picture of the recently defeated Muhammad Ali (a black United

Front?); it said, "You're still our champ." The overall strategy? "Survival pending revolution."

WITNESS PUTS SEALE'S CO-DEFENDANT IN MURDER VICTIM'S ROOM

The *Times* headline missed the point of the state's opening.

Why had the government called a witness sympathetic to the defense first, or at all? Did they have only the police and Warren Kimbro and George Sams? And need more witnesses from anywhere? But then, why push this case over the millions of dollars and the years?

The defense had the psychoanalyst Jay Katz, of the Yale Law School, standing by as an expert witness to attack Sams' competence to testify. Did this force the prosecution into its puzzling strategy? Were they afraid of what Garry would do to Sams?

THE THIRD DAY (MARCH 23, 1971)

A half day. The motion for a new psychiatric examination of George Sams is denied. The prosecution is looking for its next witness. Garry's cross-examination of Margaret Hudgins is minimal. He cannot get her to expatiate on the free clinic, hot breakfast, clothing program or community control of the police. Only George Sams, with drugs, with a gun and shouting orders is invoked.

GARRY: Were you scared of George Sams the whole time?
A: Yes.

The fisherman who found Alex Rackley's body comes on. The defense offered to stipulate, but Mr. Markle said he wanted the jury to get the "flavor" of the testimony. Five pictures of the dead body are introduced. "Why five?" Garry asked. "None of this has anything to do with Mr. Seale or Mrs. Huggins, it's cumulative, prejudicial and inflammatory to show *five* photos."

There, in the 8-by-10 photographs, were the shrubs and trees of the swamp where Alex Rackley had ended. Some of the black jurors only looked at the first exhibit.

Miss Martino, the young social worker, was studying Bobby and Ericka. Number 12 peered at each picture, her blue-knit head bent low. All the jurors looked to be dressed in their best. Some of them could see over Ericka's shoulder as she wrote notes and poetry.

Then a fireman and State Trooper Leonard confirmed the finding of the body, and the judge dismissed the jury, leaving the defense two hours for lunch and a conference.

In the ghetto:

"I don't think he had anything to do with it. It don't seem like it to bring him in to it, with the same member of the same organization. He don't have people killed."

"It seems like a long, long, long, long, long; just goin on, on, on, on, on—somebody must know somethin, you know. The man has his punishment if he did what they say he done. If God would give us justice we would be in a bad fix. If you got to go to jail, all right, but it don't make sense to keep a person in jail *forever* just goin over and over, over and over, over and over, over and over, over and over, over and over. If he hasn't had his punishment now I don't know when he's goin get it."

"Well, ladies and gentlemen, counsel has finished a little earlier than expected so you're free until tomorrow morning. It's nice weather, a little cold for March, but a blue sky."

The state had not yet "connected" the prisoners with the crime. The prosecution's daring opening move had miscarried somewhat, but, on the other hand, the defense had not drawn anything memorable from Peggy Hudgins as Garry had planned. They all looked glum and a little afraid.

One rejected juror said, "People like me couldn't give 'em a fair trial. Nothing against the people themselves. I am biased against any group that's out to overthrow the government. I was with

Russians for two weeks in World War Two, and I saw how their system works. We fought with the French and I saw how their system works. Whether it be the Lettermen or whatever. They deserve a fair trial, but I couldn't give it to them. It's not the people themselves."

In the ghetto:

"I came to the city shortly after it happened. You hear a lot both pro and con. The jury has a heavy burden. I am one of those diehards who does not want to give up on the system. I still have a little hope. It might be in vain, but I don't want to turn it loose right now."

THE SIXTH DAY (MARCH 26, 1971)

DON,

I've been working at the jail in that isolation cell for two months now on "decent housing fit for shelter of human beings."

You know I'm a draftsman, mechanical but mainly architectural. I learned quite a lot about building from my father who is a master carpenter. Ever since I was around 12 years of age I've been dealing with building homes and carpentry work. . . .

So, Don, I've put together some beautiful designs, but the Party now is moving to obtain the land and funds to get supplies, materials and equipment to start building this cooperative housing by the square block with some kind of people's factory building going up with every two or three square blocks. We'll be trying to do this in 20 or more cities around the country within a couple of years.

But one of the main factors about this cooperatively owned housing is that there will be no pig mortgages on the land and housing at all, and the people will be living on a standard and decent level that will show the pig power structure and landlords, show them up for what they are—pig exploiters. (I wish I could talk to you and Jan and show you specifically how this can, will, and must be done. The implementation of decent communally owned housing fit for shelter of human beings. You'll have to see it.)

But there are a lot of renegading Jackanapes who are now denounc-

ing the survival programs, even denouncing the selling of Party newspapers which inform the people about how to go about and sustain
people's revolutionary struggle. These same counterrevolutionary divi-
sionary Jackanapes want only to talk about some "higher level"—so-
called higher level which amounts to an ignoring and denouncing the
people's numerous survival programs which are programs, when imple-
mented, actually sustain the people's revolutionary struggle. Survival
programs are the first signs of a beginning self-determination by all
people toward political enfranchisement. Even the heroic beautiful
revolutionary fighting people in Vietnam, they have numerous survival
programs which sustain the revolutionary peoples' struggle WINNING
there.

BOBBY SEALE

Seale had just had a meeting with Huey P. Newton, and as he
entered he addressed the audience. "We got a new project! Decent
housing fit for the shelter of human beings. I'm designing it in
prison. They can't stop me." Unknown to the pundits, he had
made the decision to make his position public: Bobby Seale would
work together again with Huey Newton on the second five-year
plan of the Black Panther Party. The crisis of the rhetoric seemed
to be on the way to resolution.

In the audience was David Dellinger, suffering from an old anti–
Korean-war wound garnered in a putative peace march of long
ago. Officials from the Communist Party were present. William
Patterson, who forty years ago that week, on March 25, had
plunged into what became known as the case of the Scottsboro
Boys raised his fist to salute the young prisoner. Ericka entered
smiling. Each day her hair looks different. Today she wears a
pretty Indian band. She touches Bobby.

One of the state's chief witnesses took the stand. Warren
Kimbro had grown up in the New Haven poverty program. Shortly
before the murder of Alex Rackley he had turned his apartment
into a Panther headquarters. He was tall, thin, weakly handsome.
In the box he kept moving. He had smiled at Lonnie McLucas
when he testified against him, but he did not look at Bobby Seale
once. Another defeated black man in a suit and tie. (George Sams

had referred to him as "a punk," and once, when the judge called him Mr. Rackley, Kimbro shuddered.)

MARKLE: Now when you say "discipline," what do you mean?

A: We started to beat him again.

Q: And who did that?

A: Well, all of us down there. There was myself, George Sams, Lonnie McLucas and George Edwards. . . .

Q: And who was present also in the room?

A: The same group that came down in the beginning.

Q: That's George Sams and Ericka Huggins?

A: Right, all of us.

Q: And then what, if anything, happened?

A: George said, "Get some hot water," and Lonnie went upstairs and Ericka went upstairs and Lonnie came back down with the hot water. . . .

Kimbro was placing Ericka at the scene, but just.

On the morning of the eighteenth, Kimbro said he got up and went downstairs to the living room, where he saw Ericka telling Alex Rackley (who had arrived from New York the night before) that he shouldn't be sleeping in the office, that the least he could do would be to spend the time reading. She handed him a copy of the *Military Works of Chairman Mao*. Rackley said that he had never learned to read, that no one would teach him. Ericka told him that if he really didn't know how, all he had to do was ask and a sister would teach him. Sams (who had come in at the same time as Kimbro) said that Rackley had lied to Ericka and would have to be "disciplined."

Kimbro said that they ordered Rackley to stand up and both he and Sams beat Rackley with their fists and that Sams got a stick and hit him with that. Rackley fell down on the floor. A little while later, Sams stopped beating him and told him that he was expelled, and asked him where he would like to go. When Rackley said that he wanted to go to New York, Sams ordered Kimbro to call the bus station to find out what it would cost. He later gave Rackley the money and Rackley left the house, only to come back a few minutes later to ask for his coat. Kimbro said that they looked all over the house, but could not find the coat, and Sams said that he didn't think Rackley wanted to leave, and that they were going to take him to the cellar for more questioning.

Several times Rackley almost got away. If only he had left. Did he have a reason for not leaving? Could there have been a conspiracy to murder if Sams told Rackley to leave?

Q: Did there come a time, after you had gotten the tape recorder downstairs, that Mrs. Huggins came downstairs?
A: Yes, after the tape recorder was down there.
Q: And was a tape recording made?
A: Yes.
Q: And you have heard that tape recording?
A: Yes.

The prosecution might not, but the jury would draw a clear distinction between torture and tape recording—or would they?

TORTURE OF RACKLEY DESCRIBED AT TRIAL

By Lesley Oelsner

Warren Kimbro, the man who has admitted firing the first shot at Alex Rackley the night he was murdered, described graphically today how Rackley was beaten and tortured by fellow Black Panthers three days before his death.

First, said Kimbro, the prosecution's fifth witness against Bobby G. Seale and Ericka Huggins, Rackley was hit with fists and a "Panther stick" until he "fell to the floor and started crawling around."

Next—after he was given and then denied a chance to leave Panther headquarters—Rackley was placed in a noose, beaten some more, bound to a chair and gagged, according to the testimony. Finally, he was scalded with "several pots" of boiling water, followed by some cold water, to "cool him off," the court was told.

Mrs. Huggins was present during all the water-throwing, Kimbro said. [Italics added.]

This was a typesetting mistake. Lesley Oelsner's original copy for *The New York Times:* "*but* Mrs. Huggins was *not* present during all the water-throwing, Kimbro said."

At this point a two-day fight over the admissibility of the tape was begun with the jury excused.

PANTHER BID TO SUBPOENA FBI DENIED

Huey P. Newton and his party were being trailed by two F.B.I. vehicles. Panther agents were watching the F.B.I., everybody took pictures of everybody else.

In court, Katie Roraback was unable to get the judge to rule that she had a right to question the federal involvement in the raids on Kimbro's house in 1969. In none of its suits in federal court, either, had the defense ever been able to get *one* federal agent to make an appearance. Stylishly dressed, sideburned young United States attorneys swore that the F.B.I. had nothing that had been seized at 365 Orchard Street in May of 1969.

Outside court the surveillance was clear enough. A "liberated" F.B.I. document mailed to the Panthers and the media stressed that there were "plenty of reasons" for increased surveillance, "chief of which are [that] it will enhance the paranoia endemic in these circles and will further serve to get the point across there is an F.B.I. agent behind every mailbox." These "top dressers"—as Mr. Hoover called his new agents from the Vietnam officer corps—could be seen in doorways in their inexpensive raincoats.

Only Katie could argue for the suppression of the tape, as it, theoretically, affected only her client. She now had seventeen cartons of evidence carted into the court. Boxes were piled everywhere. Subpoenas had been issued for twenty-six members of the Orchard Street raiding party.

Like W. C. Fields, Katie would pause and then plunge her arm into a bag or box and come up with a scrap of paper that had been seized in the search by the policeman on the stand. Katie had looked at every single item. She was formidable.

There were typewriters and mimeo machines, the children's clothing, the posters and leaflets—all the properties of a Black Panther Party political office. Now abstracted and tagged these two years, the adding machine and posters lay with the baby clothes in a ring of dusty boxes.

The judge and State's Attorney seemed in physical pain, a *grand mal* of male chauvinism as Katie, the super *woman,* and David Rosen, the sorceress' apprentice, handed out the sad, dead inventory.

Bobby Seale chuckled at the mad rummage and then slept peacefully as Katie stalked through the mounds of millenarian debris with a sly smile hidden on her dust-smudged cheek.

Deep in the second day, Mr. Markle began to scream his demands that the relevance of all this be shown. "She has a theory," the judge would say.

"Two tubes of vaseline?" Katie asked, and Ericka began to laugh. It went on. Katie with her yellow-foolscap inventory (the court reporter and the clerk whom everybody liked were now completely hidden by the Ionesco-like phenomenon) advanced, covering the police witness Consiglio or Ryan, with dust. David Rosen staggered after her as Garry closed his eyes. But the point was made: the police had had time to get a search warrant on the night of May 21, 1969. Now it was up to the judge as to whether or not to allow the tape.

The state stuck to its major rationale. A trusted female informer had told them exact details of the torture and murder. Thus, the police had cause to enter the premises without a warrant; and they could not be forced, in this court, to reveal who she was.

Stephen Ahern, the brother of New Haven's former police chief, swore under oath that Warren Kimbro's wife was not the informer.

Ahern, who directed the warrantless search and arrests in May, 1969, testified against a motion by the defense to suppress any evidence seized in the course of that search. Under direct examination by Mr. Markle, he told the following story of the late night of May 21, 1969, and the early morning of May 22:

At 12:45 P.M. (5/21) Ahern received a phone call from Nicholas Pastore in the Intelligence Division of the New Haven Police Department telling him that Pastore had received information that an automobile was going to be used to transport either a person or a body from 365 Orchard Street. Ahern put out a pickup on the car, on the "hot line."

At 8:00 P.M. (5/21) Ahern got a phone call from Detective Vincent DeRosa, who told him that a body of a "male Negro" was found in a Middlesex swamp. He had been shot in the head. Ahern called some detectives and told them to contact their informants to see whether any of them could supply any information linking the body to the man who he had been told was being held at Orchard Street. He said also that he received a call from the morgue in Middlesex Hospital, saying that a note was found in one of the pockets of the victim's pants, addressed to "Chairman Bobby," from Ericka.

At 10 P.M. (5/21) Ahern met with an informant who told him that a subject called Brother Alex had been tortured at Orchard Street, and that the proceedings of the "trial" given him had been recorded.

At 11:40 P.M. (5/21) Frances Carter was picked up by the police and brought to Ahern "to be interviewed." She told him that she was the secretary of the local chapter, and that she had been at the Orchard Street headquarters on and off throughout the period of May 19–20. She said that she had seen Rackley's wounds, and had been told about him by Lonnie. She identified a photograph of Rackley taken at the morgue, and mentioned Ericka, Sylvia Kimbro (Warren's wife), Lonnie and some children. She said that there were weapons on the premises. She also mentioned the tape recording done in the basement.

At a little after 12 midnight (5/22) Ahern gave instructions to the men he had called for the raid, and gave them bulletproof vests and told them to be careful because there were children present. He received another call, from police at the morgue, who said that the press knew about the body. He asked them to stall the press, but was told that they couldn't do that.

At about 1 A.M. they proceeded to Orchard Street. DeRosa entered the premises by force after having received no response to his announcing that they were police. The police entered, arrested everyone present, including Ericka. They seized the gun in a second-floor bedroom and the tape in the basement.

When the raiding party arrived at Orchard Street, they passed the living-room window to get to the door. They did not notice that it was open. The door, which they broke a window in so that they could enter by force, was unlocked. When they did enter they found Ericka sitting in a chair with her baby and both Kimbro and Peggy asleep.

Although Ahern said that he told police to arrest everyone in the house, he himself did not arrest Sylvia Kimbro, whom he found upstairs. He said, this was because he had been given information by her lawyer that she was not involved and disapproved of the Party. He said he never met her before that night.

Would high officials risk perjury to protect an informer? De-Rosa had testified in the McLucas trial that the informer claimed to have gotten the details from Warren Kimbro himself!

It was warm enough now to hold a press conference on the Green. Ron Stevenson of the Communist *Daily World* read a telegram that had been sent to the Black Caucus of the United States Congress. The caucus, after a two-year-wait, was to see the President.

As part of effort to obtain larger courtroom citizens and journalists call to attention of congressional black caucus the denial of adequate access to the Seale-Huggins trial. Democratic rights of press and public violated in framework of racist repression. Judge refused response to petition signed by 800 urge black caucus personally witness this situation.

Next, David Dellinger read a statement of European support. He left to meet privately with Huey Newton. The plan: issue a final call to the movement—"Come to New Haven." Send agitators through the May Day's antiwar capital throngs with an ultimatum: Come to New Haven.

CALLEY GUILTY

MANSON, GIRLS GUILTY

THE SEVENTH DAY (APRIL 13, 1971)

The tape recorder was set up, and Warren Kimbro returned to the stand after a ten-day recess. Miss Goldson, the Avon lady, had had a bad case of flu, and Dennis Adams, the old black man, was hospitalized, having fallen down a flight of stairs—

PROBE CONCLUDES PANTHER JUROR'S
INJURIES WERE ACCIDENTAL

—he was out; an alternate had to be chosen. (His head was cracked in the fall. That head that he had nodded and shaken "yes" for all those years and might have nodded and shaken once more for Bobby and Ericka; the defense mourned him.) The clerk put his hand in a box and came out with Mary Armstrong's name, the first alternate, a black woman. The defense breathed.

Kimbro, a Catholic, thirty-seven years old, in suit and tie, walked and sat as if he were on trial. His body image was tortured, he walked under a burden, and once, when Garry rose to make a point, Kimbro snarled, "You should have been there that morning to cross-examine him." Kimbro had been cool and affable when he testified against Lonnie McLucas, but now he frowned and shifted constantly; Garry took careful note, searching out the vulnerability. (It was true, someone should have saved Rackley in 1969. The state and the town blamed the twenty-one-year-old Ericka.)

During the long break Katie, along with David Rosen's wife, Kathy Emmett, and other women, had been busy arguing the Constitutional right of abortion. Now she asked that the tape not be played because background voices were not identified on the transcript that Mr. Markle insisted on passing out to the jury. From then on the jury was excused every few minutes as Katie and Garry found a rhythm of objection: if Kimbro mentioned Ericka, then Garry objected that it was hearsay for Bobby, and vice versa.

At last the tape recorder, which the defense had shunned as an infernal machine, was turned on by Corporal Schultz.

VOICE: Testing, testing, one, two, three. Testing, testing, one, two, three. Testing, one, two, three. Testing, one, two.

ERICKA HUGGINS: This is Ericka Huggins, member of the New Haven Chapter Black Panther Party, Political Education Instructor. On May 17, at approximately ten o'clock, Brother Alex from New York was sleeping in the office, that is a house that we use as an office . . .

The jury, like good children, turned the pages of the transcript in unison. Bobby surveyed the scene and Ericka wrote. The tape turned:

. . . So then the brother got some discipline, you know, in the areas of the nose and mouth and the brother began to show cowardly tendencies, and began to whimper and moan.

After recess, Number 12 came out of the jury room minus her white 1930s hat; her rhinestones and a big cross for Easter season shone on the wide, wine-colored bosom. Except for Miss Martino, they all picked up their scripts again where Garry had interrupted them.

Ericka's voice came from the tape; in the background the baby, Mai, could be heard crying. Ericka sounded mechanical and hoarse. Why had they called her down? Garry would suggest an answer on cross-examination. Bobby and David Rosen hung halfway over their table trying to pick up the coaching voices of Sams and Kimbro in the background of the basement. Gary scored a sharp point when he forced the prosecution to replay one section three times and admit that Ericka had said, "You're lying *again*," and not "You're lying, *nigger*," as the script showed.

It was, curiously, the F.B.I. that had made the written transcript from the original tape recording. How had that mistake been made? Kimbro watched Garry making notes for cross-examination.

During the time he grabbed George and tried to fight back and was kicking, kicked Warren, kicked me, you know, dis— discombobulated the whole office and began to cry real tears.

Ericka was done. David Rosen had definitely spoiled part of the state's effect by arguing that the tape was like a show, but that the jury could not see the backstage management of George Sams and Warren Kimbro. Denied, but the impact was vitiated a little.

Then the dead man spoke. Like a Japanese morality ritual, the machine sent the sad, lost, forlorn voice of Alex Rackley through that courtroom of cruelty where no one could see or hear everybody else without twisting and turning and straining.

Q (*Male voice*): What's your name?
A: My name is Alex, Alex Rackley. I was a member of the Black Panther Party. The people that—the pigs that they put in the party to infiltrate the party this is their name: Janet Serno (phonetic); Steve or Steed (phonetic).

Q: Who?
RACKLEY: Steve or Steed: Akbar or Agbar (phonetic).
Q: Who?
RACKLEY: Jack Bright.
Q: What's Akbar's real name?
RACKLEY: Jack Bright. And the other informant, you know, Lonnie Epps, the brother that turned himself in to the pigs and was set at a hundred thousand dollar bail at first, then they let him all the way back down to ten thousand dollar bail and then the pigs let him go.
Q: How you know all this?
RACKLEY: I've been—people—like I keep my eyes and ears open, I mean, I listened to everything what people say.
Q: What people?
RACKLEY: What?
Q: Name names, nigger.

Part of a Yale basketball game that had been on the spool mercifully interrupted the thick pants and barely stifled sobs, then the mélange of names and "pigs" played on.

Q: How you know this? How you know that?
RACKLEY: I—there's the telephone in the office is bugged and the one next door in the restaurant you can hear when the brothers sometimes you can hear what the brothers in the restaurant is saying by dialing 391 only all the telephones they's pick up the lever and dial and you hear them talking to the pig.

This was to have been the state's *coup,* but Garry and the defense had counterattacked with a relentlessness that left Mr. Markle scowling and paler than before his quick holiday in Barbados. Yet the jurors said later that the tape was very damaging.

THE EIGHTH DAY (APRIL 14, 1971)

When Bobby and Ericka enter, the audience stands and gives the raised-fist salute. Ericka half covers her face. She is carrying a yellow daffodil and a blue crocus and two books by Hermann Hesse. Bobby is lugging a prepublication copy of John Gerassi's *The New International,* which is dedicated to Charles R. Garry and Huey P. Newton. Visiting old friends are shocked at how thin Ericka is.

Bobby sits reading his article in *The Black Panther*.

. . . I am the Chairman of only one party . . . So all I have to say to the people is that you know where it's at. We're going to stick in solidarity. There're a bunch of jive renegades and jack-a-napes around. But later for that. Just later for that. Let that ride, cause we got survival to get on with, and a People's revolution to mobilize. And we got political prisoners to free all over this land.

He is happy. The Party is moving again. Emory Douglas, the Panther artist, is drawing mops and groceries in the hands of Welfare Mothers; the mops are reminiscent of the thousands of guns that made him famous as the angry artist of the Left. George Jackson is writing, week by week, about the "inner city communes," while Seale is designing them in Montville prison.

The cover story of the new paper has been prepared by the Panther Ministry of Health:

BLACK GENOCIDE

Sickle Cell Anemia

GENOCIDE: THE SYSTEMATIC KILLING OR
EXTERMINATION OF A WHOLE PEOPLE

In Western and Central Africa, where there is a high incidence of Malaria—particularly the most severe type of Malaria, Plasmodium falciparum, a natural immunity against this dreaded disease was built up in some of the People. Since the Malaria germ attacks the red blood cells, some Western and Central Africans began to develop an immunity to the germ. The actual shape of the red blood cells in these people began to transform. Instead of being the normally round, donut shape, their blood cells became elongated into a sickle-like shape.

When the Euro-american slave traders invaded the African continent and forcibly removed the people from their homeland to the U.S., the people naturally began to be affected by this new environment. That is, what was once an advantage in their homeland, became a disadvantage in this foreign environment.

"Your Honor, please tell the jury why I'm standing. (I don't crave the exercise.) Your Honor says I can't make a standing objection, that I have to object specifically to this testimony that is hearsay and not in the presence of Mr. Seale." Finally, he stood during the entire last part of Kimbro's testimony; the figurative cross-examination had begun early. There was by-play and the jury beamed on Garry as he deferred to the court, distracted the witness and rankled the prosecution. So far, to the jury, he was more real than the defendants.

The old Swede looked on kindly; number 12 permitted herself a mint and took off her pink pillbox hat—she could appreciate the "work" of the counsel. Garry made some little joke about David Rosen being his lawyer; Bobby slapped Garry on the back. There was life at the defense table. ("I would have hugged Schultz but . . .") Katie and Charles had found a rhythm now, the four-month *voir dire* had bridged their natural temperamental distance. He gave her a cup of water as she persisted in her way. Katie's cross-examination was quiet and brief. She stood behind Ericka so that Kimbro had to look at them as if in a portrait. Kimbro was more friendly with her; it was Garry that put him up tight. Katie's last question was about Jon's death and the baby and— ". . . Mrs. Huggins trying to get back on her feet?" Markle objected, and Kimbro looked away.

The judge called a sudden recess.

Tight Security Veils Arrival
PANTHERS END EXTRADITION FIGHT

Rory Hithe and Landon Williams were being arraigned in the courtroom next door. They had waived extradition from Denver and came in giving the fist salute, but no one knew whether they were loyal to Oakland or Algiers, as the so-called split in the Panthers was being designated by the press.

PANTHERS FEAR GROWING
INTRAPARTY STRIFE

The *Times* coverage of the trial was on page 87 some days, but "the split" was being kept carefully alive near to page one.

In the bright afternoon sunlight, with the branches dancing at the window, Garry began his cross-examination. There was no apparent order or chronology to the attack. He worked in a low key.

Q: . . . now you never at any time saw Mr. Seale at 365 Orchard Street where your house was and also Party headquarters?
A: No, I can't recall.
Q: . . . now, before we go to Yale, did you talk to him? . . .
A: Yes, I did.
Q: . . . he asked you what kind of an audience it would be and what kind of people are those at Yale, isn't that right?

Then came the first Garry *coup de théâtre:* "Now, if your Honor please, I have at this time the tapes of Mr. Seale's speech, two tapes, and . . ."

The state had had its famous basement tape complete with transcripts for the jury. Garry ripped open a package, there were copies for the jury *and the press.*

THE NINTH DAY (APRIL 15, 1971)

VOICE: Testing, one, two, three. Testing, one, two, three.

The tape of Bobby Seale at Battell Chapel plays for seventy-seven minutes:

BOBBY SEALE: . . . and the Minister of Defense, Huey P. Newton (feedback, man), the Minister of Defense, Huey P. Newton, went to the streets and he got some niggers off the block that's used to robbing banks; he got some niggers off the block that's used to going for themselves and don't give a damn about nobody else because they've been living in a wretched condition for 400 years; he got some niggers off the block that deal dope, working for their own individualistic interests; he got some niggers that was going through the same shit that Malcolm X went through all his life, and gave them some political perspective, and outlined a ten-point platform and program that said we wanted land, we wanted bread, we want justice, we want some peace, we want some full employment, we want some decent education—and told these niggers that they going to have to work in a organized set, stop that jive-ass, petty-ass, chickenshit robberies and bullshit, get organized, and Huey P. Newton put what Malcolm X said to do on a higher level—Huey P. Newton, brothers and sisters, people, put this shit, in case you didn't know it or not, into motion. Mr. Huey P. Newton.

Imitations, patter, passionate exhortations: a virtuoso performance that has at least Miss Martino looking around and several black jurors shaking with suppressed mirth. It had taken four months to get a jury ten years younger than the average and almost half black that could respond to this strange and fabulous oration—a Garry jury for a Seale speech.

And we told you we weren't no black racists, and we had a lot of principle behind not being black racists—'cause we wouldn't stoop, Huey P. Newton says, "We will not stoop to the level of a low-lifed racist pig who would murder and hate a person because of the color of his skin. We wouldn't stoop to the level of a Ku Klux Klansman just to hate a person, just because of the color of his skin. We wouldn't do that same shit. Couldn't do it. It was wrong.

Sounding like Dick Gregory, then Martin Luther King, Jr., then Malcolm X; then a last, long peregrination in cultural anthropology.

. . . The problem is—is that you have to understand that Superman is a punk. You have to understand that the comic book . . . comic books you been reading . . . that started this shit off. This is the kind of education you're getting. You're getting a comic book education—Batman and Robin—that's what you started off. . . . I'm showing you not only are black people brainwashed with this same shit, all of you, every group . . . are brainwashed with Superman, Batman Betty, Veronica and Archie and Jughead comic books. You started off that way. [Applause] And they run that little jive, chicken-shit, middle-class, puritanical line down. They start you off with that and they project that same shit in the same books you're studying. The same shit, just on another level. Superman's a goddamn punk! In other words, Tricky Dick Nixon with his H-bombs and his atomic bombs and his antimissile and his anti, anti, anti, antimissile and his anti, anti, anti-tank, anti-tank, anti, antimissile who's playing Superman is a motherfucking punk. [Applause]

. . . You know, you see the pig with his .357 magnum, his handcuffs, his walkie-talkie, his billy club, and whatever the hell else he's got . . . that's a utility belt—Batman. [Applause] That's all it is. And little Robin, the new pig that just got on the force is running around hollering "Holy cow." Here, meanwhile, is Batman telling him that, "Well, you know how these niggers are." But then you say well wait. What has Superman and Batman got to do with niggers? I'm going to tell you what they got to do with niggers. I ain't seen Superman or Batman, nobody, save no black, Mexican-American, or any colored people in this world ever in them goddamn comic books. The punk's been in the comic books for over forty years. And he don't even relate to replenishing the earth.

. . . Superman does not relate to replenishing the earth, if that's another fact that you been brainwashed with . . . replenishing the earth—My god! The Omnipotent Administrator told you to go forth and replenish the earth. Superman, the punk, aint even tried to relate to no chick shit; he ain't kissed Lois Lane yet. He's been in that comic book for forty years. He's been in the comic books for forty years and he ain't tried to kiss Lois Lane yet, not even get a passionate arousing, you know what I mean? And as far as I'm concerned—about Lois Lane—she's just a frigid little stupid bitch. [Laughter] That's all she is. She thinks, she thinks . . . now [I'll show] how stupid she is . . . she thinks that Superman has a steel penis. [Laughter] But even when we look at the pictures of Superman in the comic books, it don't even show a print of a penis on him. Now you think that's nasty, don't you. Well, it's not nasty! I'm trying to get you unbrainwashed so you can start looking at reality. 'Cause that's what's going [to] have to happen. People [are] going to have to start opening their minds where we can stop relating to this comic book politics that's going on all across the country—punks running around here telling you that Superman is out to save the free world, and that's . . . ain't nobody but Tricky Dick Nixon telling you the same shit. Goddamn government been up here, the U.S. Government and federal governments and local governments been here for how long? Hundreds of motherfucking years! And they ain't one time, not one time, set up a free breakfast for children program. That's only one program the Party's trying to get together. Not once! If you get rid of that comic book rhetoric and that comic book politics out of your head and start looking at reality like Malcolm X had to look at it, like black people have to look at it, like Mexican-Americans have to look at it, like the Vietnamese people have to look at it, like the African people and all the other oppressed people of the world have to look at it, you'll begin to see something—that they been jiving you, jiving you. Grow some long hair! Do any goddamn thing, but just don't relate to that ruling-class system.

All the while a pig was being defined "as anyone who helps the aggressor," Warren Kimbro sat hunched up on the witness stand.

Visiting writers and lawyers like Mark Lane were astonished that Garry had gotten the tape in. He had "naïvely" demanded equal tape time in the same way he had secured the better table for the defense months ago.

The burning images, the tense passion must hang over the rest of the trial. Now Bobby's testimony will be explication on the free-wheeling text of the speech. Number 12 adjusts her green knit cloche hat, wipes her glasses, digests the "motherfuckers."

. . . Alprentice Bunchy Carter was in prison with Eldridge Cleaver. He's dead now, and he was murdered by some black pigs, brothers. Bobby Hutton is murdered; he was murdered by some white pigs. Alprentice Bunchy Carter wrote a poem, and I'm going to say this to the brothers: This is the message for the night. Alprentice said:

In niggertown, in niggertown, the streets are made of mud;
Infested with rats, bats, and bugs.
In niggertown, in niggertown, the streets are made of brick.
Ask any livin' swingin' dick that happens past.
In niggertown, in niggertown four little children kneeled
to pray in Jesus name
BO-O-OMMM!
Four little children dead and Jesus never came.
I know you say you're scared, you're tired of this shit,
you suckapaw son-of-a-bitch.
If you would, you'd ball your mitt.
So brothers, do something niggers if you only spit.

A SEALE WITNESS SHIFTS TESTIMONY

Kimbro's Version of Killing
Aids the Prosecution

That is what the defense must overcome before letting Warren Kimbro go back to Brooklyn, Connecticut, prison and George Sams. Kimbro's new testimony had taken the defense off guard. Unlike his testimony in the McLucas trial, Kimbro was now saying that everyone knew that Alex Rackley was to be killed and that *Ericka Huggins* said, "Don't use your car, Warren. It's too well known." But yesterday's surprise testimony was today's incredibility. Every contradiction will come back as a motif in Garry's summation.

After the spectacular tape play, Garry is conservative. He simply builds up points of contradiction and incredibility, walking slowly around the room looking up at the paralyzed hands of the wall clock.

Q: . . . Is there a person named George Sams there (Brooklyn, Connecticut) with you?
A: Yes.
Q: And how often do you get to see Mr. Sams?
A: Oh, every day.
Q: . . . when was the last time that you discussed anything with reference to the case?
A: Probably yesterday, when he asked me how I was doing.
Q: How did you answer him?
A: I told him I was doing all right.
Q: . . . Now, I believe you talked about the fact that there was someone in the kitchen, a man in the kitchen, when you left?
A: Yes.
Q: Who was that man?
A: I don't know his name.
Q: Was that man angry?
A: I couldn't say.

Who was the unknown man? An informer? Would he appear to testify?

On redirect Ericka began to cry silently, the tears caught the fading brightness of the afternoon light.

MARKLE: And where was Mr. Rackley at that time . . . when you went to Battell Chapel?

RORABACK: . . . this really has nothing to do with redirect.

MARKLE: I'm just showing the contrast, your Honor, of what happened at the speech, the verbiage, and what's occurring at the house . . .

GARRY: Your Honor, I think that's misconduct!

Then it got ugly.

Q: And you were asked whether or not Mrs. Huggins had ever spoken of how her husband had been killed?

A: . . . She had told me that she heard the news on the radio. . . . I think one of the sisters told her, "How did she take it?" She said, "She just offered everybody coffee at that time."

Q: . . . Did she tell you whom they had been shot by?

A: By Ron Karenga's US organization at that time.

Q: . . . And whether or not Ron Karenga's US organization is white or black?

A: It's black.

GARRY: Your Honor, I wonder if we can have a recess?

Garry was the first to notice Ericka's grief. (It had come back, December, Los Angeles, 1968; and how she had comforted them, before the police broke in and put a gun to Mai's head.)

> noises
> sounds
> unspoken words
> feelings repressed because
> the prison walls are also
> soul walls
> barriers
> if only all barriers could be removed
> and we could walk/talk/sing
> be. . . .
> free of all psychological, spiritual
> political, economic
> boundaries

> all of us all the freedom lovers of
> the world but especially
> right now—prisoners.
> Ericka

Katie made him pay on re-cross-examination.

Q: So that you did not say that Mrs. Huggins said this about your car in your statement to Sergeant DeRosa, and you did not say it in your testimony in the McLucas trial, is that right?

A: No.

Q: And this is the first time you said it, when you testified here in the last several days?

A: The first time I said it here, yes.

Q: And this is approximately two years after this alleged conversation took place?

A: Yes.

Q: And approximately fifteen months after the first statement you gave concerning—

A: Yes.

Q: And approximately nine months since you testified in the McLucas trial?

A: Yes.

Q: And you are claiming that your memory is better today. . . .

A: Somewhat, yes.

Q: Who has refreshed it for you, Mr. Kimbro?

A: Myself. Two years going over and over and over and over and over.

Q: And adding and adding and adding and adding and adding?

He made a show with "clearer and clearer and clearer" but he was used up.

The long day ended on an angry exchange. Seale's tape had been a bit much for Markle, and Judge Mulvey seemed out of sorts.

GARRY: I would like to know who the next witness is going to be so that . . .

THE COURT: Do you care to inform him, Mr. Markle?

MARKLE: No, sir.

THE COURT: . . . Mr. Garry, I have no right to ask the State's Attorney . . . you know that.

GARRY: No, I don't know that.

THE COURT: Well, you know it now!

THE TENTH DAY (APRIL 15, 1971)

But the next witness is not a surprise or George Sams, only a doctor to talk about a "dead male negro" and show color slides.

Bobby walks in and sings out "Good morning, Big Man" to the powerful figure, one of the first Panthers, in the press section. Seale was jubilant, the new Panther paper had arrived.

ON THE DEFECTION OF ELDRIDGE CLEAVER FROM THE BLACK PANTHER PARTY AND THE DEFECTION OF THE BLACK PANTHER PARTY FROM THE BLACK COMMUNITY

"For a time the Black Panther Party lost its vision and defected from the Community. With the defection of Eldridge Cleaver, however, we can move again to a full-scale development of our original vision . . ."

The Black Panther Party defected from the community long before Eldridge defected from the Party. Our hookup with white radicals did not give us access to the white community, because they do not guide the white community. The black community does not relate to them, so we were left in a twilight zone, where we could not enter the community with any real political education programs; yet we were not doing anything to mobilize whites. We had no influence in raising the consciousness of the black community and that is the point where we defected.

We went through a free speech movement in the Party, which was not necessary, and only further isolated us from the black community. We had all sorts of profanity in our paper and every other word which dropped from our lips was profane. This did not happen before I was jailed, because I would not stand for it. But Eldridge's influence brought this about. I do not blame him altogether; I blame the Party because the Party accepted it.

Eldridge was never fully in the leadership of the Party. Even after Bobby was snatched away from us, I did not place Eldridge in a position of leadership, because he was not interested in that. I made David Hilliard administrator of programs. I knew that Eldridge would not do anything to lift the consciousness of the comrades in the Party. But I knew that he could make a contribution; and I pressed him to do so. I pressed him to write and edit the paper, but he wouldn't do it. The paper did not even come out every week until after Eldridge went to jail. But Eldridge Cleaver did make great contributions to the Black Panther Party with his writing and speaking. We want to keep this in mind, because there is a positive and negative side to everything. . . .

Huey P. Newton had spoken and there was as much self-criticism as there was anything else. On the back cover a woman sat holding a child with an empty plate. Both had big tears running down their cheeks and they had no guns. The artist confessed, "it is my belief that we black people need gas and electricity on cold and dark days; doctors and medicine in times of sickness; breakfast, lunch and dinner in times of hunger." Emory Douglas too had come home from an Algeria of the mind where niggers died alone in shoot-outs with the pigs of destiny.

The naked black meat with the death traumas in it. This is the second set of pictures and his clothes again, too. The jury is getting annoyed by the time the envelope with his underwear is handed around. Yes, Alex Rackley is dead; a dead nigger, but who is to blame?

Everything is, if possible, more unclear. Every once in a while— during a long silence as they passed some jacket or picture around—the swamp and the frightened men with Sams started to get real. Then Rackley was standing there, and he must have known when Sams handed the gun to Kimbro. The incredible waste of it; years later and here was the underwear being passed around still again, and no end in sight and starting May 10, the court in San Francisco was only going to give Huey Newton week-to-week continuances in order to force Garry from one courtroom to another without letup; but that would be a relief, because Garry was heartsick over *Alex Rackley* every time he really thought about it, and he found it obscene that Markle and the state should be Rackley's official defender.

Court adjourned early. That meant someone important for Tuesday. Garry was speaking in Chicago and at the University of Illinois, but before leaving town he had to make a local headline to spoil Mr. Markle's weekend. The week before it was "Garry Tells Panther Story in Bridgeport," and now it would be "Garry Suggests Elimination of Prison System."

The final insult which must have reached Mr. Markle was Garry's, "When the fix is equal, Justice prevails."

But events were catching up with Garry's strategy. Confidence in the F.B.I. was going down by the numbers—

BOGGS SEES PERIL
TO U.S. FROM F.B.I.

BERRIGAN LAWYERS SAY FBI STILL
TRYING TO PUT CASE TOGETHER

Then he had received certain documents in the mail:

STOLEN FILES SHOW FBI
SEEKS BLACK INFORMERS

BOSTON, April 7—The Federal Bureau of Investigation has been recruiting informers, ranging from bill collectors to apartment house janitors, in an effort to develop constant surveillance in black communities and New Left organizations.

Under a program begun in 1968, agents were ordered to cultivate informers who could move into high levels of radical organizations, but later directives from Washington warned that some informers had been attacking policemen and urged "control" of such activities. . . .

And Senator J. William Fulbright had come to New Haven.

FULBRIGHT SEES STRONG TREND
TOWARD AMERICAN DICTATORSHIP

and finally, as always

Area Figures Soar
UNEMPLOYMENT HITS NEW HIGHS

THE THIRTEENTH DAY (APRIL 23, 1971)

Sams!

George Sams, Jr. The name is a savage joke. "Jr." Nothing, son of nothing; nothing, Jr. There are millions like him in the ghettos of the Third World; they do not exist until through an act of violence they materialize for a split second before sinking again beneath the level of history.

When Huey P. Newton later took responsibility for the disaster at New Haven, he wished for Sams to have psychiatric help; but even that, he added, was impossible in this "sick American culture."

Now Sams exists. An act of violence has been reified by the state in order, the defense insists, to bludgeon the Black Panther Party through its Chairman. Sams exists because his deed is encased in rhetoric, on paper, on tape recording, perhaps on film. He is a creature of the government now, as Whittaker Chambers called Harry Gold and the lunatic witnesses of the '50s. Sams is defined now, for all time, not by his act in arranging the torture and killing of Alex Rackley but by his *testimony* about it. He exists in the motions of the defense as they recapitulate his pitiful biography of nihilism.

According to a brief included in defense motions:

Prosecution witness George Sams, Jr., was born in Mobile, Alabama, on April 23, 1946. At birth he weighed barely two pounds. His parents, known alcoholics, deserted him at three months of age, and he was placed in the care of foster parents. Until two years of age, George Sams, Jr., apparently remained a very sickly child.

Little else is known of his early youth. Sams apparently progressed in the Mobile, Alabama, public-school system until he reached the sixth or seventh grade. At that juncture he left his foster parents and went to live with a foster sister in New York City. There he went as far as junior high school before running away from home. At approximately fifteen years of age he participated in a robbery at knife point. His participation included beating the victim over the head with a clenched fist when he refused to turn over all the money. Sams was adjudged a juvenile delinquent and ordered to the Wassaic State School in New York State, an institution he entered on July 14, 1961.

An "intelligence examination" which was administered at that time resulted in a test score of 64. On August 15, 1961, he was diagnosed a "moron." In addition, the Personal History entry on the admitting records indicated that Sams had a "tendency to lapse into mumbling verbal communication and was extremely hard to understand." Furthermore, "he was considered dangerous on losing his temper." His retention and immediate-recall capacities were listed as "poor."

Within ninety days Sams was transferred to the detention ward of the institution, because of his alleged "assaultiveness." According to the school report he "beat up other prisoners for no reason," seized a coprisoner, Calvin Smith, threw him on the floor and "stomped on his face" and, finally, stacked eight tablespoons together and "hit patient Musil over the head for no reason." The report is replete with incidents including Sams's "throwing chairs blindly around the dining room" and concludes with the following: "Every day this patient comes up with something to cause a disturbance on the ward." It is of significance to the defense motions that the reporting psychiatrist indicates that Sams "when interviewed . . . acts very innocent." In the final report of the institution, dated February 12, 1963, Dr. Salinger diagnosed Sams as "mentally retarded" and "unimproved."

Sams was then adjudged by an appropriate court to be An Alleged Dangerous Mental Defective pursuant to Section 134A of the Mental Hygiene Laws of the State of New York. He was then transferred to the Eastern Correctional Institution at Napanoch, New York. While Sams tested somewhat higher in the intelligence examination given him upon entrance to that institution, the senior psychiatrist, Dr. James S. Fleming, notes in his admitting report that Sams is an "unstable, inadequate and immature individual who reacts to his feelings of rejection with incorrigible, hostile and aggressive behavior." He adds that close supervision and guidance are necessary until Sams gains more adequate control "of his primitive anger and rage." On November 23, 1964, Sams left the Eastern Correctional Institution. The concluding report characterizes him as "a behavior problem, being loud and boisterous and argumentative in his reactions." However, there is a note of optimism in the final report with the hope that he "should show further improvement with increasing maturity."

However, subsequent events showed an increase, not a decrease, in a continued pattern of antisocial behavior. After leaving Eastern he moved with his foster family to Detroit, Michigan. While working there in an automotive firm he received a blow to his head of unknown severity. Evidently he applied for workmen's compensation for that injury. On January 26, 1966, he was adjudged guilty of tampering with an automobile in Highland Park, Michigan, and given a three-year probationary sentence. Less than sixty days later, Sams attempted to break and enter a grocery store situated next to the apartment in which he lived. The establishment he sought to rob was owned by people he had known for approximately six or seven months. Upon leaving the premises he was observed by the police and shot several times, once at the base of the skull and once in the back. The skull injury required major surgery. The hospital records indicate that there were "multiple metallic foreign bodies scattered through the right antrum and a big piece of metal . . . at the base of the skull." When Sams was incarcerated in the State of Connecticut on the charge arising out of this incident, the admitting records indicated that the foreign bodies were still lodged in the antrum portions of the brain. The injury left Sams with a malady described as nerve deafness in his right ear. In the personal history he gave to the admitting personnel at Connecticut State Prison he indicated that he suffered from "fainting spells."

During the McLucas trial Sams acknowledged that he had a tendency to forget events after drinking or smoking marijuana, and indicated to Dr. Miller that he blacked out when he drank wine.

Sams's conduct after joining the Black Panther Party in 1968 earned him the nickname "Crazy George." In August of 1969 he knifed one Mark Johnson in the leg at a party in Oakland, California, and was promptly dismissed from the Party. He was subsequently reinstated only to commit a brutal physical assault on another Party member, Jerry Tanaka, on May 3, 1969, in San Francisco. An eyewitness reported that Sams was laughing hysterically as he beat and attacked Tanaka and stopped only when ordered to do so by a superior officer in the Party. Other episodes of brutality committed by Sams included a physical assault upon Brea Nora, a member of the Black Panther Party. He bragged about being a participant in the murder of a policeman in New York or Detroit known as "Two-Gun Pete." In the instant matter Sams confessed to ordering the throwing of boiling water upon the body of Alex Rackley and pleaded guilty to second-degree murder. While awaiting disposition of this matter it is reported that he assaulted an inmate in the Brooklyn State Jail, in Connecticut.

In his examination report Dr. Robert Miller, the state psychiatrist, indicates that he was singularly impressed by Sams's "affability and politeness." He concluded it was noteworthy that when he entered the room Sams "was ensconced in what he thought was the most comfortable chair. Upon being introduced to me he immediately, in a friendly but not obsequious fashion, offered me the chair." In his testimony at the trial the doctor explained the significance of that act: "Obviously he, in the course of growing up, had learned to treat his elders with some respect." Although Sams had recently pleaded guilty to second-degree murder, confessed to being a party to the throwing of boiling water on the body of another individual and acknowledged the beating of Tanaka in his testimony of May, 1969, Dr. Miller concluded, on the basis of his interview, that Sams's antisocial behavior "appears to have diminished in the reasonable recent past." And he was legally "competent," said the Babylonians.

He was bigger than life, more real.

"But I have never got outside that circle. I have never broken out of the ring of what I have already done and cannot ever undo," he thinks quietly, sitting on the seat, with planted on the dashboard before him the shoes, the black shoes smelling of Negro: that mark on his ankles that gauge definite and ineradicable of the black tide creeping up his legs, moving from his feet upward as death moves.

This was even more true for Sams than for Faulkner's Joe Christmas.

Sams was like Richard Wright's Bigger Thomas—"Confidence could only come again now through action so violent that it would make him forget." Malcolm X, and others now in the Black Panther Party, had awakened from their nightmare; George Sams, Jr., had become his.

After Sams's perfunctory recital for the state ("Ericka Huggins brought down the first bucket of hot water . . . and it was true that the New York twenty-one were going to blow up the places at that time . . . Chairman Bobby came upstairs and came into the room . . . and he asked Rackley was he a pig . . . Chairman Bobby seemed to get an attitude, 'What do you do with a pig? A pig is a pig. Do away with him. Off the motherfucker.' . . . pulled the trigger; daylight came through the fog, and Alex turned around and fell on the ground"), Garry started in on him, and something ghastly happened after a few discontinuous exchanges.

Q: How old are you, sir?
A: What did you say, Mr. Garry? What did you say?
Q: May the question be read back?
A: . . . Today I became 25 years old.
Q: . . . Before May 19, 1969, weren't you told by Mr. Seale that you are not to be around any of the Party headquarters?
A: No, sir.
Q: And as a matter of fact, isn't it a fact, sir, that you always made

sure that you were never around when Mr. Seale was around any part of the Party functions?

MARKLE: I'm going to object to this.

THE COURT: Sustained.

Q: And isn't it true that on the nineteenth of May, 1969, you didn't go to hear Mr. Seale because you were afraid that Mr. Seale would know you were there? . . . Now, you said you first went to New York about the 12th of May?

A: Somewhere around the last of April; around about the 12th of May . . . (Garry shows him McLucas transcript.) . . . Late April or May, I'm not sure.

Q: There is not a word in there about "late April" is there?

A: It could have been.

Q: . . . You show me where it says "late April."

A: . . . I'll tell you what, you look around somewhere else, Mr. Garry, and you might find it . . . you asking me specifically what happened, second-for-second . . . I didn't keep up with the days you know.

Q: Didn't you used to use heroin?

A: When I was about twelve, yes.

Q: Is it true that you said, "I have every intention of destroying the Party, the Party, period"?

A: No, sir.

Q: You didn't say that?

A: No, sir.

Q: So if it's in this tape recording of yours, that's an incorrect transcription, is it?

THE WITNESS: Could I have some water?

Q: Are you taking Thorazine?

A: I don't know, Mr. Garry. I just go in the Medic Room and tell them, you know, describe to the doctor that I can't sleep, I'm suffering from some migraine headaches. And the doctor prescribes something for me, I don't go into asking him what he's giving me. And if he give me any drugs, and if it's too powerful—I think I have it for the record to the institution that I don't want any drugs. So the doctor just give me something to go to sleep. They don't work.

THE WITNESS: . . . I have nicknames, like Crazy George, Madman, Detroit George—several names—I had the name Dingee Swahoo, which was an African name.

THE COURT: Dingee what?

THE WITNESS: Dingee Swahoo.

THE COURT: All right.

THE WITNESS: It's an African name, and I had the name that

Chairman Bobby and David Hilliard gave me, which was Madman No. 1, which was in San Francisco. This is what we had, these are the names that we had, just like you have a nickname, Mr. Garry, you know people call you a nickname, basically.

Q: What else?

A: They call you, Mr. Garry, "Farry." [He had gotten a laugh in the McLucas trial by calling the attorney Koshoff, "Foshoff."]

Q: What other names have you been known by?

A: That's about all I can recall. No, lately I have been called No. 1 Agent. I have been called Rats, Snitch—a lot of times, you know, basically, it's—Rats, Snitch, Agent—lots of times, you know, these is—to me these names are just that people be misled by, because they don't know no other thing. Somebody push the rhetoric and they follow it. It means not that much to me.

Q: You have also been accused, for many, many months prior to your being arrested, as being a pig, have you not?

A: Yes.

MR. MARKLE: Object.

Q: . . . Who went with you to get the marijuana here in New Haven where you got beat for $15?

A: I just don't think that I should continue, you know, in this case, which you trying to use people as they are and paint them, that I should continue to use young ladies' names in this testifying case. You know, it's not my—you know, reasoning that really I want to testify against Sister Ericka. As you notice in all my testimony, I try to protect most of the sisters in the case anyway, because the only thing they was doing was the same thing I was doing, and that is following orders, but it seemed though, Mr. Garry, you want to pretend everybody had they own piece in the crime, and everybody was following orders, and that's just what I was doing, Sister Ericka was doing—Chairman Bobby give the orders, and we follow them. The Central Committee gave the orders, we followed them, and everyone—I just don't appreciate, you know, you trying to paint certain people to be doing certain things, because the man runs on our policies or we had policies—like they tell you to don't smoke weeds, and Chairman Bobby drinks "Cutty Sauce" (*sic*) all the time and the members smoke weeds, and they tell the society they don't do these things, but the true members, they know different, and this is the reason I particularly don't care to continue, you know, to, you know, be testifying on sisters and brothers in the Party, because the real responsibility lie on the leadership, and I'm a Party member, and that's why I am accepting to the truth, Mr. Garry.

Q: . . . You say Bobby Seale drinks "Cutty Sauce"?

A: Man—

THE COURT: Cutty Sark?

THE WITNESS: He constantly—"Cutty Sauce," liquor, he drinks all the time. He was drinking when he came to the rally at Yale. Warren Kimbro tells the Chairman to put away the liquor, and you think he put it away? This man tell the members not to drink, and he drinks all the time, he does the same thing, and if you do it, he gives—he's on the stage at the rally hollering about members smoking weeds, and he's drinking "Cutty Sauce," the liquor in the bottle, and I don't think that's fair, Mr. Garry.

. . . The same rules they set, they break. This is the whole argument between Eldridge Cleaver and Bobby Seale. They break their own rules and regulations. They break them, you know, and you are here trying to paint people as—the Black man is dead, I'm not denying it. This man gave the order to kill that man, and that's the simplest—this is as plain being, like, as I can.

What you want to do is paint me as a monster, and every member dies in the Party. The Party put them in the paper and say they are agents, and there ain't a member ever resign at the Party. That person just do not go out of the Party and nothing said about it. Every member who go out of the Black Panther Party, something is wrong of some kind, he's an "Uncle Tom," a sick nigger of some kind, an agent, and there ain't a member that can resign without being intimidated by the people in the Black community, you know, for lying, Mr. Garry.

You know the Party is lying. You're lying. I just—I'm not going to be no martyr. I'm not going to be no martyr for the Party. I have never been a martyr. I just speaks my own mind. Bobby don't like it. When I first came to San Francisco, he tells me, he says, "Who are you? What are you here for?" I said, "I am here to see Don Cox." He says, "My name is Chairman Bobby. You supposed to see me," and because I refused to see this man, he got the attitude he wants to move on, and he called me a "East Coast nigger." This man, hey, the Party is known—you know, it's about time for you to stop going around here and playing on people. I'm stepping up, because it can't work with me, or any other member of the Black Panther Party. I happen to be one that survived and not to get killed in the Black Panther Party, and I have made up my mind I am going to expose the truth to everybody, and if I have to, if I have to, I can prove the fact that you are on the Central Committee, you are part of the same Panther Party that goes around promulgating and using the Blacks and Whites, and I would do it, Mr. Garry, and this is a fact, and you are wrong.

Q: Why don't you go ahead and do it?

A: Well, the Black Panther Party—and see that you are on the Central Committee. You know, I expect—you sit there and tell these lies and you try to incriminate people. You can't do it with me.

Q: I'm on the Central Committee of the Black Panther Party?

A: Yes, you are the lawyer of the Central Committee of the Black Panther Party. You make the decisions. You make just as many decisions as the other people in the Black Panther Party. You get up and you represent the Party as if you have been in there for twenty years, you don't know nothing. You know that's a fact, you do it all the time, and you did it on the David Frost Show. You got on the David Frost Show and said the police killed the Panthers. You know the Panthers killed some of the Panthers.

John Huggins—what happened to John Huggins? What happened to Brother John—

From the bowels of the courthouse a group of prisoners was being led in singing hymns. The rough chorale drifted dimly up into the courtroom, where the man whose mother had said he was "fit for the garbage can" was led hulking in, after a merciful recess, for another session. The pitiful bravado that he had displayed when trying to spar with Garry was gone. He walked like the "field nigger" that he had used to boast of being back in the days when Eldridge Cleaver deified the madmen and the bad niggers.

Since the terrible ten-minute eruption, Sams had sunk into himself, he sat sideways facing the window, the hand with the handkerchief in it shielding his face.

Garry worked carefully lugging up the contradictory transcripts from old hearings and statements to confront George Sams, Jr., with himself. But Sams was impeaching himself now almost from sentence to sentence. He was not lying. He simply was no more responsible for his words than he was for his actions.

He had begun in an institution, he was in one now, he would end in an institution. He would be brought out, from time to time, to eat raw meat like a geek in a carnival. The state would get a few more days' work out of him.

The nigger from Alabama (he is very black and looks like a Scottsboro boy) is stamped "competent" by the psychiatrists, the judges and State's Attorney, the police and the F.B.I. But unlike Prospero—who said, finally, of Caliban, "this thing of darkness I acknowledge mine"—the state takes no responsibility for him. The whole instant case turns on whether or not the Panthers used Sams, but there is no doubt about the state's use of him. George Sams and Alex Rackley are interchangeable pieces of black meat in the chain of logic that the Panthers call "The New Haven Railroad."

Garry's hand trembles turning the pages of the wild old testimony; this is the kind of broken monster that he could defend and explain: Sams's complete deracination, the long torture house of racism. But the state has no shame over the use of this man—who looks like a nineteenth-century African, somehow an "older" body image than the "modern" Panthers on the front row of the gallery.

Mr. Markle has had an extra chair installed for the convenience of his long-haired son, who is here on his school spring holiday, watching the coon show.

Compared with how Garry handles his "villains" in other cases, this is simply technical impeachment and damnation:

Q: Well, isn't it a fact, sir, isn't it a fact that you told, under oath, that the word "off the pig" as used by Rory Hithe was a slang expression?
A: . . . Yes, sir.
Q: Sir, you remember Mr. George Edwards?
A: Yes, sir.
Q: You beat him up, too, didn't you?
A: I slapped him, yes.
Q: And tied him up?
A: No, sir.
Q: You had him tied up?
A: Yes, sir.
Q: You ordered it?
A: I suggested it, yes.
Q: You ordered it?
A: Yes, sir.

Sams is punchy; he mumbles his answers at random. The motes of late light are on Garry's white hair and George Sams's natural, which covers some old bullet slugs. (He said he had "an iron plate in his head," but X rays showed only the slugs, and then he said he *thought* he had an iron plate in his head.)

Now, Garry is finishing, and Sams will be handed over to Katie Roraback for more. It is a judgment on everyone, this ruined nonentity. No one had been prepared for the pity and terror of him.

After two years and two million dollars, all the raids and arrests, the state had finally unveiled its evidence. Sitting there, sweating through the cheap jacket that they had bought for him, he is evidence of some other unspeakable crime of which he is both the victim and the witness.

Almost every answer has to be read back. The pale court reporter with the New England accent produces an almost psychedelic version of Sam's run-on street rhetoric and heavy accent, something out of Joyce or Beckett signaling the death of language.

He did not "keep up with the days," he said, and here he sat on his birthday, which he did remember along with his garbage mother, and he had told some girl that he had raped somewhere that if he ever saw his mother he "would cut her throat." It was his birthday, and the collar on his stiff new shirt stuck up over his coat.

Bobby Seale watches him. Here is the Stagolee that the Black Panther Party was formed to save. There is a part of George Sams in every Panther, there must be—without a renaissance in these damned creatures there can never be a revolution and that is why the Panthers for so long could not give up their bloody rhetoric. Well, they had paid for it now: in the "split" no more than in George Sams, who had taken the language literally. Now he sits there trying to make it all make sense and the sheriffs laugh openly at his spectacle.

Was he, on top of everything, a government informer? Garry kept trying but the court blocked his way.

Q: . . . Well, you were working under Stokely Carmichael at that time, were you not?
A: . . . Yes, sir.
Q: And so, when Stokely Carmichael left the Black Panther Party, you decided to move in and destroy the Black Panther Party yourself, isn't that right?

A: No, sir.

Q: When was the last time that you had talked to Stokely Carmichael?

What cynicism and sadism could produce these men and then use them to try to drag back down into hell those who had broken out? Sams, a soul on ice at last, if the trials ever end, sweats in the four-o'clock sun.

CATHERINE RORABACK: . . . And one of the reasons you came up that Saturday night was to bring some posters and so forth for the Bobby Seale meeting Monday night, wasn't it?

A: No.

Q: No?

A: No.

Q: Do you remember Warren Kimbro going out to the car to get some posters and other stuff from the car?

A: No.

Q: . . . And when was it, exactly, that Landon Williams announced, in your words, as you put it, I believe, let everybody in the house know that Alex Rackley was under suspicion?

A: I think that was—that was just before I left the house, just before I left, then he told me to go get the reefer, I think.

Q: Now, you are going back and saying he did say something else. Before you said the first thing he said to you was to go get the reefers?

MR. MARKLE: I object. That doesn't mean nothing was said. That's being unfair to the witness.

THE COURT: Cross-examination. Let her go. Go ahead.

Q: Isn't it true, Mr. Sams—

A: That is true, Miss Roraback.

Q: —that you said before that—

A: Yes, Ma'am.

Q: And now you are correcting that?

She smiles and he, gratefully, seems ready to admit to anything. But she must bring out the "book" against him, too, and force him to read his testimonies past.

Once she calls him "Mr. Rackley." He closes his eyes. That is the truth. Dead in different swamps. The singing of the Gospel hymns down in the basement has stopped. Not just Alex Rackley, but God himself is dead, here in New Haven, where He started in the New World.

The judge adjourns early. No one, not Mr. Markle nor Corporal Schultz, wants to ask any more questions of this unreconstructed Stagolee who sits brushing mindlessly at his pants.

THE FOURTEENTH DAY (APRIL 27, 1971)

Out in the world, on the Green, some few drunks sat watching the pigeons wheel and the students' frisbees spin. On the flesh of this spring world, *The New York Times* and the Liberal Establishment raised their printed abstractions: Panther pathology.

The Black Panther trials in New Haven and New York have disclosed some appallingly brutal infighting among these militant groups, entirely apart from the charges at issue. . . .

This, as the jury in the case of the New York Twenty-one was about to go out.

Now the press section in New Haven understood what had been plain since November: the Panthers were not news, a dying street gang that represented no one. The editorial referred to "eight persons" in the death of a "West Coast official." But the eight had been already identified by the *Times* as Sam Napier's *colleagues*. They had come to New York to make his funeral arrangements.

SLAYING OF PANTHER
BLAMED ON POLITICS

RAIDERS SEIZE 8 FOR QUESTIONING
IN KILLING OF PANTHER

In Oakland Huey Newton "preached" another funeral:

M U R D E R E D
SAM NAPIER

One Word Is A Thousand Words To A Thousand Ears. Sam Napier Spread The People's Word. Even Now We Hear It Resound Ten Thousand Times.

"CIRCULATE TO EDUCATE"

Sam Napier, Black Panther Party, Intercommunal News Service,
Circulation Manager, Murdered by Fascists,
April 17, 1971, New York, New York

FOR SAM A
BROTHER/FRIEND OF THE PEOPLE

i remember now that sam used to call me sweet sister
and his voice had a ring to it like music/sort of a
soft-fast-hardworking voice (always a smile to it tho)
    like his soul was—soft yet strong
fast, yet not bypassing the
needs of the people/the FREE-dom of the people/
                      hardworking—yes he was
too symbolic of all we stand for dedication
                          love self less ness
seems as tho this country, america, wants to wipe out
all the samuel napiers
    jonathan jacksons
    bobby seales of the whole world
seems as tho we have a *whole lot* of work to do
             love to give, freedom to give. good brother,
. . . i cannot be there/chairman bobby cannot so—on that, i place
a kiss upon your forehead and a dandelion in your hand
(a dandelion because they grow wild/free/rebellious over the earth)
(like the people—poor people/oppressed people.)
. . . this may be said many times, but from us it is sincere—
you will not be forgotten, we love you, sweet brother
              we love you/

                                  Ericka

On the back page a picture of two old men discussing "Free Health Clinics Now." In their hands, canes.

Sam Napier had been one of the keys to Panther literature distribution, and his loss was very heavy to them. As in the case of Fred Hampton and Jon Huggins, the police had arrested the victims.

Their funerals were "colossal events"—Huey Newton's term—forced without prior announcement on the Panthers, who had once chosen the time and place of revolutionary drama. These colossal events over a five-year period were all that the *Times* really knew; the inner-city communes of Bobby Seale and George Jackson (autonomous ghetto collectives of two thousand people) would break unknown on a public that had been told about the "cooling" of the ghetto in the same way that they had been informed that the "peace movement" had melted away. But 2 percent of the population had demonstrated against the war that spring of 1971 (2 percent, Einstein had calculated once, is sufficient to make a revolution), and the "objective conditions" of rage and hope, in the ghetto, as the trial moved toward its climax, were incomparably sharper than at any time since the Civil War.

The pigeons settled on the grass, the headlines prepared the public for more "culture shock."

Denounces Seale, Garry
SAMS EXPLODES IN WITNESS BOX

Mrs. Huggins' Remark Also Mentioned
**SAMS QUOTES SEALE SAYING
TO 'OFF' PANTHER RACKLEY**

SAMS: SEALE ORDERED RACKLEY SLAIN

**SAMS TESTIFIES SEALE ORDERED
PANTHERS TO MURDER RACKLEY**

**WITNESS LINKS SEALE TO HOUSE
WHERE MURDER VICTIM WAS HELD**

**DEFENSE CONTINUES TO GRILL
KEY PANTHER WITNESS SAMS**

WITNESS DENOUNCES SEALE AND PANTHERS

PANTHER TELLS OF DEATH ORDER

**SAMS SAYS HE WAS CALM
WHILE TORTURING RACKLEY**

Inside, in the time capsule of the rhetorical courtroom, nothing else but "the case" existed. The only conduit between the world and the court was the press, and they, of course, could satisfy no one.

Sams came on, one last time, in what looked like a borrowed sheriff's jacket. He sat in his borderline fugue (among his medications was "cough medicine," though he never coughed) baring his gums autistically. Katie would bring up some past record of his, he would turn the pages heavily, breathing through the mouth. In the courthouse basement they were singing again, just a few voices, discordant.

As it went on, it looked as if Sams had fallen asleep. He would deny, then, as Katie picked up the book, he would give in. "Mr. Sams," she would say softly, and he would give his grinning wince. All the most damaging contradictions Charles would pretend not to hear and then ask the court reporter to read back for the jury.

Q: Now, Mr. Sams, going back to that Sunday morning . . . at 365 Orchard Street . . . I believe you said that Ericka Huggins threw a book at him?

A: Yes, Ma'am.

Q: . . . I show you page 1283 of the transcript in the McLucas trial . . . you said that time that she threw it over to Mr. Rackley —it was not that she threw it *at* him.

A: Yes.

Q: . . . Who brought the first bucket of hot water down?

A: . . . Ericka Huggins.

Q: Do you remember making a statement in Toronto . . . that it was Mr. McLucas that you said got the hot water?

A: . . . Yes.

Q: . . . Upstairs in the bedroom . . . Ericka Huggins was not present there?

A: No.

Q: . . . And was there anything in his mouth?

A: Tape. His mouth was taped up and gagged.

Q: Do you remember saying on . . . "I think he was ungagged"?

A: Yes, I remember. Yes.

Q: . . . By the way, Mr. Sams, when you gave your statement to the

FBI . . . you did not state . . . that Ericka Huggins told Maude Francis to try to seduce Mr. Rackley, did you?

A: No, Ma'am.

Q: And on August 16 . . . August 21 . . .

A: I probably say "Sister Ericka" or . . .

Q: Mr. Sams, you talked about conversation . . . between yourself, Landon Williams, Rory Hithe, and Ericka Huggins . . .

A: Yes, Ma'am.

Q: . . . no mention of that on your statement of August 15, 1969?

A: It's true, though.

Q: . . . August 16, 1969 . . .

A: No.

Q: August 17 . . .

A: No.

Q: August 21 . . .

A: No.

Q: . . . at the Bobby Seale bail hearing?

A: No.

Q: . . . at the McLucas trial?

A: No.

It was meticulous, devastating cross-examination. The state's case was now in jeopardy.

Then Sams was gone. He had sent the state psychiatrist a Christmas card that was, said the doctor, "a plea for help." These trials were his therapy, and the next one, with this new set of contradictions, would be geometrically cruel. The big crowd, swollen with off-duty sheriffs, watched him trudge out in his splay-footed way. Where was Sams's lawyer?

"It's a wonder steam didn't come out of my ears," Harry Gold said after his testimony in the Rosenberg case. The history of political trials is replete with "psychopathic personalities," but most of them—like Gold or David Greenglass, Ethel Rosenberg's brother—gained some sick notoriety or security from the government for their pains. George Sams, who turned the pages of those damning transcripts like a seven-year-old, had been had.

Katie had tried to prevent this torture before the trial began.

ARGUMENT

POINT I

WHERE THE DEFENDANTS ARE ON TRIAL FOR THEIR
LIVES AND REASONABLE GROUNDS EXIST TO DOUBT
THE COMPETENCY OR CREDIBILITY OF A KEY
GOVERNMENT WITNESS DUE TO HIS LONG PREVIOUS
HISTORY OF MENTAL DISTURBANCES AND ANTI-
SOCIAL BEHAVIOR, THE COURT SHOULD ORDER A
FULL AND THOROUGH PSYCHIATRIC EXAMINATION
OF THE WITNESS BY A QUALIFIED PSYCHIATRIST
SELECTED BY THE DEFENSE.

"Defendants herein are charged with capital offenses. It is
anticipated that the key witness for the government will be one
George Sams. His credibility may very well determine the outcome
of the trial.

"George Sams is and has been in the sole and exclusive custody
of the State of Connecticut, being presently incarcerated at the
Brooklyn State Prison. At the request of the Court he was examined for approximately two hours by an employee of the State of
Connecticut, Dr. Robert C. Miller. Dr. Miller's examination was
performed without the benefit of the current prison records, a
previous psychiatric evaluation rendered by Dr. Benjamin Marks,
of Detroit, Michigan, and the medical records related to the brain
injury and accompanying surgery. The neurological examination
took approximately fifteen minutes. None of the personal history
which was orally related by Sams was checked for accuracy.

"To compel these defendants, who are on trial for their lives, to
contest the most crucial factual issue in the case solely on the basis
of the cursory examination of Dr. Miller would virtually strip them
of their Sixth Amendment right to prepare an adequate and mean-
ingful defense. As recently stated by the New Jersey Supreme
Court in *State v. Butler,* 143 A2d 530:

When reasonable grounds for doubt as to a person's mental capacity as
a witness becomes known to the parties and to the Court, and lives
may depend upon his testimony, the proper administration of justice in
the public interest ought to stimulate a cooperative, voluntary effort to

establish a means of mutual solution of the problem. *State v. Butler,* 143 A2d 530, on page 553.

"In *Butler, supra,* the trial court's refusal to afford the defendant a psychiatric examination of the government's key witness led to a reversal of the first-degree murder conviction.

"The existing case law of this and other jurisdictions, as well as the published opinions of the leading experts in the respective disciplines of law and psychiatry, ordain that, under the circumstances of this case, 'the proper administration of justice in the public interest,' *Butler, supra,* demands a new and thoroughgoing psychiatric examination of Sams by a qualified and competent clinical psychiatrist selected by the defense."

At the outset, the use of a single court-appointed psychiatrist, particularly one employed in an administrative capacity by the state, has fallen into disrepute. In a thoroughgoing review of the legal problems posed by the witness with a mental history entitled "Psychiatry, Psychoanalysis and the Credibility of Witnesses," 45 *Notre Dame Law Review,* 238 (1968), Professor David B. Saxe, Professor of Law at the City University of New York, concludes:

The neutral or court-appointed psychiatrist concept has recently fallen into disrepute, as such psychiatric experts often display a fairly mediocre level of clinical competence. 45 *Notre Dame Law Review* 238 on page 251.

Even more critical of their use are the psychiatrists themselves. Dr. Bernard L. Diamond (Garry's colleague in forensic medicine and law innovation), a psychiatrist who has written extensively in this area, authored an essay directly on point: "The Fallacy of the Impartial Expert," which appeared in 3 *Archives of Criminal Psychodynamics* 221 (1959).

The frequent use of court-appointed psychiatrists was analyzed:

. . . They are often drawn from the ranks of administrative psychiatry, an area deficient in psychoanalytically oriented therapists. They are less inclined to probe deeply, more inclined to uncritically accept surface manifestations, and are prone to interpret the legal criteria for

insanity is a narrowly restricted way. [Emphasis added.] 3 *Archives of Criminal Psychodynamics* 221, on page 228.

Psychiatrists employed by the state in a full-time administrative capacity, particularly state hospital superintendents, such as Dr. Miller, are especially ill suited for the role of a neutral, qualified expert:

In a criminal case the adversary to the defendant is the People of the State. The institutional psychiatrist is a full time employee of the People of the State . . . The hospital superintendent, as a permanent State employee, with ambitions within the State bureaucratic system, may be totally identified with authority of the State. He may be an excellent hospital administrator, yet be completely out of touch with modern psychiatric attitudes toward criminal behavior. 3 *Archives of Criminal Psychodynamics* 221, on page 233.

The dangers inherent in allowing the jury to consider as the sole aid to the fact-finding process the testimony of a single so-called neutral psychiatrist are poignantly noted:

When actual partiality is masked as impartiality, the judge and jury are deceived and misled. 3 *Archives of Criminal Psychodynamics* 221, on page 230.

Diamond concludes by calling for a return to the "traditional adversary system" of distilling truth from a contest of opinions:

. . . To utilize a system in which the expert witness is labeled as "impartial" in no way eliminates the shortcomings: *it merely conceals them from the jury and creates the illusion of psychiatric omniscience.* Such illusions may be good for the public relations of psychiatry, but they are not good for the administration of justice. 3 *Archives of Criminal Psychodynamics* 221, on page 234.

In dwelling on the importance of a long-term and probing diagnosis of the sociopathic or psychiatric personality, Dr. H. A. Davidson, a psychiatrist and supervisor of the state mental hospital in New Jersey, wrote:

To make a diagnosis requires the assembly of large amounts of historical data about the patient. *The important point is that the doctor cannot diagnose psychiatric personality by tests, x-rays or personal examination.* He can diagnose it only by an analysis of the total life history.

It should be noted that all of the commentators are in agreement that the sociopath and psychopathic witness can easily pass the test of competency. It is for that reason that the courts must give the party challenging the credibility of such a witness additional latitude for a full exploration of the witness' psychological makeup. *Psychiatric Evaluation of the Abnormal Witness,* 59 *Yale Law Review* 1342 (1949–50), *Testimonial Capacity,* 39 *Boston U. Law Review* 172.

The defense concluded: "By any test Dr. Miller's examination does not satisfy that minimal requirement. Accordingly, the defendants should be accorded the right to a new and thorough psychiatric examination by an expert of their own choosing."

"May I approach the witness, your Honor?" Now Garry had a cop to fight. After the pathetic cases, Kimbro and Sams, here was something to push against.

In his new light-blue suit, polka-dot tie and blue shirt he began on "Mr. Witness."

Mr. Witness was a New Haven County detective named Pastore, who had been assigned to Markle's office as the trial began. His testimony was short: he saw, he said, Bobby Seale enter 365 Orchard, where Alex Rackley was detained, at 11:20 P.M. on May 19, 1969, after the speech at Yale. That was all. That plus Sams was the state's case against Bobby.

Garry strode around Pastore in a tight, vicious circle. A note of Pastore's about "colored males" was held up to constant ridicule as identifying Bobby Seale. Garry, the linguistic critic, kept calling attention to Pastore's manufactured reconstruction of events on the cloudy, rainy night two years ago. The stabbing interrogation and response was like the stychomythia in a Greek tragedy.

After court the defense drove out to 365 Orchard. As they were measuring the distance from where Pastore's unmarked car had been to the Kimbro apartment where Rackley had been held, a squad car drove up and a police photographer emerged to tell everyone to move.

Garry, scowling, stood his ground for the series of photographs.

Later that night the defense returned. A black man stood where Pastore had placed Bobby Seale. His face was a blank. Even under the apartment light the shadows swallowed up a black person. Now Garry had to debate whether to bring the jury there at night.

THE FIFTEENTH DAY (APRIL 28, 1971)

The judge: "Whose picture?" The courtroom erupted in incredulous laughter. There, looking like a vodka advertisement, was Charles R. Garry in the middle of the prosecution's new photographs. Garry, arms crossed, in his new blue outfit, stared out at the jury as the *defense* entered the photos—that Pastore had brought to court—as *their* exhibit.

Garry, all in gray, toyed with the earnest detective for a while. Now was the time: The state must call its surprise witness (*nobody* had ever again mentioned Sylvia Kimbro, she had been abstracted out of everyone's litany of names at 365 Orchard; they said Sams had liked her) or rest.

"The state rests, your Honor."

Bobby Seale whirled in his chair to look at Mr. Markle, his eyes bulging melodramatically.

Garry left fast. He was flying to Berkeley to speak with Congressman Paul N. McCloskey at Law Day ("May Day!" he shouted) ceremonies. On the Monday, a Chicago federal appeals judge had called a meeting of the old Chicago conspiracy, and Bobby Seale was at the center of that script too.

There Garry would try to meet with the prosecutor who was being fined each day for contempt of court by a judge who had been Mayor Daley's law partner, for seeking to obtain an indictment against the Mayor's State's Attorney and police officials for obstructing justice in connection with their investigations of the raid in which Fred Hampton and Mark Clark were shot to death.

STATE'S ATTORNEY IN CHICAGO APPEARS
BEFORE SPECIAL PANTHER JURY TODAY

HASSLE SNARLS CHICAGO
PANTHER DEATH PROBE

On Tuesday would be the arguments for a directed acquittal. On Wednesday the defense would begin the presentation of its case.

In the ghetto too, the verdict had long since come:

Stokely Carmichael speech. I was there and he rapped about the ideology of the black people, that Pan African shit. And I feel that's wrong. I, for one, don't know a damn thing about Africa; since it's here, we built this country, and it's here I think we should take advantage of it 'cause it's here.

I also look at the Jewish Defense League and the Black Panther Party. The Jewish Defense League same thing as the Black Panther Party. I've never known the Black Panther Party to hold no one. They're the only ones to show the black people what's going on.

The only thing I know about the split is what I read in the paper about the split with Cleveland. I met Miz Huggins when she first came to New Haven and I really respect her.

THE SEVENTEENTH DAY (MAY 7, 1971)

COURT RULES SEALE BEARD CAN REMAIN

MOTION TO DISMISS CHARGES
REJECTED IN PANTHER TRIAL

Garry returned from Berkeley and Chicago sleepless and exhilarated. The defense was ready to begin. *"Vi et armis,"* he brayed, as he greeted the regulars waiting in line.

The state had called eleven witnesses, but only the unsentenced Kimbro and Sams and the detective, Pastore, meant anything.

Ericka looked bright-eyed, her hair was up, and Bobby looked lean and restless.

Young Craig Gouthier was called up out of the audience to the stand. A former Panther, he had been in New Haven on May 19, 1969.

Gouthier and the second witness, Valerie White, had *both* parked their cars across the street from the Kimbro apartment at 365 Orchard Street. They both had returned to the apartment after the Seale speech in Battell Chapel in hopes of meeting Seale. They had waited "thirty to forty-five minutes," but Chairman Bobby had not come.

Here was great economy: if Gouthier and White were parked across from 365 Orchard, then Detective Pastore could not have been there and seen Bobby Seale enter, and if they had waited in vain with a crowd of people for a talk with Seale, then Sams was a liar.

More than fifty people had crowded into the Orchard Street headquarters that night after Seale's rousing speech. There they had waited for more than thirty minutes, until midnight.

It was clear that the state, when it made its arrest of Bobby Seale in August of 1969, had assumed that any number of that hectic crowd of May 19, 1969, would be available to testify that Seale had entered and gone upstairs. Then, upstairs, Sams would report the Seale-Rackley confrontation. But two years later, no one, not even Warren Kimbro, who had confessed, would put Seale at the scene; not even Sylvia Kimbro, who had been up-stairs all the time.

RORABACK: Now, what happened after you were there inside the house?

GOUTHIER: Well, after I got inside of the house, I guess about five or ten minutes after I was there, George Sams was telling everyone that a lady had called about her kid being lost and they wanted everybody to go out and find her. Before I could leave, Warren came over and asked me not to leave, that he wanted me to take him somewhere.

RORABACK: So you stayed there at the office?

GOUTHIER: I sat down in the living room and read papers.

RORABACK: And approximately how long were you there, if you remember?

GOUTHIER: I guess I was there about forty-five, thirty-five, forty-five minutes.

RORABACK: During that period of time, did you see anyone else enter the house or leave the house?

GOUTHIER: There were other people who came in, and by the time they could get in the door, George Sams was sending them out to supposedly hunt for the little girl that was lost.

RORABACK: And during that period of time while you were there at 365 Orchard Street, did you see my client, Mrs. Huggins?

GOUTHIER: No.

RORABACK: Did you see Mr. Seale?

GOUTHIER: No, I didn't.

Recross-Examination by Mr. Markle:

MARKLE: You said the ideology of the Panther Party was to love people, right?

GOUTHIER: To love the people and serve the people.

MARKLE: Serve the people?

GOUTHIER: Right.

MARKLE: And to take care of them and nurture them, right?

GOUTHIER: Not all of that.

MARKLE: Not all that?

GOUTHIER: No.

MARKLE: Just to love the people?

GOUTHIER: I said, the ideology of the Party was to serve the people and love the people.

MARKLE: Serve them, and love them? So that it would be a violation of Black Panther Party policy, according to ideology, to tie a prisoner up, wouldn't it?

GOUTHIER: Yes.

MARKLE: And to bind his hands, wouldn't it?

GOUTHIER: Yes.

MARKLE: I show you state's Exhibit A, and I would ask you, that condition of that man is a violation of the Panther ideology, isn't it, that hanger around the neck?

GOUTHIER: Yes.

MARKLE: And that string on that man's hands—and I show you state's Exhibit C—is a violation of Party ideology, isn't it?

GOUTHIER: Yes.

MARKLE: And so that if people who were Panthers—and I show you state's Exhibit D—that represents a violation of Party ideology, doesn't it?

GOUTHIER: Yes.

MARKLE: And so, that if people were present at that time and saw a man in that condition—Panthers—they would be violating the ideology of the Party, wouldn't they?

GARRY: Just a minute now, if your Honor please. That's argumentative and it's assuming facts not in evidence. He's asking for the opinion and conclusion of this witness.

MULVEY: I think I'll sustain it.

GARRY: Now, after the speech you came back to Orchard Street, how long did you remain there before you left?

WHITE: About thirty-five minutes.

GARRY: About thirty-five minutes?

WHITE: Yes.

GARRY: Now, how did you get to the Battell Chapel?

WHITE: We went in a Volkswagen bus.

GARRY: And you came, did you come back in a Volkswagen bus?

WHITE: Yes.

GARRY: And during all that time that you were gone to the speech, your Studebaker remained where it was?

WHITE: Yes.

GARRY: Is that right?

WHITE: Yes.

GARRY: Do you recall what the weather was like when you returned from the Battell Chapel?

WHITE: It was damp.

GARRY: It was what?

WHITE: It was damp. I'm not sure whether it just got through raining, or it was beginning to.

GARRY: And while you were at the headquarters of the Black Panther Party on Orchard Street, during all the time that you were there, did you ever see Bobby Seale there?

WHITE: No.

GARRY: Did you at any time see Mrs. Huggins there?

WHITE: No.

GARRY: Miss White, I have discussed this matter of your testimony on two different, three different occasions, have I not?

WHITE: Yes.

GARRY: And it's been within the last three or four days?

WHITE: Yes.

GARRY: Isn't that correct?

WHITE: Yes.

GARRY: I never saw you before, is that correct?

WHITE: No.

GARRY: And at my behest, we went out to the scene yesterday at Orchard Street?

WHITE: Yes.

GARRY: Do you remember that?

WHITE: Yes.

GARRY: I show you here Exhibit—Defendant's Exhibit No. 22—and ask you if that photograph of the scene brings to your mind anything?

WHITE: Yes.

GARRY: What does that—speak up louder so that everybody in the courtroom can hear you, Miss White, please—

WHITE: That's where my car was parked. (Indicating)

GARRY: And when you say your car was parked there, is there anything in that picture that draws your attention to it?

WHITE: The tree.

GARRY: The tree?

WHITE: Yes.

GARRY: That's the tree? (Indicating)

WHITE: Yes.

GARRY: Were you parked where that automobile is, or was your automobile forward or more backwards?

WHITE: About the same, where this car is. (Indicating)

MARKLE: Was there a lot of talk around the house that Mr. Seale was coming to the Kimbro apartment while you were waiting between a half hour and an hour?

WHITE: Yes, I heard some people saying that they were waiting for him.

MARKLE: They were waiting. Did anybody go outside and look for him?

WHITE: I don't know. I think so. I'm not sure.

MARKLE: And during that period of time that you were on the premises, did you see a Mr. June Hilliard?

WHITE: I don't think so.

MARKLE: You don't think so?

WHITE: No.

MARKLE: And you came to the conclusion that George Sams was weird, that was your first impression of him, is that right?

WHITE: Yes.

White and Gouthier made good defense witnesses. Gouthier was plausible. Unlike Kimbro and Sams, who had rattled off names and times, the soft-voiced former Panther remembered that it had been before midnight when he parked where the detective, Pastore, had said he was staked out—because the "ice cream store was still open." Later he had taken Kimbro on an errand; he knew how long it took, because he was afraid his wife would be upset at his being out so late. This rang true to the jury, the way people really remember the passage of time after two years.

Then Katie read the end of the Panther Ten-Point Program to the jury. The words were comfortable in her strong New England mouth:

. . . Prudence, indeed, will dictate that governments long established should not be changed for light and transient causes; and, accordingly, all experience hath shown that mankind are more disposed to suffer, while evils are sufferable, than to right themselves by abolishing the forms to which they are accustomed. But, when a long train of abuses and usurpations, pursuing invariably the same object, evinces a design to reduce them under absolute despotism, it is their right, it is their duty to throw off such government, and to provide new guards for their future security.

Markle attacked both witnesses, talking so fast that the judge had to slow him down. But these were not combative witnesses like Kimbro and Sams, they simply quietly insisted.

Finally, the prosecutor forced the police photographs of the dead Rackley on Gouthier when the ex-Panther said that the philosophy of the Party was to "love and serve the people."

Now came Linda Young and Shirley Wolterding. Linda Young's African names (Ukale Bethea and Kupenda) completely stymied the proper Maine court reporter. Their testimony was a chorus against George Sams, Jr.:

GARRY: Miss Young, during the period of time that you knew Mr. Sams, was there ever a discussion regarding Mr. Bobby Seale?
YOUNG: Yes, many times.
GARRY: And what did he say regarding Bobby Seale?
MARKLE: I am going to object to this.
MULVEY: No, I'll let it stand on the question of veracity and credibility.

MARKLE: May I have an exception, your Honor?

MULVEY: Exception may be noted.

YOUNG: At one time, when I first met him, he said that he loved Bobby Seale and Huey Newton, both, and then, another time, when he was very upset over the fact that he had been expelled at one time for stabbing someone, he said that he hated and resented Bobby, because it was him who had him purged, and if it wasn't for Stokely, he'd never have gotten back in, and that he would get even one day.

GARRY: I have no further questions.

GARRY: You stated to Mr. Markle that you stayed out of Mr. Sams's way. Why did you stay out of his way?

YOUNG: Well, he attempted to rape me and he beat me once.

MARKLE: When he attemped to beat and rape you, were you not living with him at the time?

YOUNG: I was not living with him. I was living at a house where he was living.

MARKLE: Didn't you tell the ladies and gentlemen of the jury and me that you were living with him?

YOUNG: I was living in the same house. I'm sorry if I gave that impression.

MARKLE: I have no further questions.

MULVEY: You mean you were not living with him?

YOUNG: He was in the same house. I was not—how do you—I was not staying in the same room. We were living in the same house. Does that clarify it? I don't understand. Is there a problem?

Recross-Examination by Mr. Garry:

GARRY: You never at any time carried on a husband-and-wife relationship with Mr. Sams?

YOUNG: No, never, not at all.

GARRY: All right.

GARRY: Did you have a conversation with Mr. Sams after he came back from New Haven?

WOLTERDING: . . . Oh. He said that he suspected three persons of being pigs. I told him I knew nothing of it. He became very violent and told me he would give me what he had given Alex Rackley, and I had better respect him as a man. Prior to that, he had punched me in my face, and I was crying about my face, and he said, "You should have seen Alex's face." He said, "Bang. Bang. You should have seen that motherfucker's face," and he said that he offed him because he thought he was a pig, and that if he ever suspected me of being a pig, that he would off me as well.

GARRY: Now, you knew Alex Rackley, did you not, Mrs. Wolterding?

WOLTERDING: Yes, I knew Alex quite well.

GARRY: And what kind of a person was Alex Rackley?

WOLTERDING: He was unsophisticated, like a baby, a child, you know. He was very, very naïve and very—almost like an "eager puppy," you know?

GARRY: Did anybody in the New York Chapter—the Chapter that you were involved in—ever thought or suspect or said, that Alex Rackley was an informer and/or a "pig"?

WOLTERDING: No . . . and George sent out for some heroin, and when the heroin came back by someone that he had sent, he asked me in front of the people, would I—he said, "Here, take some." And I said, "No." He pulled me into another room, and he pulled out a knife and said that I was his "woman," and that I shouldn't embarrass him in front of his friends. And that I'd better go out and take some of the dope. He also wanted to appear to be a big shot, so I guess— (Objection by the Prosecutor)

The press was changing its tone. It was all coming down to Sams's credibility.

**DEFENSE WITNESS TESTIFIES SAMS
SOUGHT TO 'GET EVEN' WITH SEALE**

**WITNESS SAYS RACKLEY BEATEN UP
BY SAMS BEFORE MURDER IN STATE**

**EX-PANTHER TRAINEE CLAIMS SEALE
NOT AT HEADQUARTERS**

At lunch, Garry ate a sandwich on the Green and watched the peace demonstration. Panthers with buckets circulated through the crowd collecting money for Lonnie McLucas' $60,000 bail and sold the new Panther newspaper.

STERILIZATION—ANOTHER PART OF THE
PLAN OF BLACK GENOCIDE

Garry talked his politics and read the papers.

JOBLESS RATE UP SLIGHTLY IN APRIL:
NEGRO LEVEL RISES

POOR IN NATION RISE BY 5%,
REVERSING 10-YEAR TREND

11 MAYORS WARN HERE OF COLLAPSE
OF U.S. CITIES

An old black man sat on a sunlit bench talking to two Panthers. "Trying to help the nation of colored people. Like a lodge give you certain rules. I'm seventy. The old law, in those days, everything changed, the years changed. God law never fades away. Young generation now different from when I came up. Everything changing. They used to drag 'em around and hang 'em, when you all was small, weren't born."

SEALE IS PRAISED AS PEACEFUL MAN

Priest Tells Jury 'Arming'
Doesn't Involve Weapons

In walked an Irish Catholic priest and a handsome black Episcopalian father and a beautiful black woman. These were Eugene Boyle, Earl Neil and Elaine Brown. They had flown in from San Francisco to testify.

RORABACK: Now, on January 17th of 1969, did you have occasion to attend a meeting at the University of Southern California—the University of California?
BROWN: Yes, I was there at a meeting.
RORABACK: And was Mr. Huggins there as well?
BROWN: John Huggins, Jr.?
RORABACK: Yes.

BROWN: Yes, he was there.

RORABACK: Was Mrs. Huggins present?

BROWN: No. She was at home with their newborn child. The baby had just been born about three weeks before.

RORABACK: And after that meeting, what happened, Miss Brown?

BROWN: The meeting closed, and the majority of us were about to leave, to go into a thing—there were approximately 75 students there, students of UCLA there at the time, and I remember having an appointment myself with an attorney, and I was about to leave, to go and see the attorney, and I went to find a car, and when I wasn't able to find the car, I came back downstairs—the meeting was on the first floor of the building—and I spoke with John Huggins and also with Alprentice Carter, and after I spoke with them, I went upstairs to where they had told me I would probably find the person I was looking for to drive me, and in a matter of about three minutes I was back downstairs where people were running and screaming, and we could hear shots being fired, and as a result, in the few moments, people were saying that John was dead, and the people that I was with, we were unable to accept this, and we were not able to get into the room, so we went to the hospital on the grounds there at UCLA, and when we arrived at the hospital, we waited approximately— (Prosecution objection: sustained.)

RORABACK: And, eventually, did you go back to the house where you and the Hugginses and others lived?

BROWN: Approximately two and a half hours later, yes, we went back to the house where we had all lived.

RORABACK: And at that point, did you see Mrs. Huggins?

BROWN: Yes. We came to the house, and she and the baby were there, and we spoke with her.

RORABACK: And you were the one who told her about her husband's death?

BROWN: Yes. . . . I told her that John had been killed, and she looked down at the floor and said that she thought so due to a conversation she had with someone earlier, several hours earlier, and she suggested that everyone was upset, and she seemed to want to busy herself, and she made some coffee and began to pack away some of the baby's things, due to the fact all of us wanted to get the baby out of that particular house at that particular time.

RORABACK: And—

BROWN: So that's what we did.

RORABACK: And did Ericka Huggins then leave California at that time?

BROWN: No. Approximately twenty minutes after we arrived at the house, the police, Los Angeles Police Department, came to the house, approximately 75 to a hundred, en masse—

MARKLE: I'm going to object to this, if the Court please.

MULVEY: Sustained. It's not responsive. The question is a simple one, did she leave California at that time?

BROWN: She did not.

RORABACK: Can you tell me, Miss Brown, what sort of person Miss Huggins was—Mrs. Huggins was, prior to the death of her husband?

BROWN: Very open, and always sort of warm and—and friendly. I don't know how else to say it. Very warm to other people, and open, and always involved in open exchange with people.

RORABACK: And after the death of her husband, was there any change in her?

BROWN: Yes, there was.

RORABACK: And what was that?

BROWN: She became very withdrawn. It was difficult, when we would talk, for us to have a conversation that didn't eventually lead to her discussions of John and how much she missed him. And that would basically be all she would talk about, most of the time.

The judge and the priest could have been related. Father Boyle was frustrated, he was not allowed to expatiate. Garry was livid.

MULVEY: Is that Boyle or Doyle?

BOYLE: Boyle. *B* as in *boy*.

MULVEY: All right.

GARRY: Father Boyle, would you tell us what denomination you are the clergy for?

BOYLE: I am a Roman Catholic priest.

GARRY: Father Boyle, would you tell us some of your occupation that you have been involved in?

BOYLE: Well, I am, first of all, the pastor of Sacred Heart Church in San Francisco, which is at the address I just indicated, which is in the western addition or Fillmore district of San Francisco. I am also Chairman of the Commission on Social Justice for the Archdiocese of San Francisco. I am Co-Chairman of the San Francisco Conference on Religion and Race and Social Concern, and I am also on the San Francisco Conference on Religion and Peace, and I serve on a variety of other boards of agencies dealing with human relations and human rights.

GARRY: Father Boyle, in connection with your work and your occupation in the vicinity of San Francisco and the Bay area, have you had occasion to come in contact with Bobby G. Seale?

BOYLE: I have.

GARRY: And do you know Mr. Seale personally?

BOYLE: I know Mr. Seale personally.

GARRY: And have you worked with him in community work with Mr. Seale?

BOYLE: I have worked with Mr. Seale.

GARRY: And has your church been involved in any Panther activities, Father Boyle?

BOYLE: It has. Our church has been the center for one of the Black Panther breakfast programs for children since March the 10th, 1969.

GARRY: This was instigated and you were contacted by whom to put this in operation?

BOYLE: I was contacted by Bobby Seale and by David Hilliard.

GARRY: And they personally contacted you?

BOYLE: They personally contacted us.

GARRY: Now, are you familiar with Mr. Seale's reputation for truth, honesty and veracity in the Bay area?

BOYLE: I am.

GARRY: And what is that reputation?

BOYLE: Very good.

GARRY: Are you familiar with Mr. Seale's reputation in the community, in the area, in the Bay area of California, the Bay area— the northern part of California, as to his propensity for peace and quiet?

BOYLE: I am.

GARRY: And what is that?

BOYLE: Well, I would say that the Black Panther Party in—

MARKLE: I object. I want to know about Mr. Seale.

MULVEY: You were asked about Mr. Seale, Father.

BOYLE: All right. Mr. Seale's propensity for the kind of activity that you had mentioned is, I feel, very high. In other words, I firmly believe, having dealt with Mr. Seale on a number of occasions, that his interest is in serving the people—

MARKLE: I am going to object. He testified to what it is.

Cross-Examination by Mr. Markle:

MARKLE: That would not affect your judgment of him, is that correct?

BOYLE: What would not?

MARKLE: The fact that he has a Bad Conduct Discharge.

BOYLE: No, not necessarily, in itself. I would have to know the background reasons for it.

MARKLE: If it has to do with using disrespectful language to an officer and also drinking on duty, would that affect your judgment?

BOYLE: Not simply in itself, no. I would never make a judgment on any man on one particular instance of that kind.

MARKLE: Are you familiar with the fact that in 1966 he was arrested and convicted for battery on a police officer, and I believe it was in California?

BOYLE: Well, I certainly am familiar with the fact, with the general knowledge of the fact that Mr. Seale has a background, a police background, and what I am trying to say is that in the ghetto, in the Black community, a man without a police record would not be normal.

MARKLE: Father, that may be, but you testified that he has a propensity for peace and quiet, and that would not affect your judgment of him?

BOYLE: No, it would not because I can give you—

MARKLE: In—

GARRY: Just a minute.

MARKLE: He answered me.

GARRY: He is entitled to finish his answer, your Honor.

MULVEY: He answered the question. He wanted to do a little ad-libbing with a "because." That's not permitted.

Father Neil's voice rang out. When Bunchy Carter and Jon Huggins were assassinated, Father Neil had preached the sermon to the huge throng. Now he cast his spell over the jury.

GARRY: Father Neil, would you please tell us what your denomination is that you are a clergyman for?

NEIL: The Episcopal Church. I am an Episcopalian priest.

GARRY: Would you tell us a little bit about your background?

NEIL: Presently, I am rector of St. Augustine's Episcopal Church in Oakland, California. I graduated from Carlton College, Northfield, Minnesota. I am a graduate of Seabury Western Theological Seminary, Evanston, Illinois. I have served churches in Wichita, Kansas, and in Chicago. Presently, I am a member of the National Board of the National Committee of Black Churchmen, a member of the

National Board of the Union of Black Episcopalians. I am Chairman of the Bay Area Union of Black Episcopalians, and former Vice-President and National Vice-President of the Episcopalian Society for Cultural and Racial Unity. During the Selma-to-Montgomery march in 1965, I was in charge of orientation for the Southern Christian Leadership Conference. I have done extensive civil-rights work in Mississippi, in voter registration. This past year I was a member of the Alameda County Grand Jury, 1970 Alameda County Grand Jury, and last year I was included among one of the 10,000 Outstanding Young Men in America in 1970. I am also a lecturer at the University of California at Berkeley on the History and Development of the Black Church and of the Black Family.

GARRY: Now, Father Neil, how long have you known Mr. Seale?

NEIL: I have known Mr. Seale intensively and intimately for a period of three years.

GARRY: And what was your first contact with him?

NEIL: I first met him at my church.

GARRY: That's the St. Augustine's Church?

NEIL: That's right, in Oakland.

GARRY: You have a breakfast-for-children program there, do you not?

NEIL: That's right, the breakfast-for-schoolchildren program began at St. Augustine's under the co-sponsorship of our congregation and of the Black Panther Party.

GARRY: And you have worked closely with not only Bobby Seale, but with the Panthers themselves?

NEIL: That's correct.

GARRY: And you were also a close friend of Martin Luther King?

NEIL: That's correct.

GARRY: Did you go to his funeral?

NEIL: Yes.

GARRY: Did Mr. Seale go with you?

NEIL: That's correct. We went down to his funeral in Atlanta, Georgia.

GARRY: Father Neil, in the years that you have known Mr. Seale, are you familiar with his reputation in the community regarding the truth, honesty and veracity?

NEIL: Yes, I am.

GARRY: What is that reputation?

MARKLE: I will object unless we get what community.

GARRY: The Bay area of Northern California?

NEIL: Yes, I am.

GARRY: And what is that reputation, Father Neil?

NEIL: It's an excellent reputation.

GARRY: What is his reputation—strike that. Do you know his general reputation in the community for peace and quiet?

NEIL: Yes, I do.

GARRY: What is that reputation?

NEIL: Mr. Seale is regarded as one of the foremost upholders of peace and quiet in the community, in the Bay community, Northern California community.

GARRY: And I am going to ask you now, on your own personal relationship, one-to-one relationship with Mr. Seale, as to how you personally ha e found him on the question of truth, honesty and veracity.

NEIL: I found Mr. Seale to be a very honest person, with a tremendous amount of integrity and truthfulness.

GARRY: And regarding your own personal experience with Mr. Seale as to the question of peace and quiet, have you, yourself, formed a personal opinion in this regard?

NEIL: Yes, I have.

GARRY: And what is that personal opinion, Father Neil?

NEIL: That opinion is that if anyone can keep peace and quiet in the community, then Mr. Seale can.

GARRY: And you have actually seen this demonstrated?

NEIL: I have witnessed this and experienced it.

GARRY: Would you give us some examples?

MARKLE: Objection, your Honor.

MULVEY: No examples, counsel. Sustained.

GARRY: Exception, your Honor.

MULVEY: Exception may be noted.

MARKLE: . . . And if he said, when he was here, that "The revolution is on. We want some solidarity. We don't teach you how to cuss. We're talking about people arming themselves." Is that peaceful talk?

NEIL: It most certainly is.

MARKLE: I have no further questions. Thank you, Father.

GARRY: Father Neil, you have heard Bobby Seale speak on many occasions, have you not?

NEIL: That's correct.

GARRY: And when you said that "That certainly is," in response to the question that counsel gave you, what did you mean by that?

NEIL: I meant by that—

MARKLE: Your Honor, I am going to object to this. I asked him the question and he answered that it was peaceful talk. What does he mean by it—

GARRY: I am entitled to find out.

MULVEY: Overrule the objection.

MARKLE: May I have an exception?

MULVEY: Exception noted.

NEIL: I mean that this is peaceful talk as defined by oppressed people, oppressed Black people and oppressed White people, oppressed yellow people, oppressed brown people, oppressed red people, because what we mean by "revolution," oppressed peoples mean by revolution, is that a change needs to come about, that a change is in process, and one must arm himself to bring about this revolution, and when one speaks of arming one's self, one speaks of arming one's self to the political arena, to the social arena, in the sense of alleviating and changing social conditions through trying to relate to each other, as human beings, that these are the kinds of arms that oppressed people are talking about, and that oppressed people will only take up the arms of weapons, of such firearms, only when they are forced to do so, but when we speak of arms, we are talking about these other means first, the means of arms that oppressed people have always engaged in through the time of Frederick Douglass, W. E. B. DuBois, A. Philip Randolph and Doctor Martin Luther King, up to the present.

GARRY: I have no further questions.

The jury were on the edge of their seats. The tension was rising—David Rosen was as pale as a Romantic poet—when Mrs. John Huggins, Sr., rose from the front row of the spectators' section and took the stand.

HUGGINS: Between November, 1967, when I had seen Ericka last, and January, 1969, when I saw her again, she had moved to California, had married my son, had a daughter, and had lost her husband.

RORABACK: And when she came back in January of 1969, was that to the funeral of your son?

HUGGINS: Yes, it was.

RORABACK: And, thereafter, where did she stay?

HUGGINS: She stayed with us.

RORABACK: I see. And she began to live with you here in New Haven?

HUGGINS: Yes; as of January 23rd.

RORABACK: And was the baby with her as well?

HUGGINS: Yes, she was.

RORABACK: Now, Mrs. Huggins, can you tell me what her condition—shall we say—her condition was after she came back in 1969?

HUGGINS: When she came back in 1969 she was very withdrawn, and quiet, and shy.

RORABACK: And was that a contrast to the way she had been previously?

HUGGINS: Yes, it was. I thought, in '67 when I first met her, she was a very friendly, open type of person.

The prosecutor bowed to the tremendous pride and barely cross-examined.

MARKLE: And was she in the company of someone rather constantly at that time?

HUGGINS: I don't have any way of knowing.

MARKLE: And you don't know whether she was going with Mr. Kimbro or not at that time?

HUGGINS: No, I do not.

Now Ericka's mother came forward.

RORABACK: Are you the mother of Mrs. Ericka Huggins?

JENKINS: Yes, I am.

RORABACK: And did Ericka grow up in Washington, D.C.?

JENKINS: Yes, she did. She was born in Freeman's Hospital in Washington, D.C.

RORABACK: Did she attend school there, Mrs. Jenkins?

JENKINS: Yes, she did.

RORABACK: What schools did she attend?

JENKINS: She attended Richardson Elementary School, Kelly Miller Junior High, and McKinley High School.

RORABACK: During that period of time, did she engage in any activities around Washington?

JENKINS: Yes, she did. She participated in the school activities in elementary school and she was a Girl Scout and in junior high school she was in the art club and she was an editor of the school newspaper.

RORABACK: Did she do anything outside school?

JENKINS: Oh, she was a member of the church.

RORABACK: Right.

JENKINS: And she attended Sunday school and she was a member of the junior choir.

RORABACK: In the community itself, did she do any work with children at all?

JENKINS: Yes, she did voluntary services with the church, and also in high school she volunteered her services to take the less fortunate kids to shop on Sundays at the different stores that were provided for them.

RORABACK: Now, after she finished high school, Mrs. Jenkins, did she go somewhere else to school?

JENKINS: In the summer, before she went to school, she volunteered her service with the recreation department. I mean she wasn't paid, she volunteered her services.

RORABACK: Was that sort of a summer-camp arrangement?

JENKINS: It was a community—in the community center.

RORABACK: That was with younger children?

JENKINS: Yes.

RORABACK: And then she went away to school?

JENKINS: Yes, she went to Cheney.

RORABACK: Where is that?

JENKINS: In Pennsylvania.

RORABACK: Is that a teachers college?

JENKINS: Cheney Teachers College. I think so.

RORABACK: And after she had been at Cheney, did she transfer to another school?

JENKINS: She transferred the second year to Lincoln University.

RORABACK: Was that also in Pennsylvania?

JENKINS: Yes.

RORABACK: And did there come a time when she left Lincoln?

JENKINS: Yes, she left Lincoln in her third year, in November of the third year.

RORABACK: And where did she go?

JENKINS: She went to California.

Ericka was smiling through tears. It had been another life.

The week ended when a young photographer yelled over Mr. Markle's objection that it was impossible to see what the detective had said he saw on May 19th at 365 Orchard Street.

JUDGE AT SEALE TRIAL BARS VISIT
AT NIGHT TO OFFICES OF PANTHERS

NEW HAVEN, May 7—The jury in the case against Bobby G. Seale and Ericka Huggins was barred today from making a nighttime visit to the area of the apartment where Mr. Seale, national chairman of the Black Panther party, is alleged to have given the order to kill Alex Rackley.

The defense had asked permission to take the jurors there in an effort to rebut testimony by a prosecution witness—Nicholas Pastore, a county detective, who said he saw Mr. Seale enter the apartment at 11:20 P.M. on May 19, 1969. . . .

Garry had played an important card. Only Bobby and Ericka remained now to testify for themselves.

What about Ericka? The death penalty, the High Court had said, was not cruel or unusual, and of the 648 people on death row, seven were women.

> This woman's house goes up in
>   flames probably
>   dull reddish/grey ones
>   . . . it is only a hut . . .
> South Vietnam doesn't care
> About her sad eyes
>   her children's naked thighs—
> South Vietnam has been tricked
> Into believing they have won
> (When if winning were
> near for that side, America
> would claim fame) that is all
>   They care about—I know.
> I have read between the
>   lines of so many faces
>   in so many places for so
> long—I read The New Haven
>   Register too
> (This sister's soul cries out.)
>   Ericka

SEALE TRIAL NEARS FINAL DAYS

The Eighteenth Day (May 11, 1971)

She, Ericka, walked slowly toward the stand—in her long, serpentine, green dress—partaking of the qualities of a guerrilla, and an adolescent girl in a hand-me-down formal with a black shawl and a homemade necklace, beautiful skin and hair. She could have been Pakistani or Hindu and at the same time someone in a nineteenth-century photograph.

Only some of the jury looked at her as she began her story in a clear, low, girlish voice. ". . . I wanted to work with children, poor children . . . It depressed me . . ."

(Her attenuation, abstraction was clear. Ericka the teacher, the saver of the weak, had been powerless in May of 1969 to rescue the childlike Alex Rackley, so, now, she appeared exhausted, even guilty, with none of the passion that had animated and informed her testimony earlier in federal court.)

". . . I wanted to get into special education. I wanted to teach retarded and birth-defective children . . . I was a member of a writers' club, a drama club . . ."

(In May of 1969, she had totally failed her ideal of herself. Playing the role of a Panther moll, she had had to pause again and again when the interrogation tape was being made, but Sams and Kimbro would always prompt her.)

The black jurors all watched her as she sat washed in blue sunlight speaking so low now that even the court reporter could not hear. (Number 12, all in black, watched the lawyers.) Once, when asked if there had come a time when she had met Jon Huggins, a glorious smile seemed to well out from her heart.

Charles Garry took her a cup of water but she sank lower into her remembering of Jon and Alex Rackley.

It was so quiet that a telephone could be heard ringing somewhere. She was testifying for her life now, pulling memories in through the blue windows, smiling at the mnemonic device of Katie's questions: ". . . did you move into a house with a number of people . . . By the way, Mrs. Huggins, at that time were you pregnant . . . and eventually, you did have a child born, is that correct . . . and it was a girl? . . ." (Yes, yes, yes, yes, yes, yes . . .)

Then the story of the murder of Jon at U.C.L.A., again, and the aftermath. The jury is excused and Katie explodes: "The three-week-old baby was *searched* there! I'm going to ask it! That's highly relevant!" "I am ruling on that question. You are not going to ask whether the baby was searched in Los Angeles, California, on January 17, 1969!"

So the jury never heard the details but when Katie questioned her about New Haven days the flat exhausted tone that she used to describe the funeral told something. "Thought occupied the rest of my time," she said, that and taking care of Mai.

She and the baby had gone to stay with the Huggins family, but before long she was teaching a political education class for the new Connecticut Panthers and starting an experimental children's school.

Q: What school do you attend?
A: Huey P. Newton Intercommunal Youth Institute!
Q: Can someone tell me what the schools were like that you went to before?
A: I didn't go to school.
Q: You didn't go to school before?
A: I kept messing up, and I wanted to quit.
Q: Why did you want to quit?
A: It didn't have nothing I wanted. . . . The reason why I didn't go to school is that I didn't like what the pigs were teaching me, and I got kicked out of school a few times 'cause I was messing up.
Q: How were you messing up?
A: Just wasn't doing my work, and tearing my papers up.
Q: How come?
A: 'Cause I didn't like the way my teacher was teaching me. . . . I didn't like it 'cause all they was teaching us, especially in my history class, all they be teaching us is about George Washington and Abraham Lincoln. And I kept getting suspended for cussing at the teachers and telling them I didn't want to do this and that, that work they be giving us. And one time I was reading about Angela Davis and he grabbed my book and tore it up. And I cussed him out and then I got suspended for that. And I always used to get suspended for not coming to school on time. And I just stayed out of school. And I didn't like it 'cause when I be sitting in the class, I could see that they were telling lies. . . . Over here they don't be getting no sticks to beat you. And they don't be teaching you lies like they used

to do. And they used to make you read those baby books and stuff, and not like over here, where they be teaching you about Malcolm X and Bobby and Huey. . . . Little Bobby was killed three years ago by the pigs. And now on the news media, they saying that the pigs didn't, this ex-pig, that works someplace, talking about he putting everything together, talking about Little Bobby wasn't murdered. He said that when Little Bobby was coming out of the house, he had his hands up and he was walking, 'cause he had tear gas and everything in his eyes. And they say that he didn't try to get away, he stumbled and his hands fell and the pigs lost control of their guns. And they trying to say this is a justifiable homicide. And like they saying the same thing about Mark Clark and Fred Hampton.

Q: Why else do people leave the Party?

A: Because they be saying the Party is moving too slow and they be talking just like Eldridge: Let's pick up guns and shoot pigs right now. They don't know that the people aren't educated enough. They going to be skipping from A to Z, instead of going A, B, C.

These were young black "drop-outs and kick-outs" from the new Panther school in Oakland. Would Ericka ever teach there? The children were speaking in the new Black Panther newspaper that had arrived with Huey P. Newton and David Hilliard as they entered for their fifth visit to this trial. Newton had other good news: the first clothing and shoe factories were ready to open; the new Bobby Seale clinic had been started by black doctors; a broadening of the free food program; an employment center for emerging convicts. On the cover of the paper was the prophetic face of last week's witness, Father Earl Neil:

THE ROLE OF THE CHURCH AND THE SURVIVAL PROGRAM

"Then shall the King say unto them on His right hand, come, ye blessed of My Father, inherit the kingdom prepared for you from the foundation of the world: for I was hungry, and you gave Me meat: I was thirsty, and you gave Me drink: I was a stranger and you took Me in: naked, and you clothed Me: I was sick, and you visited Me: I was in prison, and you came unto Me."

—Matthew 25:34–36

The Reverend Charles Koen was coming from embattled Cairo, Illinois, to preach a "Revival for Survival" for Bobby and Ericka on that Sunday. In the corridor, Huey P. Newton had begun to compare and contrast Christian transcendence and dialectical existence when the sheriffs signaled the end of the recess.

Sams had called Rackley "a Maryland farmer," Ericka said. Mr. Huggins, Sr., told Huey Newton later that Sams walked as if *he* had never had shoes on before. (The last things Sams had said to Ericka were that if he ever found his mother he would kill her and that he had a steel plate in his head.)

Sams and Rackley were a terrible team, with Sams constantly picking on Rackley. Ericka had watched it all until the hot water. She had "nudged" Rackley awake, had "handed" him a book, then watched the beating go on until the hot water. "The water was brought downstairs. George Sams took it and poured it into Alex's lap."

"What did you do?"

"I got nauseated."

A juror had a coughing fit, and it was time for lunch. Once the judge had had to say, "You are wasting your time if the jury doesn't hear what you have to say." When she moved slowly and numbly out for the lunch that she would not eat, he seemed to look at her with some concern or pity.

Later she described George Sams in a towel, with his hair braided, sitting on the floor playing with a gun. The days of May, 1969, slipped by, and each day the horror grew as the scalded Alex Rackley lay tied to an upstairs bed, unfed and unwashed, in his own waste and finitude. And she, downstairs, tending the baby and going through the motions of Party work.

Once, after the torture, on Saturday, she had confronted Warren Kimbro: "Why was all this necessary?" He had looked at her, confused and unable to answer. When Bobby Seale came on the Monday, she had started to say something—"There's a brother—" but she was cut off.

Garry finished up with his antistrophe: "Did you at any time conspire to kidnap . . . murder . . . harm . . ." (No, no, no, no . . .) And on Monday night, she had returned to Kimbro's apartment after the speech and had left Bobby Seale dozing in the car for twenty minutes. He had not entered.

It was the state's turn. The cross-examination would have to be savage to salvage either case.

In the corridor, a sheriff pointed out Huey P. Newton to a beefy priest, saying, "He's killed a lot of people." "Is that so?" asked the father with a look of boyhood on his big red-and-white head.

"All the phones in the courthouse are bugged." A serious, quiet reporter from the Yale newspaper had just heard voices coming out of his pay telephone receiver.

ERICKA HUGGINS TELLS
PANTHER PARTY GOALS

MRS. HUGGINS CLAIMS
TAPE CONTAINED LIES

THE NINETEENTH DAY (MAY 12, 1971)

>   . . . i watched you grow (not sizewise)
>   and learned a little, we both learned—
>   a little 'bout world things
>   money things
>   war things
>   ackshally 'bout america things REVOLUTION things
>   and at 806 w. century
>   learned a lot
>   loved a little (like our girlchild) and elaine bunchy
>   franko gee and all
>   and they told me you were gone
>   spine severed and i learned a little 'bout brother
>   things and sister things
>   'bout r e v o l u t i o n things 'bout death things
>   and i lost a lot
>   i was inside
>   i was thrust out of warmth

into cold, into reality
i was born (from lovewomb)
   i grew a little
   i died a little
and in jail
   i learned a little
       left
and in here
   i learn a lot
   hate a little
   cry a little (for our girlchild)
and i am inside . . .

                                Ericka

"Testing, 1, 2, 3." It was George Sams roaring into the tape again, as Mr. Markle insisted over defense objections on playing the tape again. This time the tape sounded much worse. Ericka was told to say "stop" wherever she was coached; a few times she lifted her finger.

Now Markle scored time after time. In the front row, Huey P. Newton sat watching unhappily. Ericka would not fight. Her horror at it all was palpable, but Markle had become the voice of her own fierce superego as he cleverly found an inner resonance with her, convicting her for her mortal sins of omission against the illiterate Rackley whom she should have taught to read. What difference did it make that George Sams had held a gun on them all? What about on Sunday or Monday or Tuesday?

Q: Did you call your in-laws to tell them what horrendous acts had just happened? Did you?
A: No, I didn't.
Q: And did you call any clergymen to tell them the horrors that had taken place in that basement . . .
A: No.
Q: And no one discussed getting any assistance for Mr. Rackley, is that right?
A: No.
Q: . . . On Monday morning, did you call anyone to assist Alex Rackley?

A: No, I didn't.

Q: . . . You didn't even go upstairs to see how he was . . .

A: Not that I remember, no.

Q: . . . You didn't feel that you could talk to a "brother" about what had happened at that apartment that made you nauseous?

A: Well, you see, it's very hard, first of all, for a woman to be heard by men . . .

Katie darted an exhilarated look toward the gallery. Radical women exhaled in pleasure. The jury, except possibly for Marilyn Martino, was unaware that a major defense theme—of Katie's and Ericka's—had been announced.

SEALE WITNESS:
'I Tried To Tell'

She was tied to the witness chair now, like Rackley to the bed, as Markle beat her with the nothingness and dereliction of 1969.

In the corridor, DeRosa, the head of intelligence for New Haven said, "Yesterday she was the Virgin Mary, today she's a *vampire!*"

Huey P. Newton left with the Hugginses to visit with the beautiful child, Mai, now almost three years old, who called him "Hooey" and stared at his bullet scar. The little girl was a clock: the mother, Ericka, had been in prison a long time.

Outside, it was stifling, tornado weather. The court and its halls were lavatorylike in the weather.

> sitting here thinking of 2 million ways
>   to break out
>   to be half free
>   on the streets—out there—
>   to take what's ours by right—
>   complete freedom . . .
> sitting here with noise—laughter and people
>   prisoners—women—oppressed women
>   prisoners all around me
> sitting here wishing i had the keys
>   i think of you and i smile
>   i see your face and i wish i were near you

i see you smile and i hope you know
   that
   i miss you 'cause you wd
be nice to talk to\laugh with\
to listen to\touch\to
love . . .

                          Ericka

THE TWENTIETH DAY (MAY 13, 1971)

On redirect it was better. Ericka in "American" clothes looked more real, broad-shouldered, full-breasted, and Katie in a light summer dress seemed youthful, too. The burden was lifting, the moral masochism was less:

. . . Detached? . . . Well, for me it's, it's depression, a feeling of futility; not being able to correct or handle a certain situation in any manner. And when I feel that way I sort of withdraw from things. And sometimes I actually don't, you know, hear with more than my ears: I might hear things but I don't internalize what I'm listening to or participate in activities around me. [Pause.] It also involves a certain amount of escape, in pushing, pushing what's happening into the background.

The demoralization, the perfect futility of 1969 was becoming real to the jury. Markle had purged her just enough.

She said the telephone lines were tapped at Panther headquarters and so she hadn't told Elaine Brown, because the "part of the government" that was tapping might very well be involved. The black jurors leaned forward, but that was all. Garry's extralegal chorus of attack on the F.B.I. had surfaced in the courtroom, before the jury, at last, but the golden opportunity had faded back into Ericka's silence and responsibility which she could not share with the F.B.I. For, while she was innocent of Rackley's suffering and death, she was guilty of her own finitude and powerlessness during the May two years ago. Everyone knew that she was in the past as she smiled out through the bulletproof glass, through the heavy new branches of the trees.

Once again she was questioned about her silence, but she did not say that "in-laws," "clèrgymen," the rest, all led back to the police. Nor that the "male chauvinism" that had intimidated her had reached its crisis in the expulsion by Huey P. Newton of the Party's "infantile" Left wing, or guessed at the use of government *provocateurs* as part of the conspiracy against the Panthers. But no one knew that Garry would yet get his chance to take up these themes.

Markle piled it on on re-cross-examination. He stuttered over the question of what Ericka's relationship to Warren Kimbro had been; Corporal Schultz, who had been getting heavier over the six months of trial, looked up from his "notes" for the first time. The prosecutor was already trying the next case—

COURT HEARING SLATED JUNE 8 FOR
LAST PANTHER DEFENDANTS

—and as he argued querulously with Ericka about the where-abouts of Landon Williams and Rory Hithe at different times the jury gradually lost interest.

At the recess, unnoticed, May, 1969, was acted out *in statu nascendi:* she came down from the stand and went to the defense table. She and Bobby were alone (the lawyers were whispering at the bench). She leafed idly through a yellow legal tablet (as she had gone through the motions of selling newspapers, et cetera, two years ago instead of crying out and saving Alex Rackley). She was blocking out all the new pain of the old past, just as she had done then, until Bobby reached over to touch her, and she wept.

In the overflow of spectators and the world press, Charles R. Garry rose—"The defendant, Bobby G. Seale, rests, your Honor." Bobby Seale beamed around the frozen tableau.

The state stood asking for time for "out-of-state witnesses" for rebuttal. Ten o'clock tomorrow morning, the judge said.

The shocking strategy had been agreed upon by Garry and Huey P. Newton: they would not put Bobby on the same stand. The taped speech at Battell Chapel before a cheering crowd was more than could ever be worked into a courtroom, which was too small for Bobby's rhetorical gifts anyway. The dialectic of consummate legal technic was complete: the great oration injected during the state's case, and now the sensational refusal to dignify George Sams and what the defense saw as his crack-pot rendition of the state's B-movie conspiracy theory. This was Garry's "one-two" punch, in headlines as big, at last, as on May 22, 1969.

**PANTHER DEFENSE RESTS: SEALE
NOT TO TAKE STAND**

The Twenty-first Day (May 14, 1971)

The "witnesses from out of state" turned out to be Mr. Carlos Ashwood, who hesitated when the clerk requested his address but then produced 240 Centre Street, New York City—which happened to be the headquarters of the New York Police Department, by whom Mr. Ashwood was employed. He was one of the undercover men in the case of the New York Twenty-one! Flanking him as he entered were two others from the same case.

(In New York the District Attorney had had all the black undercover men take a bow when the case against the Panthers had opened; at the end he had called them "geniuses." That jury, after eighteen months of evidence, had not even deliberated through dinner.)

**JURY ACQUITS NEW YORK PANTHERS
OF BOMB PLOT**

**13 PANTHERS INNOCENT ON ALL
CHARGES**

**REACTIONS TO PANTHER VERDICT:
JOY, SURPRISE, SILENCE**

**THE PANTHER VERDICT: JURY
TELLS WHY**

JURORS JOIN HAPPY VICTORS
AFTER TRIAL

The cases had begun together and they were ending that way. It had cost New York two million dollars, too. Then there had been millions in bail and a year of pretrial search for a judge to reduce it and the longest trial in New York history and a sobering glimpse of the city's Bureau of Special Services, the feared BOSS.

To all of this legal pathology and metropolitan scandal the reaction of *The New York Times* was

13 PANTHERS HERE FOUND NOT GUILTY ON
ALL 12 COUNTS

on page one, while on the editorial page there was

THE PANTHER ACQUITTAL

The acquittal by a New York jury of the 13 Black Panthers who had been charged with conspiracy to bomb police stations and department stores should put to rest the unfounded but frequently heard comment that it is impossible for a black militant to get a fair trial in the United States. The outcome of this trial in New York State Supreme Court also exposes as a fraud the Panthers' noisy and noisome oratory about the "fascist" nature of justice in America.

Nothing that was heard during the long trial made the Panthers' paramilitary posturing, their confused totalitarianism and their morbid internal squabbles any the less offensive. But the jurors recognized that these were not the issues before them. They properly resisted the temptation to turn the proceedings into a political trial. In doing so, they protected the defendants' rights and punctured the propaganda balloon of the Panthers' radical supporters. Incidentally, they also scuttled all efforts at self-justification on the part of the two defendants who jumped bail.

But the jury's verdict also stands as a timely reminder to officialdom that the charge of conspiracy is extremely difficult to prove, and tends to be viewed by the general public as a dragnet kind of device—which it often is—used by authorities more eager for political conviction than for criminal justice.

"It was not the system," said Charles R. Garry when the *Times* called him in New Haven, "it was the jury that gave them justice." His own vulgar translation of this weighty concept was, "The fix was equal."

The "Twenty-one" lawyers had lost nearly every motion and every objection, had gone through forty-three judges in the attempt to get their clients out of the Tombs prison or together for conferences, but they had won the case mainly, according to the jury, because of agents like Mr. Ashwood. When a black lawyer who represented one of the Panthers had asked Ashwood if he had "seen the defendants try to kill anybody, or bomb anything, or do anything" the answer was always "No."

Garry just toyed with Ashwood on cross-examination. "Where are your notes, sir?" "Where does it say that in *your notes,* Mr. Witness?" "You did not write these notes up yourself?" (The notes described breakfast-for-children meetings; and once, when the Officer of the Day was ten minutes late, everyone "kicked him in the ass"—to which the offender, himself, had shouted "Right on!")

A long conference at the bench; summations on Tuesday, instructions to the jury on Wednesday. Everyone tries to read the moving lips around the judge. Garry relaxes in the witness box; it had been offered to Katie and when she refused on grounds of "male chauvinism," Charles had accepted gracefully.

The crowd waited, as they did every day, to wave to Bobby and Ericka as they were driven away from the back of the court building. As the state trooper's car swept by, Bobby held up the New York *Daily News* with its huge headline.

ALL 13 PANTHERS ACQUITTED HERE

THE TWENTY-SECOND DAY (MAY 18, 1971)

Charles R. Garry arose at dawn as usual. After yoga, vitamins and a glance at yesterday's mail—

DEAR MR. C. GARRY:

Very Interesting show the other night. I was watching and listening to your malarkey. You are a shyster like Kunstler. That's all!

Yours truly

A QUIET LISTENER

and the news on the front page of the *Times*—

STOCK PRICES SINK IN BIGGEST
SETBACK OF LAST 11 MONTHS

NORTH VIETNAMESE CAPTURE KEY LAOS
TOWN NEAR TRAIL

JOB OUTLOOK BLEAKER FOR CLASS
OF '71

—he emerged from his monastic cell at the Yale Law School, impeccable and immaculate for the battle, in a dark-blue suit, blue-striped shirt and a tie with a red design.

On Grove Street there were pickets; Yale employees were on strike. (Over a century ago, in the smug New Haven of clocks, rifles, carriages, locks, tools and rubber goods, William Graham Sumner of Yale had led the counterattack on labor that followed the Civil War.) The strikers were already in place. Garry snapped the "power" sign, all elbow and fist, *en passant,* and lugging the huge briefcase started for court again. On the right the big fake-Tudor Yale architecture, built by works programs in the '30s, was rosy in perfect late New England spring; on the left the looming Asiatic gate to the cemetery: *The Dead Shall Rise.* He glared at the huge legend over the entrance, then let his gaze come back to earth with a passing coed.

Members of the Chicago conspiracy were holding press conferences all over the country. Bail was being raised for Bobby, against the old Chicago contempt charges. William Kunstler and Leonard Weinglass, the lawyers, were on their way to New Haven to demand a permit for vigilers to sleep on the Green while

the jury was out. John Froines was everywhere, a frantic bear for
Bobby. Stew Albert and other Yippie antiheroes were headed for
the courthouse.

"A stupid and cruel zero" is how the Panthers characterized the
case in their press release calling on people to come to New
Haven.

Markle and Schultz had changed chairs. Markle would argue
first *and* last because, in theory, the state's burden was very great
because of the "presumption of innocence."

The jury came in in bright costumes—number twelve all in pink
and mother-of-pearl, the old Swede with a bright tie.

A 'SENSELESS MURDER,'
MARKLE TELLS JURORS

Bobby Seale entered, very lean and elegant. Ericka's hair was
wild again; she would not make it easy.

> some peoples lives begin easily
> end easily and the shit in
> between flows easily
>   not for me—
> it seems that from birth
> i was meant to deal with hard things
>   like obtaining freedom
> but i realize that i am no different
> that my life tho filled with tears
> and a little suffering is no extraordinary thing
> i realize that the hard way is the best way
> that change never comes overnight
> that i should never hope for my personal freedom nor
> anyone's individual freedom till all are free—
> i realized this and i found out that the black panther
>   party knew it too—i joined
>   i am still suffering
>   we all are
> but winds of change are blowing
> i know because of the revolutionaries and most of all

the people—
the wretched of this earth
will be free

Ericka

"This is not a case of police versus Panthers or black against white. This is a murder trial . . . I beg you to remember Alex Rackley's murder. . . ."

The prosecutor dwelt on Ericka's crimes of omission, hardly mentioning Bobby. He kept referring to the example set for the "young Panthers"—as if these were code words for the "good Negroes" versus the "bad Panthers." The hanger from around Rackley's neck was produced and of course the pictures of the corpse in the swamp.

Katie put her watch down, poured a cup of water. She stood in her light, inexpensive summer dress with legs planted firmly.

"My client is not charged with the crime of silence." Bit by bit, with a kind of sad eloquence, she confronted the jury. "I rely on you. Don't forget about Ericka Huggins. Remember who my client really is and what she tried to do in this world." She used only a portion of her time. The entire affair had been unspeakable to Ericka from the beginning. Little by little her silence was encroaching on the rest of them.

"Mr. Garry."

"Thank you, your Honor. Mrs. Huggins, Miss Roraback, Mr. Seale, Mr. Rosen, Mr. Markle, ladies and gentlemen of the jury."

He began with Ashwood. "The prosecution is a desperate man and he is using desperate means, but perjury should not be one of them." He made the state pay for Ashwood.

He strode about. He leaned on the table, the hips were at an angle, the big shoulders driving the hands like uncanny and tireless machines. The voice was stabbing—"Not one single person! Not one. Not one single person has corroborated George Sams. In two years not one person. They went to the speech at Yale, they knew what he looked like, they came to Orchard Street to see him. He wasn't there and *not one single person says he was!* In two years they couldn't resurrect one!"

When he finished smashing on the jury rail, he spoke in a low resonance. "You are the conscience of the community. . . ."

Mr. Markle's son sat watching as Garry finally, after six months, turned to the State's Attorney: "The prosecution told you that this was not a case of black versus white. I don't look upon it as black versus white, but I do go back historically—and this is where the undercover agents come in—that the establishment in New York and other places don't seem to have enough confidence that black people can run their own institutions, they have to have informers and agents and stool pigeons paid by the establishment to curtail the activities and to create chaos and suspicion between brothers and sisters, and if anybody is responsible for the death of Alex Rackley, it is the establishment that creates this kind of a situation where an organization that is seeking to have breakfast for children, to eradicate hunger, and to eradicate . . .

"You know, I have been waiting since this trial started—as I have been waiting since I have analyzed some of the testimony in the McLucas case—for that man to tell me or to tell this court and to tell you, when was it that Bobby Seale was allegedly—allegedly said to George Sams, 'Kill Alex Rackley,' or whatever the terminology was. I have been waiting to hear that. I thought I was going to finally hear it in the opening statement this morning, his opening argument, where he ranted and raved, raged and raved, just like his cross-examination of Mrs. Huggins, where he ranted and raved about what she didn't do, but never talked about what anybody did do. I have been waiting to find out when Mr. Seale was supposed to have gone into 365 Orchard Street and told all of this to Mr. George Sams. I presume you have been waiting to find that out yourself. . . .

"What does he want you to do? To guess and conjecture on suspicion that something may have happened? Are you going to take the word of the man who has been talking to you this morning, where he is dragging a new person that none of you ever heard of before—that's David Hilliard—he mentioned David Hilliard being there on two occasions, he mentioned it twice, that David Hilliard was there. There is no excuse for this kind of conduct on the part of the prosecution. Or is it so important to get Bobby

Seale, who is chairman of the Black Panther Party; or is it so much a part of a scheme and a device to get him, no matter what the situation may be; or is he depending on the hysteria that goes on regarding Black Panthers in order to get a conviction? You draw your own conclusions, but I have heard the evidence just like you have, and I have been waiting—and I have been waiting patiently —and when he rested his case the other morning or the other afternoon, whenever it was, I was dumbfounded. I hadn't heard anything, and he rested his case and he hasn't got the audacity, the decency, ladies and gentlemen, to dismiss this.

" 'I want you to dismiss and acquit Mr. Seale.' But no, he doesn't do that. He has to get his last ounce of blood; he has to keep this man in misery until you decide, the conscience of this community, to acquit him, and I expect you to do that. I expect you to do that, because I think that that's the type of a jury that we picked. It took us long enough to pick you. . . ."

He was at the end of one of his shortest summations. One big hand gyred down to light on Bobby Seale's shoulder, at rest it trembled as he said:

"Well, he (Sams) is more to be pitied, I am sure, and I am sure I would have compassion for him, which I do, if it wasn't for the seriousness and how it affects and who it affects, when beautiful people are involved, when the life of an innocent person was taken, and I personally don't like any form of killing and neither does my client, but when I see the state using the type of a witness against the background of a man like Bobby Seale, where a Father Boyle, a Catholic priest, he talks about the beautiful man that this man is, his character, his integrity, his belief in peacefulness, truthfulness, integrity. . . .

"I said to Sams, 'Long before May, you were considered to be an informer yourself, were you not?' He said, 'Yes.' When you have got this kind of a man, I don't know what you call him. I don't know whether he is sick or ill, but, anyway, he is a by-product of our society. He is the by-product of the racism that we have lived in day in and day out for 350 years in this country. I feel sorry for George Sams, but I am not going to permit the sorriness that I have for George Sams, a person who is in this kind of a category, I won't permit him, for his own manipulation, to send my client to the gallows on a conviction of any kind, not when I have the type of client that Father Boyle talks about and Father Neil talks about.

"Again, I want to say to you, the matter is going to be in your hands. It is going to be upon your conscience, because you are the conscience of the community.

"Your role is as judges of these facts, that is your responsibility. It took a long time to get you. It's been a long time for both defendants. They have gone through an awful lot for a crime that they did not commit or even thought of committing.

"Thank you."

It was Markle's turn again. He kept on. He brought out the pictures again, everyone was turning against Alex Rackley now, he had been killed a thousand times over during the trial. Bobby Seale, the critic of style, closed his eyes, everyone else stared blankly in hate. It was too much. It had been two years ago almost to the day, there was no more life in the public memories.

"Is it conceivable that George Sams could be that stupid?" pleaded Markle, and Bobby Seale laughed lightly. The jury was not following the names and dates anymore. Markle's nasal whine persisted—"*A conspiracy is a group. It's like a bunch of grapes squashed together and if the drippings get on someone, that's their problem.*"

One of the women jurors looked as if she might go mad. "Ericka Huggins could have been a big man . . . Seale and the rest of them, Oakland sent George Sams . . . they all went crazy . . . animals . . . no kindness . . . not one . . ." He was ranting into the afternoon of the hot late spring, "Bobby Seale, not Stokely Carmichael, has to take responsibility for George Sams."

(What George Sams stood for—in his unreconstructed and terrific atavism—had finally riven the Black Panther Party. Huey P. Newton's purge of the ghost and revenant of George Sams would go on long after New Haven.)

"My reputation doesn't depend on getting Seale. I'm only doing my job."

Finally, the Manson Family and the My Lai Massacre got in, too.

"They all wanted a piece of Alex Rackley. They had him in the palm of their hands. They played God . . . I am the only voice now, for Alex Rackley." The state had certainly had its piece of the "Maryland Farmer," as Sams called him. Rackley's death had become a legal, political and news-media trap for Bobby Seale and the whole Black Panther Party.

Arnold Markle and the state were not the voice of Alex Rackley. Ericka Huggins was. Her monosyllables on the witness stand, her monumental silence and grief, these are his voice and its echo. The mean, opportunistic superego of the State is dwarfed by Ericka Huggins' conscience. The State indicts and prosecutes in the *name* of Rackley. Ericka is immured in his lost flesh and blood; he has entered her conscience through the skin.

"Who knows how many Alex Rackleys we have saved?" Garry wanted the Prosecutor cited for misconduct for that final remark, but it seemed much more likely that it would be Huey P. Newton's purgation of the "infantile Left"—with its seductive, suicidal rhetoric and the liability to criminal adventurism and government infiltration—that would "save" many a future Alex Rackley.

PART III

THE

VERDICT

"The finding or decision of a jury on the matter submitted to them"

The First Day (May 19, 1971)

Two years before, Bobby Seale had spoken at Yale in honor of the birthday of Malcolm X. Now he sat tipped back in his chair with his long curling lashes drooping as the judge instructed the jury: ". . . follow the law even if it is wrong . . . or it leads to chaos . . . well-being of life and property . . . law is made to protect society and the innocent, not the guilty . . ."

Sketch artists were at work. Now, for some reason, they were not stopped; Ericka stared at her lilacs, a sheriff had searched them. The judge wound his way through the labyrinth of "guilty intent" or "evil purpose." By this rhetoric the "stranger" was delimited. Western guilt and judgment is as metaphysical as it is rhetorical, the judge's words are the architecture of the Western superego; was Dostoevsky correct? Did the crime bleed through from the rhetoric itself?

On the Green the vigil had begun: Stew Albert, one of the nonleaders of the Yippies, was reminiscing about Berkeley and Bobby and the days of the middle sixties. The Yippies were thinner now, and Ho Chi Minh's birthday was celebrated collectively with that of Malcolm, and Bob Dylan had surfaced as Robert Zimmerman, it was rumored that he was a supporter of Rabbi Meir Kahane and the Jewish Defense League: the 1960s were as dead as Dallas or Memphis, and Stew Albert and Jerry Rubin, Tom Hayden and Art Goldberg and Martin Kenner were on the New Haven Green remembering the future.

In the corridor, Garry held court; he would never once leave. He told stories about the old days—" . . . before the war, in Portland, I defended thirty-nine guys for . . ."

Katie Roraback's dreams through the last part of the trial were ironic: "I see myself and Charlie walking out of the courthouse, down the front steps and into the sun. Bobby and Ericka are between us—and then the security men step up and haul Charlie and me off to Montville and Niantic!"

THE THIRD DAY (MAY 21, 1971)

In the corridor the "Chicago Conspiracy," except for an ailing Abbie Hoffman, were in a hairy huddle; ten feet away their respective F.B.I. "tails" were also being reunited in their own particular style.

The jury deliberates from 9 A.M. to 6 P.M. and exits to a singing, banner-waving "Free Bobby, Free Ericka" throng.

In the McLucas case the jury had been hung, deadlocked, until the judge gave them the "dynamite" charge, requesting the minority to reconsider their position; in Connecticut this transaction is called the "Chip Smith" charge, after a regional antihero of the past.

The new Black Panther newspaper was rushed to the Green—

THE PEOPLE'S FIGHT AGAINST
SICKLE CELL ANEMIA BEGINS

Farmers from Alabama—

MESSAGE TO THE BLACK PANTHER
PARTY FROM REVOLUTIONARY FARMERS

—and workers from Boston—

INTERVIEW WITH THE UNITED
COMMUNITY CONSTRUCTION WORKERS

—and while Bobby Seale waited for the verdict, he was talking with a British-American architect about his new plans and designs for the inner city.

There were "FOOD FOR CAIRO, ILLINOIS" and "MOTHER'S DAY—CHICAGO."

And, finally, statements from Gerald Lefcourt and William Kunstler on their "victories" in the cases of the New York Twenty-one and the Harlem Five.

Lefcourt:

Way back on April 2, 1969, the government launched its attacks with the indictment of the "21," following soon thereafter with the indictment of the "Chicago 8," then in May, 1969, the New Haven Chapter of the Black Panther Party was indicted for murder, and in a phony hunt for George Sams, the government attacked and destroyed offices of the Black Panther Party in several cities across the nation and finally indicted Bobby Seale also for murder in Connecticut. These attacks culminated in the killings of Fred Hampton and Mark Clark on December 4, 1969, in Chicago, Illinois. Besides Ericka and Bobby, Angela Davis and Ruchell Magee, the Berrigans, in Harrisburg, and countless others around the nation, the government has been attacking ever since.

Kunstler:

These cases do not mark the beginning of the Golden Age of Universal Justice. But they do give heart to us all and indicate that some fights can be won if we are together with ourselves and determine to resist oppression until we destroy it or die in the process. And, hopefully, they will teach other juries in other places that there is truth to the cries of the persecuted and that the system will often stoop to the pavement in order to preserve itself and its mythology.

All this was complemented by stories in the *New York Post* on the new Panther-church coalition and another setback for Eldridge Cleaver.

PEACEFUL PANTHERS MAKE HUEY PURR

FREED PANTHERS PLAYING THE MIDDLE IN PARTY FEUD

312 I AGONY IN NEW HAVEN

Now the jury wanted *all* of Ericka's testimony reread. Katie urged that a woman be allowed to do the reading but three court reporters took turns stridently recreating the soft, lost tones.

After three hundred pages and a loud argument offstage, in the jury room, they sent a message that they were satisfied and that they did not need to hear the tape again either.

Rumor circulated that it was 9 to 3 for acquittal for Ericka. The three white holdouts were supposed to be Number 12, who was forced on the jury; Number 1, the hard-working postman, who had been chosen in November; and Number 11, the tense little red-haired woman who looked as if her face were melting under the strain.

The tension was beginning to show; Corporal Schultz slammed down his legal pad. There was no question that the jury was fac-tionalized now. When they went out again their screeching could be heard into the hall, then they were quiet.

As if by stage direction an agent with a subpoena appeared to revive the exhausted hallway tableau.

On the Green, Stew Albert, "Chief of Staff" of Y.I.P. (Youth International Party), held a press conference. Flanked by Charles Garry, old friends from Berkeley and an eager drunk, and using the royal *we,* Albert categorically denied the bombing of the Capitol in Washington, D.C., and other charges. He, the Yippie who had helped dream up the People's Park experiment in California, moved over to the knot of F.B.I. agents and began pointing them out to the media. He would take a lie-detector test, he said, and challenged the government to do the same. "Also," he said to the man from the Los Angeles *Times,* "I am not guilty of the Los Angeles earthquake."

The Communist Party was releasing a letter from Angela Davis to Ericka Huggins, but the media wanted Stew, Jerry and the "heavies" of the new old Left.

DEAREST ERICKA, SISTER, COMRADE,

All your messages have been beautiful and inspiring.

It's been a long time—over two years—since our last meeting. I recall, however, as if it were yesterday, that cold, rainy evening, submerged under sadness and rage, those agonizing hours we were stationed in the parking lot outside Sybyl Brand, anxiously awaiting your release from jail. The outrageous assassination of John and Bunchy had come so unexpectedly, engendering an atmosphere of shock, incredulity and ungovernable anger. But our paramount concern was you Ericka. Your husband, closest comrade in struggle, your love, the father of Mai, your new-born child, had just been slain by the bullets of our foes. You had been immediately arrested on a manifestly fabricated charge—conspiracy to retaliate, or something equally ridiculous. We were hurting with your pain.

While we watched your approach—you were now walking through the jail's iron gates—our silence was throbbing with inexpressible pain. And as we were desperately searching for words to convey our unyielding solidarity, it was your strong, undaunted voice that broke the silence. *You* were asking us why we appeared so thoroughly dejected. Had we forgotten the infinite fortitude the long struggle ahead would require? Your unflinching determination as you clenched your fist and said "All power to the people" prompted me to think to myself, this must be the strongest, most courageous Black woman in America. . . .

Chief of Intelligence DeRosa, dressed to kill, was watching the slow show on the Green. Jerry Rubin and Stew Albert took him on.

"Jerry, are you queer?"

"What, Vinnie?"

Albert: "I am. You want to fuck?"

Rubin: "I am, too."

"You're going to have a lot of time in jail."

"Bobby and Ericka are going to be set free."

"You're queer. I'll fuck you but you won't fuck me. . . ."

The atmosphere, muted and overcast, was getting part gay, part gallows. Garry looked a little tense: the hot water at his Yale room had run out because of the strike; Huey P. Newton's retrial was scheduled to begin in five days; Garry's own hearing for contempt was in ten days; bail on Bobby Seale's Chicago case was not yet set, and a friendly source had told Charles that the jury had decided to reopen their discussion of Seale's case. All this and there was no place for him to stand on his head as he always did in California.

Two years ago, at this hour, as the dark day ended, George Sams, Jr., was hogging an order of fried chicken at 365 Orchard Street, and Alex Rackley was seeing the sun go down, through his bedroom window, for the last time.

THE FOURTH DAY (MAY 22, 1971)

Franklin Dilger, first chosen, is ill, they say, and a short doctor with an old black bag is escorted in by a sheriff.

Dilger, the postman, is one of the three holding out, according to Garry.

A French-Canadian proletarian from Maine, Bob Gauthier, was the foreman and for acquittal; the American, Dilger, for conviction. The American working class, ruined, Tolstoy said, by the government.

THE FIFTH DAY (MAY 23, 1971)

Sunday. Glorious, high New England early summer. Bright-orange flags of Bobby and Ericka, posted by Youth Against War and Fascism, snapping in the warm-cool wind.

(Charles R. Garry is standing on his head on the Green surrounded by dogs and black kids. Tom Hayden and old friends cheer him on. Around the elegant upside-down exclamation point hover the ghosts not only of political prisoners past but the countless prostitutes [$2.50 per case or $7.50 for a jury trial] and the legion of those who had been down and out in San Francisco. The sweet, soaring music of "The Lumpen"— ". . . bullets in the air, snipers everywhere . . ."—lifts over the huge Green tableau. The cameramen crowd around to take their wire photos and ask why. Old San Francisco irregulars explain that this is how Garry communicates with the jury.)

On the glass-strewn streets of the inner city, children and dogs emerge into the clean and glowing sun. In the lockup, Bobby Seale and an architect go over the blueprints of Bobby's inner-city commune. On the Green, agents and underground press shoot it out with cameras.

Some F.B.I. agents chase a child's ball and several uniformed police do a kind of elephantine shuffle to the high *Lumpen* music—". . . snipers everywhere . . ." They seem sad, forced to be merely voyeurs to all that life force of children and the incessant running of dogs. Corporal Schultz asks Mrs. Huggins, Sr. to leave the courthouse steps—"Why don't you tell the sun not to shine!?"

In the late afternoon, the jury announces that it wants Warren Kimbro's testimony re-read. Number 12 wears no hat. The jury looks grim.

THE SIXTH DAY (MAY 24, 1971)

Chip Smith lived in Ansonia, Connecticut, in 1881. There he murdered the Chief of Police. The judge at his trial urged the hung jury to reach a verdict. They did. They hung Chip Smith.

Now Judge Mulvey tried. They stopped listening to Warren Kimbro's testimony and at 11:15 someone shouted what sounded like "motherfucker" at someone else.

At 2:45 Ericka came in with her hair up and long earrings; Bobby and his retinue of troopers entered a second later.

"We cannot reach a verdict in either case on *any* of the charges."

Mary Armstrong half stood and stage-whispered, "That's not right!"

The crowd? As in the Dreyfus Affair:

"By five votes to two—guilty . . ."—"Ah!" It burst from every part of the hall at once, half gasp, half sob—the sound with which men take wounds they half expected. Not a single word did any man articulate. Only that one choking shiver—the voice of souls that could find no words.

The judge looked sick. The hot sun made the American flag look as red as neon light. This was what he had dreaded most of all—a hung jury, a mistrial.

In the ghetto:

They don't probe down there in the Panther Party to find out what's really happening. Behind the Panther Party is a revolutionary type thing, you know, a revolutionary type thing. A war against the system. Do you believe magazines, newspapers, television. They claim to be liberals but they're not.

In the meantime, I don't believe they actually killed him. I don't think that type of guy would do that . . .

After the jury was dismissed, a friend of the defense was able to get Garry together with one of the leaders of the majority, Marilyn "Nanette" Martino. They had dinner and discussed what should be done.

Miss Martino presented the problem that really troubled her: Bobby Seale had been unanimously acquitted by 5 o'clock of the first afternoon of deliberation! After the jury became deadlocked, one person had reopened the Seale case. (They had neglected to send the Not guilty verdict to the judge, thinking to announce both verdicts at once.) The judge had impounded the note that told the final outcome.

In the case of Bobby G. Seale: 11 to 1 for acquittal.

In the case of Ericka Huggins: 10 to 2 for acquittal.

Number 12 was not a holdout, after all. The stumbling block was little Barbara Foy whom Garry had chosen for the panel because she took yoga, because somehow that had seemed human to him. Miss Foy, who sat inches away from Ericka Huggins for eight weeks, who never could look at the photographs of Alex Rackley.

THE SEVENTH DAY (MAY 25, 1971)

The "other" case was discussed as the last few hundred vigilers waited to see why the lawyers and the judge were meeting in chambers one last time.

The "other" case, the double, that the jury had never heard of: the informer; and now the feeling was that Warren Kimbro was also involved. Did that mean that the police knew that Rackley was being held? They must have, for the informer was in the house during the three days! What do the F.B.I. files reveal about George Sams? The F.B.I. cooperated in the search without warrants, where is their inventory? What part, if any, did the Yale liaison man, C. Tracey Barnes of the C.I.A., play, besides financing Bobby Seale's trip to New Haven? What happened between Sams and the F.B.I. in Canada during the two weeks after he was arrested or gave himself up? Where did all of Sam's money come from after the Rackley murder? Why did Stokely Carmichael say that he had found out that George Sams was a police agent? Was the "liberal" attack on Garry and Ericka spontaneous?

For some reason a lot of black people were drifting toward the Green. Some Panthers passed out "SELF-EXAMINATION FOR CANCER" leaflets and sold last week's paper.

Garry in gray, looking like hell, swept up the steps. He beckoned the press. He was fighting back, he was supposed to be in San Francisco to begin the retrial of Huey P. Newton on the next day, but Markle had said that the state was ready for retrial and Charles R. Garry was going to call his bluff. He struck the first blow—

NO. 15844	:	SUPERIOR COURT
STATE OF CONNECTICUT	:	AT NEW HAVEN
V.	:	
BOBBY G. SEALE	:	MAY 25, 1971

STATE OF CONNECTICUT
SS
COUNTY OF NEW HAVEN

AFFIDAVIT OF CHARLES R. GARRY

CHARLES R. GARRY, being first duly sworn, deposes and says:

1. I am one of the attorneys for the defendant **BOBBY G. SEALE** in the above-captioned case.

2. I am making this affidavit in support of the attached Motion to Dismiss upon the grounds of prior jeopardy.

3. Based upon information and belief, your affiant believes the following to be true and accurate:

a) The jury in the trial of the above-captioned case after one and three-quarters hours of deliberations on May 19, 1971, arrived at a unanimous verdict of not guilty on all charges against Bobby G. Seale.

b) The jury was ignorant of their right and duty to report their unanimous verdicts in the *Seale* case because they had received no instructions from the Court in its charge to the jury about their right and duty to treat the case of Mr. Seale as entirely distinct and self-contained and to report their verdict in his case at such time as they had reached it.

c) After reaching a verdict in the *Seale* case on Wednesday, May 19, 1971, the jury conducted no further deliberations on that day and began its deliberations in the *Huggins* case for the first time on Thursday, May 20, 1971, after concluding its deliberations and arriving at a unanimous verdict in the *Seale* case on Wednesday, May 19, 1971.

d) Not until deliberations in the *Huggins* case had progressed and become heated did a juror in the minority for conviction in the *Huggins* case threaten to reopen the *Seale* case in which agreement had been reached and withhold assent from the unanimous verdicts already arrived at.

e) The final vote in the *Seale* case prior to the time a mistrial was declared Monday, May 24, 1971, was eleven to one for acquittal on all charges except conspiracy to murder, on which the vote was ten to two for acquittal. The votes in the *Huggins* case were eleven to one for acquittal on all charges except kidnapping resulting in death, on which the vote was ten for acquittal, one for conviction, and one for conviction of kidnapping.

4. The above is submitted as an offer of proof in support of the attached Motion to Dismiss based upon prior jeopardy.

Charles R. Garry

Subscribed and sworn before me
at the City of New Haven, the
25th day of May, 1971

DAVID N. ROSEN
_____
David N. Rosen
Commissioner of Superior Court

The courtroom filled up for the last time. The defense made its obligatory motions starting with pretrial publicity. David Rosen was fine, saying, "Let us be frank, our system at this time is not prepared to handle a case as unique . . ." The prosecution was ready, as ever, pointing out that "Mr. Garry was seen in the newspapers standing on his head and . . . the state can't get a fair trial . . ."

Then, in his last argument, Mr. Markle revealed what he had denied all along. The trial was political. Referring to polarized public opinion, he said, ". . . it is not unique in this day and age . . . this is the price of this kind of trial . . . if not here, change the venue . . ." The prosecutor's sincerity was palpable, he was ready to give the rest of his life over to the obsession.

The judge began his statement quietly:

Well, first of all, as far as the audience is concerned, no outburst of any kind, no demonstrations of any kind.

I will tell counsel, very frankly, that I anticipated this motion and I thought about it considerably, and what I have to say applies to these cases only.

At the outset, I should say that I know of no more dedicated public servant than the State's Attorney for New Haven County, Arnold Markle. He is a good lawyer and discharges his duties at all times in a manner that is a credit to the State.

On the other hand, as it should be, my duties and obligations to the People of the State are different from his. It is my duty to see to it, to the best of my ability, that justice is dispensed fairly and even-handedly.

I have been involved in these cases and related cases for something approaching two years. I have, by that happenstance, gained a rather wide knowledge of the factual situation and, indeed, of the defendants themselves.

Mrs. Huggins has been confined for more than two years in this State. Mr. Seale has been confined in this State and other States for at least that amount of time. He is also faced with the problem in the State of Illinois that involves confinement. I have observed a rather remarkable change in the attitude of these defendants during the time they have been before me, and I don't think it is feigned.

I am advised by the clerk of this court that the array of jurors for this court year is practically exhausted and that the possibility of drawing a panel for these cases is practically nil. The new array will not be available until September.

I have previously heard a motion to dismiss because of pretrial publicity. Despite the obvious publicity, I denied that motion with the hope that an unbiased jury could be impaneled. Some 1,500 names were drawn and about 1,100 persons examined before a jury could be selected. It took four months.

He was reading from handwritten notes. (The defendants had changed? He was the one transformed.) The crowd was half on its feet, the State's Attorney and Corporal Schultz scribbled furiously, red-faced, pretending to write.

The State has put its best foot forward in presenting its effort to prove its cases against these defendants. They have failed to convince a jury of their guilt.

With the massive publicity attendant upon the trial just completed, I find it impossible to believe that an unbiased jury could be selected without superhuman efforts which this Court, the State and these defendants should not be called upon either to make or to endure.

The motion to dismiss is granted in each case, and the prisoners are discharged forthwith.

On page one of *The New York Times,* the case was news at last. From the biggest Left defeat since the Rosenbergs, the case had become the glad tidings—

CHARGES DROPPED IN THE SEALE CASE; 'PUBLICITY' CITED

The sound and action level was rising. Katie and Charles stood; you could hear Katie—"I request the immediate release of my client Ericka Huggins." It was dissolving now, Markle was up shouting. You could see Garry's lips moving—"I request the immediate release of my client, Bobby G. Seale." Markle was demanding something—a stay? The judge: "Denied."

The Connecticut Democratic machine had produced a man who suddenly seemed a giant. Harold M. Mulvey knew that after the longest, most expensive trial in Connecticut history, the people of the state had no more appetite. It had all become gratuitous, the judge had taken note of the years spent in prison. Several times during the trial he had looked strangely at the slow-walking Ericka, and his instinct told him that it was enough.

The federal marshals moved in for Bobby (his Chicago contempt bail had still not been set), but Ericka walked out into the hall into the purgation and dancing. The police were swept aside, Garry took a swing at someone. Ericka loomed above them as if risen, a confrontation from the Gospels, children were raised for her blessing. Though the sky was clear, there was thunder over the Green.

Big Man got her across the street to the Green. The press fought forward, with their microphones, like maniacs. "Look at the sun," Ericka said. "What will you do now?" the microphones demanded. "Live."

Possibly the other jurists who have heard your previous arguments have taken into consideration your connections and abilities through various organizations and through Hong Kong and the Viet Cong and Black Power to raise a much larger amount of bail than these poor individuals who do not have those outside big financial connections.

—Carlton Fisher, Administrative
Justice of the Eighth Judicial
District, New York State, at
bail hearing November 15, 1967.

Thus spoke Martin Sostre's judges.

The Sacco-Vanzetti judge confided that he "had fixed those anarchist bastards"; Judges Hoffman and Kaufman in the "Chicago Conspiracy" and the "Atom Bomb" trials, like Judge Murtagh in the "Panther 21" case in New York, had made a daily indictment out of their demeanor and bias. Judge Mulvey was a Solomon when measured against these men.

Once, perhaps, the judge had seen no real difference between George Sams and Bobby Seale, as the State still did not. Most of the public, including the educated class saw George Sams and Bobby Seale or Huey P. Newton as twins, indistinguishable in the American twilight. But over the two years Mulvey had begun to get to know different black people. And Garry's architectonic *voir dire* strategy allowed him to see that almost all the citizens had been blinded as he once, perhaps, was. No one had eyes yet to see or read Bobby Seale's blueprints or the souls of black people.

The white jury population was ill, congenitally ill, and black jurors—after New York and New Haven—were not going to convict any more black revolutionaries, nor would they compromise no matter how many juries they had to hang.

The polarization was complete.

PANTHER PANELISTS DISAGREE ON THREATS

PANTHER THREATS DISPUTED

"They warned me that when it was over to look over my shoulder and don't forget you have a family outside."

They had almost come to blows over the Black Panther's Ten Point Program! The Black Panthers had been on trial.

"Seale and Garry were on their way to the West Coast and a personal meeting with Huey P. Newton! The Panther campaign to register ghetto dwellers to vote and *serve on juries* was in high gear."

Also on the front page was—

Bitter At Seale, Not Judge
MARKLE SAYS COURT SYSTEM WILL SURVIVE TRIAL DISMISSAL

"This system will survive this minor breakdown in a major case" . . .

Markle, who said that he wasn't bitter against the judge or the system, did express bitterness concerning Seale and Seale's outbursts of anger in the courtroom during the trial.

"Bobby Seale's outbursts were part of the whole scheme. They were calculated. It was obvious from what happened later on when people began to buy that he had changed," Markle said.

Markle appeared to be referring to Judge Mulvey, who, in dismissing the charges, said, "I have observed a rather remarkable change in attitude of these defendants during the time that they have been before me and I don't think that it's feigned."

Markle also said that the Panthers could be a danger to national security, but not at this time.

The Panther trials in New Haven were over.

In a democracy everything is gambled on a trial where Lady Luck is a blinded Athena of Justice. At New Haven, the judge had been determined that disasters of the past—such as the Dreyfus Affair—would not be repeated. That it would not be said of them as it was of the French by Clemenceau—

Henceforth every reflecting Frenchman knows that he may be accused of any crime, condemned on evidence he has never heard of, banished, tormented in body and mind, and that hardly a soul among his countrymen will care whether he is getting justice or injustice. They happened to take sides about Dreyfus; he may have no such luck. Dreyfus, for the rights of whose case friends and foes cared nothing, happened to be a convenient stick for anti-Semites and antimilitarists to thump the other side with; he may not. Reasoning thus, will the reflective Frenchman cultivate independence of thought, civic courage, political honesty? Not he. He will make it his business in life to cultivate a safe obscurity, and shout, if shout he must, always with the largest crowd.

The results of such a lesson upon the public life of a nation are not easy to detect at once and in glaring cases; but you may be very sure they are there, and in the long run they will show themselves. The French citizen was fearful of unpopularity before; he will not be bolder now. The punishment of those who have suffered in Dreyfus' cause will not be lost on him. The timidity of a Casimir-Périer, of the President of the Republic, who suspected the truth and dared not discover it, will be emulated by lesser men. Cowardice will become a principle of public life.

The advocates had all been sincere unto the death in that case. As in Hegelian tragedy, all sides in these political trials are equally passionate and sincere.

Arnold Markle stood staring out his office window, watching "the mob" of partisans pour out of the sun into the shadows of the Roman piles of the heartless tomb of a building. Garry had hit him where he lived in his true belief. He, Markle, was like a man who had stared too long into the sun. His eyes had been pierced by the blaze of Black Liberation and now, astonished and half blinded, he staggered instinctively for the shadows in his office. The office full of civic awards and plaques from the good citizens of New Haven County, and the picture of David Frost on the wall. Blind to the vicissitudes of black America in 1971, he had chosen the fatal popular strategy of pitting "good Negroes" against "bad niggers." The proud, old New Haven *Register* was forced to bow, too, and in an editorial:

. . . But a jury immovably divided, and a judge looking in conscience at the defendants, the charges and the law, closed out with responsibility and dignity a case needlessly hampered from its start by academic emotionalism, by manipulated public controversy, and by false predictions or politicized justice.

Judge Mulvey's decision does not totally satisfy the hope that truth will be clearly winnowed from the welter of contradictory fact in a courtroom. But it serves the needs of justice—and of a Panther-weary community.

Meanwhile they were headlining—

MULVEY'S DECISION SPARKS
A NATIONWIDE DEBATE

The governor of the state took the occasion to proclaim that the dismissal proved that the "system worked" and that everyone had had a fair trial. But the judge had ruled just the opposite. It had all been for nothing and Garry, the hated street fighter with the twenty-dollar ties was walking out on the "model city" and its Fundamental Agreement. Walking out, with Bobby Seale, without a backward look.

As for "the system," Garry quoted Haywood Burns, the national director of the Conference of Black Lawyers:

It was the law which provided the onerous slave codes to govern in oppressive detail the lives of millions of blacks until their emancipation, and which turned to perform the same function through the notorious black codes after emancipation. It was the law that the architects of segregation built a Jim Crow society which is still intact a decade and a half after *Brown v. Board of Education* and more than a century after the Emancipation Proclamation.

"All that and 7,500 black men lynched in this century alone," he growled. He had become a Panther by second nature.

In New Haven someone yelled "The People won"; and others answered, "The People will always win." In Oakland, Huey P. Newton said that the power of the people had set the prisoners free. He meant the "people" on this jury and later juries and the "people" that had forced the state to spend such enormous sums of money. The "people" who had rebelled widely against the Panther trials with their conspiracy charges and secret police, these were some of the people Newton had in mind.

The Garry-Newton strategy had prevailed. The gigantic jury selection had left the judge no choice. Now the defense view was almost universal: it was impossible, in New Haven at least, to get a jury or a verdict, that is to say, a fair trial for the Black Panthers.

It was not yet time, *objectively,* for machine guns.

In the McLucas case the acquittal majority, including blacks, had collapsed. Now in New York and New Haven they had rebelled.

Part of the American Revolution was the concept of jury "nullification"; setting aside traditional directions from the court and deciding by individual conscience. Around the time of John Brown many a jury refused to uphold the Fugitive Slave Laws of 1850. John Adams, Alexander Hamilton, and others later had in mind that for all the "presumption of innocence," when the individual is in combat with the State, it is, as Camus called it, an unequal struggle.

(On the same day, in Cairo, Illinois, four black men were released from charges of attacking a member of the White Citizen Council after the jury reported deadlock. Otto Kerner and Milton Eisenhower envisioned race war if quick change failed to come; the State of Mississippi was caught purging the voting rolls of 34,000 black people; from New York and Mississippi, black people and policemen were shot down in the street at greater and greater rates. Why did this American agony seem to defy remedy?

Franklin Dilger—in his school, church, labor union—had never had to face his place in the human race, his ethnocentric blindness, his received "racism." This sober, quiet, hard working, prematurely old man of 42 became ill and vomited in the jury room.

His American institutions, leaders, had failed him, not prepared him nor helped him in any way. Now black people were saying that if they had to they would do what these leaders and institutions would not or could not do, and they would do it in the close *agon* of the jury room, over the living bodies of black revolutionaries.)

There's a war going on here. We must face the facts. I don't say which side I'm on, but there's a war on. You can feel it, sense it. When you see Mr. Markle wearing a pig on his tie, you know what's going on. Mr. Markle is on one side of the war, and he is a leader. There's no question about that in my mind at all.

Yale Law Journal reporters had interviewed the jurors after the McLucas verdict. Now, the Seale-Huggins jurors paused only to curse each other.

Katie Roraback was being toasted on all sides; and a ballet—"Clear me a space and I'll dance about Rosa Luxemburg"—had been dedicated to her. She alone had been correct about Number 12. Jennie, as the black jurors affectionately termed her, had tears in her eyes after Ericka's testimony was reread, and then she joined the majority. The fear of Jennie had been only one more instance of "male chauvinism."

At Yale, Garry was packing his junk—

DEAR MR. GARRY:

I just want to register my complaint with the thousands of others I'm sure you are receiving after your appearance on the "David Frost" show.

Rather than the outspoken, vituperative attorney one may have thought you to be, you showed yourself to be biased, obstinate and stupid. The way you antagonised the audience showed you, not Epstein, to be an agent of the CIA/FBI. . . .

. . . You are a disgrace to your profession; a neo-Fascist pig, who encourages a disregard for the law, the order that separates man from the animal. Moreover, you are a crass opportunist who is riding the wave of political dissent; exploiting the Panthers, selling out your country.

—and seventeen suits.

The third act of the Newton case was about to begin for him. Garry had won: he had exposed the class nature of the jury system, and he had helped build Judge Mulvey up for his amazing display of courage at the end. He left New Haven bloody; he had stood them on *their* heads. *The New York Times* headlines appeared to shout after him:

BURGER ASSAILS UNRULY LAWYERS

Strong Discipline By
Profession Urged

Press And Students
Are Also Chided

Defendants Favored by
Courts, Mitchell Says

As the trial began, the Harris Poll found that two out of every three white people in the United States felt that the "Black Panthers are a serious menace to the country." By 81 to 7, whites believed that the shooting of Panthers had been mainly "the result of violence started by the Black Panthers themselves." Whites believed (57 to 22 percent) that "the Black Panthers want to destroy the police and should be put out of existence."

Almost 90 percent of the black community reacted to Panther deaths by saying "blacks have to stand together."

As the trial ended, black people on juries were in open revolt. (In the Midwest a black man was acquitted after shooting down his foreman. The jury was taken to the assembly line.) Perhaps for the first time in the history of the country an American Attorney General was questioning the presumption-of-innocence canon because of the Panther trials. John Mitchell called the New Haven decision "fatuous," and the blood gleamed through the provocative rhetoric again when the Attorney General asked, "Is justice served now by shackling the prosecutor and giving more weapons to the defense?"

"Shackling"? "Weapons"? This "serious imbalance in the scales of justice" would be rectified, the Justice Department promised, and the Chief Justice himself was warmly praised for his criticism of courtroom "sophistry" and his warning that in America, "we may well come to be known as . . . the impotent society."

Mitchell: "Preoccupation with fairness for the accused has done violence to fairness for the accuser." This was just some of the ominous fallout from New Haven and the Garry-Newton strategy of "exhausting all legal means." Judge Mulvey had bowed to reality, but elsewhere, New York and Chicago, the judges were taking the *voir dire* away from the counsel, and in Los Angeles there was an uproar because the jury population was being redefined, because nonwhite juries were acquitting at too high a rate and refusing to convict in ordinary *property* cases.

Angela Davis' codefendant, Ruchell Magee, had a court-appointed attorney that the state was paying $8,500 a month; Bobby and Ericka had had a priceless legal defense. But Stagolee, Sweetback, Fast-Talking Fanny—the fateful *lumpen* were going in and out of prison as if on an assembly line, and something vital in the system seemed about to give way. It was, as the executive director of the Eisenhower Commission had described our legal system: "It does not deter, does not detect, does not convict, and does not correct."

Another strophe of the *agon* had ended for Charles R. Garry. The blasts from "high places" told him that the Tragedy without God would continue. In New Haven the scenario had gone by the Marxist book: first as tragedy (the hung jury), then as farce (the dismissal).

He glared one last time at the adjoining graveyard (*The Dead Shall Rise*), and then without modesty or vanity, without fear and without "hope," he left for San Francisco. His last words grated cruelly on what was left of the New England sensibility: "When the fix is equal, justice prevails."

On April 4th, 1972, on the Associated Press wire, Arnold Markle's pride was overthrown: EX-CHIEF SAYS NEW HAVEN POLICE HAD NO EVIDENCE AGAINST SEALE.

NEW HAVEN, Conn. (AP) —Former New Haven Police Chief James F. Ahern says he was astonished when a local prosecutor sought an indictment of Black Panther National Chairman Bobby G. Seale in the Alex Rackley murder case three years ago.

"We (the police) had no solid evidence to link him to Rackley's death," Ahern writes in a book about to be published.

"The New Haven Police Department never requested an indictment against gun (Seale), nor did we expect that (prosecutor Arnold) Markle would ask for one," Ahern says.

Markle, contacted by

telephone, said Ahern's account "is not true. He did
know. He knew I was going to
indict Seale. He never said
that he was against indict-
ing Seale."

And there was more, too, the defense was sure of that. But would the "truth" ever be known? To the Chairman of the Black Panther Party the 1972 headline was irrelevant, "We've begun our Long March," he snapped.

Bobby Seale was tired. He waited under federal guard for word on his bail, then he and Garry would go home to Oakland and Huey and the inner-city communes and history. One chapter in the odyssey that had taken him in chains from San Francisco to Chicago to New Haven, and the jails in between, was over.

The day before, when everything seemed lost, he had cheered up and consoled the sideliners with his inimitable snapping fist. Now he was dog tired—the weather was humid and electric—and as they sped him away from New Haven for the last time he appeared a kind of gay man of sorrows.

When interviewed, the State's Attorney said, "I did my job, and I am prepared to do it again."

The black jurors and Nanette Martino had a party with the Panthers and the defense. "Good Negroes" had become a fiction of the state, like the "silent majority."

Kimbro, the black Catholic, retreated more and more into faith; Sams, behind walls, raged, terrorizing even some of the guards.

Kimbro would surely be rewarded short of twenty years, but no one would dare free George Sams back into hell.

On June 23, 1971, Sams and Kimbro were sentenced to life imprisonment. But—

JUDGE MULVEY: Of course I am well aware that he (George Sams) has completely purged himself and has given out most of the details . . . He has of course been of great assistance to the state . . . and I am sure that it will be taken into consideration in another forum at another time . . . I will say a prayer for you.

ARNOLD MARKLE: I would be less than candid if I did not put on the record that when he (Sams) comes up before the appropriate board I will appear on his behalf.

In the titanomachia of the *Lumpenproletariat,* the spirit of Huey P. Newton—rebellion, resistance and life in death—had won over George Sams and homicide and suicide.

What *had* happened finally to the liberals and the "youth"? What had they run from? The corpse of Alex Rackley.

The daily and millenarian violence inflicted on the oppressed echoed and mirrored back to the public in these Panther "cases" and trials. The survival tactics of the victims are no more symbolic than the threat of violence over them. The victims do not exist as individuals with "rights" and symbolic extensions of their body in time, money, energy. They are hard pressed, they have only their bodies of flesh and blood, and the peace movement shrinks from these doomed souls, never understanding the Black Panthers or Bobby Seale or Ericka Huggins and the mighty *renaissance* locked in the unconscious of the damned.

In vain did Huey P. Newton quote Gandhi to the peace movement:

Where the choice is set between cowardice and violence, I would advise violence. I praise and extol the serene courage of dying without killing. Yet I desire that those who have not this courage should rather cultivate the art of killing and being killed, than basely to avoid the danger. This is because he who runs away commits mental violence; he has not the courage of facing death by killing. I would a thousand times prefer violence than the emasculation of a whole race. I prefer to use arms in defense of honor rather than remain the vile witness of dishonor.

Ericka Huggins is "free." (If the past were not dead, then she would not feel such grief and rage.) The past no longer exists, it is irremediable. Therefore she is free.

She too was going to Oakland (to "National," at last—except that Sams was wrong about that too; it was called "Central.") She gave that unforgettable and impenetrable smile and walked away with the child into the crazy weather of late May.

> the oldness of new things
> fascinate me like a new
> feeling about love about people
> snow, highways that
> sparkle at night, talk,
> laughter . . .
> that old longing for freedom
> that this place constantly
> renews—it all makes
> me know that humankind
> has longed to be free ever forever
> since its break from the
> whole
> maybe the longing for
> freedom will soon make
> others homesick for our
> natural state in/with
> earth, air, fire, water
> earth, air, fire, water
> not dead
> but living
> not asking for freedom—
> but free—
>
> Ericka

INDEX

Clark, Mark, 25, 138, 184, 196, 269, 290, 311
Clark, Ramsey, 107, 197
Clay, Cassius, 135; *see also* Muhammad Ali
Cleaver, Eldridge, 20, 35–36, 46, 95, 130, 193–94, 240
Leary and, 200
split within Black Panther Party and, 36, 58, 206–7, 221
Cleaver, Kathleen, 206–7
Clemenceau, Georges, 323
Coakley (Berkeley District Attorney), 104–5
"Coalition to Defend the Black Panthers," 32
Coffin, Rev. William Sloan, 74
Columbia Broadcasting Company, 31
Commission of Civil Disorders, report of, 82, 124, 146, 326
Communist Party U.S.A., 45, 217, 313
Conspiracy charge, 102–5, 305
Council of Churches, 71
Cox, Don, 254
Creem, Mrs. Abbie, 55–56
Crisis, The, 118
Crosson, Robert, 93
Crouch, Elizabeth, 139–41, 146

D

Daily News, Jackson, 117
Daily News, New York, 299
Daily World, 217, 231
Darrow, Clarence, 44, 47, 58, 103

Davidson, Dr. H. A., 266–67
Davis, Angela, 185, 189, 311, 328
Garry and, 113, 118
indictment of, 128, 163, 170–171
letter to Ericka Huggins from, 312–13
Death penalty, 85, 287
in jury selection, 59–60, 76, 80, 85, 91–93, 99, 137, 157–59
media and, 15, 168–69
Debs, Eugene, 103, 106
Dellinger, David, 225, 231
Demapolis, Deputy, 56–57
DeRosa, Vincent, 99, 110, 220, 229, 243, 313
DeStefano, Anthony, 178
Diamond, Dr. Bernard L., 265
Dilger, Franklin, 75–76, 166, 177, 314, 326
Douglas, Emory, 72, 99, 235, 245
Dreyfus affair, 184–86, 188, 315, 323
Duvalier, François, 21, 22
Dylan, Bob, 309

E

East Is Red, The (film), 148
Edwards, George, 256
Einstein, Albert, 77, 261
Eisenhower Commission, report of, 82, 326, 328
Elks Club, 55
Emerson, Thomas I., 80
Emmett, Kathy, 212, 232
Epps, Lonnie, 234

Nationalism (*cont.*)
"primitive," 21
revolutionary, 18, 20–24
See also Intercommunalism
Negritude, 21
Neil, Father Earl, 281–84, 290,
    305
Neruda, Pablo, 178
New Haven, 108–9
social structure of, 34, 41–42,
    59, 64, 86–87, 99, 106–7
New International, The, 234–35
New Orleans States, 116
New York magazine, 196, 202
New York Review of Books, 34,
    182
New Yorker magazine, 183, 197,
    202
Newton, Huey, P., 89, 92, 94,
    228, 231, 259, 292, 294
criticism of, 184
criticism of Black Panther
    Party by, 21, 99, 244–
    245, 247, 305–6
Erikson and, 168, 198–200
founding of Black Panther
    Party by, 17, 22, 40, 57,
    237
language used by, 112, 113
re-trial of, 245, 313, 317,
    326
at Revolutionary People's
    Constitutional Conven-
    tion, 113–16
split between Cleaver and, 60,
    206–7, 225, 311
statements about trial by,
    25, 100
theories of, 18, 20–21, 26, 36,
    91, 291, 325, 331

Newton, Huey P. (*cont.*)
trial and imprisonment of,
    38, 44, 46, 49, 58, 82,
    86, 93, 129, 146
Niemoeller, Martin, 71
Nigger, use of term, 109
Nixon, Richard, 23, 196, 238–
    239
Nkrumah, Kwame, 39
Noble, Vivian, 167, 186
Nonviolence, 18–19, 20

O

"Oakland Seven," trial of, 46,
    105, 146
Oelsner, Leslie, 227
O'Neill, Steven, 139–43, 150
Orchard, Harry, 103
Osborne, Ernest, 99

P

Pakacimas, John, 56
Pan-Africanism, 23
"Panther twenty-one," 17, 27,
    54, 132, 166, 201, 259,
    298–99, 321
acquittal of, 297–99
Pastore, Nicholas, 99, 220, 229,
    270
testimony of, 267–69, 287
Patterson, William, 225
Pennix, Sheila, 119
Phalen, Joseph, 56
Phantom Books, 217
Pontecorvo, Gillo, 125–26
Poole, Cecil, 197
Pope, Walter Toure, 195